Walk!
Andorra

with

Charles Davis

DISCOVERY WALKING GUIDES LTD

Walk! Andorra
First Edition - March 2005

Copyright © 2005

Published by
Discovery Walking Guides Ltd
10 Tennyson Close, Northampton NN5 7HJ,
England

Maps
Original mapping reproduced under licence from:
The Instituto Geográfico Nacional - Centro
Nacional de Información Geográfica

Cartografía original:
INSTITUTO GEOGRÁFICO NACIONAL -
CENTRO NACIONAL DE INFORMACIÓN
GEOGRÁFICA

Photographs
Photographs in this book were taken by the author,
Charles Davis, and Jeanette Tallegas.

Front Cover Photographs

The main lake on the Estany Forcats route (Walk 8)

Overlooking Estanys de Tristaina (Walk 1)

Pic de Casamanya on Walk 15

Walk 25: on the Pic de Maians route

ISBN 1-904946-04-6
Text and photographs* © Charles Davis

All rights reserved. No part of this publication may be reproduced, stored in a retrieval system or transmitted in any form or by any means, electronic, mechanical, photocopying, recording or otherwise, without the prior written permission of the publishers.

The author and publishers have tried to ensure that the information and maps in this publication are as accurate as possible. However, we accept no responsibility for any loss, injury or inconvenience sustained by anyone using this book.

Walk! Andorra

CONTENTS

Contents	3
The Author	8
Introduction	
The Other Andorra	9
Historical Sketch	10
Walking in Andorra	19
Who's it for?	20
When to Go	20
Getting there, getting about, getting a bed	21
The Walks	22
Overnighters	24
Equipment	25
Problems	27
Flora, Fauna & Environment	28
Eating & Drinking	30
Tourist Stuff: what to do on a day off	31
Language	34
Acknowledgements	34
Map Information	
Locator Maps	35
Map Notes	36
Walking Information	
Symbols Rating Guide & Notes	37
Using GPS on Andorra	38
Walking Equipment	40

WALKS IN THE WEST

1 Estanys de Tristaina — 42
4 walker, 2 hours 50 mins - 4 hours, 7 kilometres, ascents & descents 500 metres, vertigo risk, 2 refreshments (circular)
An easy high-mountain walk to Andorra's most visited lakes with enough rough ground to satisfy more rugged tastes.

2 Roc de la Cauba & Coll de les Cases — 45
5 walker, 3½ hours, 10.5 kilometres, ascents & descents 850 metres, 3 refreshments (circular)
Fabulous views and a fairytale forest.

3	**Pic d'Enclar and Pic de Carroi**	48

5 walker, 4½ hours, 15 kilometres, ascents & descents 1000 metres, vertigo risk, 0 refreshments (circular)
Either an arduous but uncomplicated climb to great views - or far and away the wildest 'walk' in the book.

4	**Pic de la Bassera (Pic dels Llacs)**	52

4 walker, 1¾ hours, 5 kilometres, ascents & descents 400 metres, 0 refreshments (circular)
Maximum height for minimum fuss or minimum height for maximum fuss.

5	**Storm In A Tea Cup: Pic Alt de la Capa**	55

5 walker, 2¼ hours, 6 kilometres, ascents & descents 525 metres, 0 refreshments (circular)
Possibly the most vigorous and vertiginous step-up exercise ever.

6	**Pic de Sanfons**	57

3 walker, 3 hours 40 mins, 11 kilometres, ascents & decents 500 metres, 0 refreshments (linear two way)
Frustrated trapeze artist? Here's your chance to satisfy unfulfilled dreams.

7	**Pic de Coma Pedrosa**	60

5 walker, 2¼-7 hours, 12 kilometres, ascents & descents 700-1500 metres, 4 refreshments (linear)
Andorra's highest summit.

8	**Estany Forcats**	64

5 walker, 5½ hours, 16 kilometres, ascents & descents 1200 metres, vertigo risk, 3 refreshments (circular)
The hermit lake: solitary, sober, and a little other-worldly.

9	**Camino Real: El Serrat to Arans**	67

1 walker, 1 hour 10 mins, 5 kilometres, ascents negligible, descents 200 metres, 4 refreshments (linear one way)
Easy riverbank strolling for all the family.

10	**Estanys de l'Angonella**	69

5 walker, 4 hours 20 mins, 12 kilometres, ascents & descents 1000 metres, 4 refreshments (linear two way)
Great Labour, Great Lakes

WALKS IN THE NORTH

11	**Port d'Incles & Estanys de Fontargent**	72

3 walker, 2 hours 20 mins, 8 kilometres, ascents & descents 500 metres, 3 refreshments (linear two way)
Traditional trading route into France; ideal for a first day, a family outing, and for those who want high mountains without heartbreak.

12	**Refuge de Coma Obaga**	**74**

5 walker, 3 hours 20 mins, 11 kilometres, ascents & descents 600 metres, 4 refreshments (circular/linear two way)
Probably the prettiest refuge in the principality

13	**Pic de Font Blanca & Estany Esbalçat**	**78**

5 walker, 5¼ hours, 11 kilometres, ascents & descents 1100 metres, vertigo risk, 0 refreshments (circular)
Ouf! - in every way; tremendous landscape, tremendous views, tremendous climb.

14	**Port de Siguer & Estany Blau**	**81**

4 walker, 3 hours, 10 kilometres, ascents & descents 650 metres, 0 refreshments (linear two way)
Smugglers' path into France and one of the region's most beautiful lakes.

15	**Pic de Casamanya + Extension to Arans**	**83**

5 walker, 3½-8 hours, 9 kilometres, ascents & descents 760 metres, 0 refreshments (linear two way + one way)
Andorra's emblematic peak. A steep, straightforward climb with the option of a very spectacular alternative descent.

16	**Vall del Riu & Riu Montaup**	**88**

4 walker, 4 hours 25 mins, 13 kilometres, ascents & descents 750 metres, 0 refreshments (circular)
A little known loop linking two torrents and three superb lakes: possibly the most memorable day you'll have.

17	**Pic de la Serrera via the Ransol Valley**	**92**

5 walker, 4 hours 25 mins, 12 kilometres, ascents & descents 1000 metres, 0 refreshments (linear two way)
Classic ascent of Andorra's third highest summit.

18	**Estanys de les Salamandres**	**95**

3 walker, 2 hours 5 mins, 7.5 kilometres, ascents & descents 400 metres, 0 refreshments (circular/linear two way)
Easy ascent with fine views of Vall d'Incles plus the option to get off path - way off!

19	**Estanys de Juclar & A Near Noah Experience**	**98**

3/4/5 walker, 5 hours, 14 kilometres, ascents & descents 850 metres, 3 refreshments (linear two way)
Andorra's largest lake plus a little extreme rambling.

20	**Estanys des Siscaró & Cap de Port**	**102**

5 walker, 5 hours, 13 kilometres, ascents & descents 950 metres, 3 refresments (pan-handle circular)
Lovely lakes and a wild, little visited crest.

21	**Northern Traverse: Incles to El Serrat** (two days)	**105**

Day One
5 walker, 3 hours 50 mins (allow 5-6 hours), 8 kilometres, 800 metres ascents, 450 metres descents, 0 refreshments, (linear one way)
Day Two
5 walker, 5 hours (allow 8 hours), 15 kilometres, ascents 600 metres, descents 1200 metres, 3 refreshments (linear one way)
Grand Hiking, great variety, and the most extravagant parade of wildflowers in a country famous for its wildflowers.

WALKS IN THE SOUTH

22	**Circ dels Pessons: Estany de les Fonts**	**111**

3 walker, 2¾ hours, 9 kilometres, ascents & descents 400 metres, 3 refreshments (linear two way)
Andorra's most spectacular cirque: easy walking in wild terrain, ideal for adventurous families.

23	**Camí de Gall: Soldeu to Canillo**	**114**

2 walker, 2 hours, 6.6 kilometres, ascents 100 metres, descents 300 metres, vertigo risk, 4 refreshments (linear one way)
Pleasant nature trail down the central valley, suitable for virtually all the family

24	**The Lazy Man's Mountain: Sender de les Tres Valls**	**117**

2 walker, 1 hour 40 mins, 6.5 kilometres, ascents 100 metres, descents 300 metres, 3 refreshments (linear one way)
Introduction to the Grand Valira cable-car walks.

25	**Pic de Maians**	**119**

4 walker, 2 hours 25 mins, 8.5 kilometres, ascents & descents 500 metres, vertigo risk, 3 refreshments (circular)
Great views round Canillo's local ski-station

26	**Refuge and Estany d'Ensagents**	**121**

3 walker, 3½ hours, 10.5 kilometres, ascents & descents 550 metres, 0 refreshments (linear two-way)
Easy walking, striking contrasts and consistently beautiful landscape - essential walking.

27	**Camí de la Canal**	**124**

1 walker, 2 hours, 10 kilometres, ascents & descents negligible, vertigo risk, 0 refreshments (linear two way)
Year round stroll for all

28	**Refugi de Perafita**	**127**

5 walker, 4½ hours, 9 kilometres, ascents & descents 970 metres, 0 refreshments (circular)
Classic valley ascent of the southern massif: a concord of wood, water and pasture.

29	**Prat Primer via Collada de Caülla**	**130**

5 walker, 4 hours, 13.5 kilometres, ascents & descents 900 metres, 0 refreshments (circular)
A very varied walk to one of Andorra's finest pastures with enough wild fruit en route to supply a small jam factory - fabulous stuff.

30	**Tour of the South: Engolasters to Illa, the Agols & Madriu Valleys** (2 days)	**134**

Day One
5 walker, 5¼ hours, 14 kilometres, ascents 1250 metres, descents 200 metres, 0 refreshments (linear one way)
Day Two
3 walker, 3 hours, 14.5 kilometres, ascents 150 metres, descents 1200 metres, 3 refreshments (linear one way)
A touch of Eden: two paths through paradise

GPS Waypoints Lists — **140**

Glossary — **144**

Appendices:

A Useful Addresses & Recommendations	**146**
B Refuges	**147**
C Long Distance Paths	**148**
D Cable-cars and chair-lifts	**149**
E Mountain Bike Routes	**150**
F Climbing Routes and Vías Ferratas	**152**
G Bibliography	**152**

Place Names Index — **154**

THE AUTHOR

Charles Davis was born in London, and has lived and worked in the United States, Sudan, Turkey, Ivory Coast, Spain and France. With the onset of middle age, he realised that the urge to roam was better satisfied by walking than bouncing about on the back of a lorry in the middle of the desert, and now divides his time between mountain tops, desk-tops and laptops. He is the author of numerous highly praised and wholly unpublished novels.

Jeanette Tallegas has spent thirty odd years labouring for the French education system, from which she has finally, gleefully, taken early retirement. Asked what she intends doing now, she resolutely replies, "Nothing". Nonetheless, she does follow the author up various gruelling mountains, frequently alarming younger ramblers who seem to assume that remote and inaccessible places are the preserve of youth.

Charles Davis is also the author of:-

34 Alpujarras Walks
ISBN 1-899554-83-1

Walk! La Gomera
(2nd Edition)
ISBN 1-899554-90-4

Walk! Mallorca (North & Mountains)
ISBN 1-899554-92-0

Walk! Mallorca West
ISBN 1-899554-98-X

Walk! La Palma
ISBN 1-904946-06-2

Walk! Axarquía
ISBN 1-904946-08-9

- published by Discovery Walking Guides Ltd.

INTRODUCTION

There are two Andorras. One, regrettable and forgettable, is a place of packaged winter breaks, hypermarkets, shopping trips, crowded towns and traffic jams. The other is the traditional, timeless, romantic, landlocked principality high in the Pyrenees, the Andorra of independent character and a cheerful contempt for other people's frontiers, of smugglers' paths and high mountain passes, of mediaeval villages and remote refuges, the Andorra of a thousand lakes, of tumbling torrents, towering peaks, splendid vistas, meadows full of wildflowers, and some of the finest paths in the Pyrenees. No prizes for guessing which of the two we explore in this book.

Andorra is a topsy-turvy sort of place, nowhere more so than in the nature of its seasons. Hectic with skiers during nature's months of hibernation, the slopes go to sleep during the summer, making it the perfect place to escape the crowds that reduce some sections of the Pyrenees to rambling motorways. This relative neglect has nothing to do with the quality of the walks, which are superb, but is the result, ironically enough for Europe's highest country (the lowest point is 840 metres above sea level), of its comparatively modest altitude. The fact that it's highest peak is 'only' 2,942 metres (Ben Nevis is all of 1344 metres!) means the sort of people for whom mountains are an adult version of standing on top of the slide and chanting "I'm the king of the castle!" tend to be a bit sniffy about Andorra as a hiking destination, gravitating instead toward the major summits of western Catalonia and Aragon. Which is all to the good for the rest of us.

Once the canard of bigger-is-better biggest-is-best is dismissed, you will appreciate why we chose Andorra for our first Pyrenean title. Tucked between the warm air rising from the Costa Brava and the 3000-metre peaks to the West, its southern orientation means it escapes the worst of the storms conjured by the clashing Atlantic and Mediterranean fronts (you'll often see a storm circling the frontier without spilling over the border), yet still enjoys the classic, dramatic landscape of the high Pyrenees. Academics sometimes cite the Pyrenees as an ideal range of mountains for study by the amateur naturalist, since you can get to know the entire chain intimately in the space of ten years! Given that this is a luxury most of us can't afford, Andorra provides a good way into the mountains, as it's a microcosm of what is seen elsewhere in the Pyrenees and can be thoroughly explored in the course of a long summer holiday. The topography is the result of erosion by rivers and glaciation creating deep U-shaped valleys and moraines (sweeps of debris) interleaved with rocky peaks, principally composed, like most areas within the central axis of the Pyrenees, of granites and slates. With sixty-five summits over 2500 metres, spectacular moraines, stunning lakes, sweeps of downland, and forests of pine, beech, birch, and poplar, Andorra is the Pyrenees encapsulated.

Though it's not so obvious from an initial glance at a map, a clear geographical logic is evident from any of the principality's central peaks, which reveal it to be a physical enclave as well as a political one, a long, southern sloping Y formed by two main valleys feathered with subsidiary gullies, gorges and dales fanning out among the surrounding mountains. Apart from the high passes, there is only one natural point of entry and that is at the southern tip into Spain, which explains the preponderant influence of

Spanish (principally Catalán) culture and customs.

Andorra la Vella

Of 65,000 permanent residents, 24,000 are Andorran nationals (the figure of 12,000 is also frequently quoted but not attributed to any source), 27,000 Spanish, 7,000 Portuguese, and 5,000 French. Despite its small size (468 km² the principality gives the impression of being thinly populated, since nearly all its residents

La Massana

are concentrated in the major towns along the **Riu Valira** with 24,000 in the capital, **Andorra La Vella**, 14,000 in **Escaldes-Engordany**, 9,500 in **Encamp**, 7,000 in **Sant Julià de Lòria** 5,000 in **La Massana**, 3,000 in **Canillo**, and 1,500 in **Ordino**.

As a result, residential land is dear, the square metre reputedly (probably apocryphally) costing more than on the Champs Elysées Despite their historical insularity and the annual invasion of 12 million tourists (pro-rata equivalent to about a billion visitors to the UK, though 8 million only come for the day), the Andorrans are welcoming and helpful, especially if you speak a little Spanish. And for all the glitz and tawdry display of the duty-free emporiums, they remain a very down to earth people. In a locally produced programme about the mytho-poetic past of the principality, it was not just the novelists, historians and folklorists that were wheeled out as talking heads, but masons, too. Imagine a British programme about, say, the cult of the country house that actually deigned to consult a living brickie!

HISTORICAL SKETCH

Historically speaking, Andorra is a curious country in that it is largely defined by the absence of the institutions governments generally regard as the vital ingredients of a coherent nation state. It is a country without a king or a president, it has no army, has *never* been to war, has never had a currency of its own, has no language of its own, no discrete ethnicity, no prison, no railway, no airport let alone a flagship carrier, didn't even have any real roads till the twentieth century, and perhaps most famously, its inhabitants don't pay any direct taxes.

Meanwhile, the topsy-turvy seasons are mirrored by a history that, at first glance, suggests national cohesion has come as much from paradox as consistency: a devoutly Catholic people who rebuffed Huguenot refugees during the French Wars of Religion, the Andorrans were equally hostile to interference from the Spanish Inquisition; a feudal state governed by princes and administered by archaic institutions, Andorra was admired by French revolutionaries as a model of responsible citizenship featuring membership in a citizens' militia and mandatory participation in public works; despite having one of the oldest parliaments in Europe and a long-standing proto-democracy of householder suffrage, Andorran women didn't get the vote till **1970** and the country's feudal institutions survived until **1993**; Andorrans have traditionally displayed a strong distrust of outsiders, yet the principality is famous as a place of refuge and, in the **1930s**, came within a hair's breadth of installing a White Russian adventurer as king; jealous defenders of the rights conferred by their own borders, the Andorrans have always regarded their neighbours' side of the frontier as a convenient fiction, the principal function of which was to encourage Andorran enterprise; famous for smuggling tobacco and selling consumer durables, they are an essentially conservative people among whom frugality and conformity were traditionally considered the highest virtues; vigorous in their promotion of the Catalán language, they can switch to Spanish or French at will and frequently speak English, too…

But in the face of so many contradictions there was one constant that, up until the **1950s**, defined Andorra, and that was its geographical and economic isolation: the first road into the principality wasn't built until **1913** and even then the Andorrans weren't sure it was a very wise idea, waiting another twenty years till they finished the second one! Doubtless geography and practical engineering problems played a part in the delay, but even so, there was an admirable and revealing lack of urgency about the project. Residing in a true enclave sandwiched between big, intermittently militant neighbours, Andorrans were bound to be a bit sensitive about contact with the outside world.

The **first settled inhabitants** are thought to have been Mesolithic cave-dwellers, though the earliest excavated remains are Neolithic, including arrow tips, flint and bone tools, fragments of ceramics and the skeleton of a woman who lived about 4000 years ago. The troglodytes were succeeded by pastoralists who built the dolmens found throughout the Pyrenees and who lived in stone huts similar to the shepherds' cabins still seen in the high mountains today. Speaking a Basque dialect, these proto-andorrans also left their toponymic mark in names like **Ordino**, **Canillo**, **Arinsal**, **Erts**, and **Certés**. The herdsmen were joined by arable farmers in around 1000 BC and that was pretty well it for the next fifteen hundred years. A text dating from **120 BC** recounts how the '' (probably a tribe rather than a nation) resisted Hannibal in the previous century, but otherwise, the gregarious, cultivated Romans displayed little interest in such a remote and wild region, preferring to sit around sunning themselves beside the spas of Cerdanya. Fired by proselytic zeal, the Visigoth kingdom based in Toledo did extend its jurisdiction deep into the Pyrenees and Andorra may have depended on the see of Urgell in Catalonia as early as the sixth century, but there is no documentary evidence of its existence as a discrete political entity for another three hundred years.

Given their rather nebulous national identity and hazy early history, it's understandable that Andorrans should have claimed at least three distinct **foundation myths**, the first featuring the original illegal immigrant - Noah. This is a common legend in the Pyrenees (Roca de Salimans in France is another well known example, the town of Nohedes being named after the great mariner) so it's no surprise that it should have cropped up in a culture that is more distinctively Pyrenean than Catalán, Spanish or French. What has been a little unusual is the variety and vitality of the legend in Andorra. The more modest chronicles claim Noah landed either on **Pic de Fontargent** or **Pic de Noe** (different sources offer different locations) and nailed a ring to the summit before sailing for Ararat, but others have gone so far as to assert he never actually left and that the remains of the ark are still preserved in the ice and snow on the mountain, though it would have to be a pretty minuscule vessel to remain concealed in present conditions.

The second legend is a variation on the Snow White theme, in which a jealous, newlywed stepmother arranges for her beautiful stepdaughter to be taken into a remote mountain valley and murdered. Struck by the innocent beauty of their intended victim, the would-be murderers did what passes for the decent thing among would-be murderers in fairy tales, and abandoned the girl and her nanny in a remote mountain valley. After several years in the valley, the two women fished from the river, as one does, the moribund body of a handsome young man. Consequent on the customary pounding and spluttering, the young man came to and recounted how he had fallen foul of a certain tyrannical woman who had married a widowed count whose lovely daughter had subsequently disappeared and…well, you get the picture. The young people had something in common, promptly fell in love and set about establishing themselves in their mountain redoubt, a union commemorated in the Toll de la Senyoreta, The Young Girl's Pool, on the **Ríu Valira**.

A more credible legend claims Andorra was a marcher state established by Charlemagne in gratitude for the mountain-dwellers' timely intervention in a battle with the Moors in the **Querol Valley** in **788**. Unfortunately, there's no trace of the original *Carta Pobla* said to have conceded Andorra's independence in **805** and even documents that do exist from later in the ninth-century are either of dubious authenticity or a little vague about the precise status of the six parishes in the *Valle Handorrensis*, the name used in the Act of Consecration when Urgell cathedral, sacked by the moors in **793**, was rebuilt in the following century. However, it's fairly clear the principality was a feudal holding of the Bishop of Urgell from about this time and that the bishops, discovering a disquieting lack of temporal power in the mitre, resorted to a family of local strongmen to 'protect' their demesne, instituting an informal alliance that was later solemnized as a co-principality. Thereafter, there are three key dates.

The first is the 8th of September 1278, Andorra's national day, when a period of petty squabbling among the interested potentates was resolved by a document confirming the co-sovereignty of the Count of Foix and the Bishop of Urgell, implicitly acknowledging the principality's juridical legitimacy. The second significant year is **1419** when the co-princes allowed that the heads of the most important households elect representatives to an administrative council, the Consell de la Terra, which would later evolve into the *Consell General* and ultimately the modern day parliament. The third and arguably most important date is **1448**, when a license was issued granting Andorra the right to hold a market and exempting the principality from taxes, thus conferring a singular fiscal identity that would not be properly exploited for another 500 years, but which would eventually become its most famous defining characteristic.

Except for one brief but glorious episode in the 1930s (see below), the episcopal part of the co-principality has been continuous and undisputed since joint sovereignty was confirmed, but the secular side had a murkier history muddled by enough marriages to make a registrar sick and fraught with multifarious claims and counter claims that were only finally settled, like so much else, by the firm hand of Henry of Navarre (Henry IV of France) who inherited the co-principality and brought it within the competence of the French head of state. There was a brief hiccup during the French revolution when the Girondins and Jacobins displayed a rare unanimity in renouncing the feudal rights inherited via the guillotine and threatened to occupy Andorra; but in the general turmoil of the times, the principal actors in Paris had neither the leisure nor, once the Terror was underway, the wit to trouble themselves with a bunch of intractable shepherds tucked away on top of a mountain, and nothing was done till Napoleon, who was considerably less squeamish about compromising himself with feudal customs, toppled The Directory and, in **1806**, recognized the principality's quasi-independent status. The French head of state has been co-prince ever since.

The seigniorial rights of the co-princes look modest enough on paper (960 francs for the French President and, for the Bishop of Urgell, a levy of 'four hams, forty breads and a little bit of wine', subsequently amended to 'one-hundred dinners every two years' then to '450 pesetas, six hams, 12 capons, 12 partridge, and 12 cheeses'), but the Bishop, whose influence was always the greater, seems to have got more than a couple of capons out of the deal, judging by another Andorran legend: **La Dama Blanca d'Aubinya**.

According to this story, there was once a castle at the Aubinya waterfall which was inhabited by a beautiful woman who always wore white and employed her occult powers to protect the principality. One night, at a time when the Andorrans were in dispute with the Bishop of Urgell, the Woman in White appeared to the ecclesiastic as he approached the principality on a lonely path, giving him such a shock (the precise technique is not described, but presumably avaricious bishops regard beautiful women manifesting themselves on remote mountains as a peculiarly menacing peril) he fled in confusion, leaving his subjects to their own devices. When, at length, he risked a second diocesan progress, he ventured into the mountains and was never heard from again. He simply disappeared. And so did the Woman in White. This may seem a strikingly convenient coincidence (*'It was the Woman in White what done it, your honour'*), but the most revealing part of the tale is its denouement. Around the same time, Andorra's livestock were being decimated by a rapacious wolf that no one could track down. Eventually however, the wolf was cornered and killed by a group of hunters (singular?: sindico de consell - factor?), who immediately started suffering terrible nightmares, in which they were dying and were confronted with the Woman in White. Begging the apparition to intercede and save them, the dying men were told she could protect the country but couldn't save it from the Bishop, who had been transformed into the wolf. Admittedly, the logic of all this is a little shaky (the wolf was dead after all!), but it does indicate a restiveness that reflects the principality's proud independence and resentment of outside control.

Life in Andorra throughout the middle ages and right into modern times wasn't exactly Hobbesian, but neither was it very easy. Isolated from the religious and political strife that ensured living elsewhere in Europe often was nasty, brutish and short, the Andorrans were also cut off from the progress entailed in these successive catharses, and from the increased wealth created by the commercial and imperial adventures of larger countries. Existence was largely defined by resisting the elements, an imperative that militated against individual liberty (there are few isolated farms in Andorra, the mountain-dwellers preferring instead to club together in small, mutually supporting hamlets) and the dissipation that characterized the urban cultures developing elsewhere. Subsistence farming and a rudimentary communalism ensured everyone in the village had the basic necessities, but that relative comfort was only guaranteed by a rigid social hierarchy and a comparably inflexible thrift, hence the elevation, noted in early texts outlining Andorran history, mores and customs, of **frugality and conformity** as the highest virtues.

These texts, the Manual Digest (**1748**) by Antoni Fiter i Rossell, a doctor of canonical law born in Ordino, and the **Politar Andorrà (1763)** by Antoni Puig, a priest from Escaldes, are often cited as evidence that the principality wasn't entirely isolated from the wider intellectual ferment of the eighteenth century, but they don't exactly constitute a burgeoning enlightenment. Fiter i Rossell was, after all, the Bishop of Urgell's representative. There were only three copies of his book, all of which were kept securely locked away, to be consulted solely by the episcopal staff and members of parliament. Its purpose was conservative rather than revolutionary. And Puig's avowed intent was to continue the work of his predecessor.

Recognition by Napoleon coincided with the first tentative **discovery of Andorra by the outside world**. Foreign travellers came to visit, notably the great Pyrenean explorer, Henry Russell, books and pamphlets appeared describing the principality, and it was even celebrated in music, the Paris opera performing Halevy's La Val d'Andorre in 1848, while Gaztambide's operetta, El Valle de Andorra, was staged in Madrid in 1852. Not that this had any great impact on the Andorrans, who continued to live much as their ancestors had done, residing in isolated communities controlled by a conservative patriarchy, surviving from livestock, logging and subsistence agriculture. Government gradually became more representative with more power devolved to the *Consell* and a ripple of the industrial revolution resulted in the development of small textile and iron industries, but the changes were so modest an Andorran resurrected from the fifteenth century wouldn't have been unduly fazed by the displacement. Frugality and conformity remained the norms.

Tobacco, at the heart of Canillo

The first attempt to introduce tourism and, by association, the modern world, came in the 1830s when a French entrepreneur suggested opening an Andorran **casino**, but seeing as how casinos aren't exactly conducive to frugality and conformity, the project was fiercely resisted by the majority of the principality's patriarchs. On the whole, Andorrans still mistrusted foreign influence, preferring foreign crops instead, so they rejected the casino and planted **tobacco**, breaking with the long established traditions of subsistence farming, and embarking on what is for many the most engaging period of their history (and certainly the most productive as far as walkers are concerned), **smuggling**. This was perhaps the first genuine seed of change in 500 years. Andorra turned to monocrop agriculture and the advantages of a duty-free economy began to accrue for the first time.

One may find it hard to square the traditional values with a contraband culture, but bear in mind that this was not smuggling by a few buccaneering mavericks working outside the law; everybody did it, so even if the virtue of frugality was diminished, conformity still prevailed. The *contrabandistas* were not professional smugglers but farmers and shepherds like everybody else who just happened to walk over the mountain once in a while with thirty or forty kilos of tobacco strapped to their back. Nonetheless, that did not prevent them becoming folkloric heroes and tales of *paquetaires* as they were called were recounted round winter fires, revelling in the way they pitted their wits against the *carabiners,* slipping over the border on inky black nights following paths they could almost literally walk blindfolded. A favourite place was **Portella Blanca** (south of **Pas de la Casa**) where one step this way or that would take you into or out of France, Andorra or Spain at will. This smuggling culture is most famous in Andorra, but in fact it was customary throughout the Pyrenees, where villages on either side of the frontier would work together and intermarry, often having more in common with their French or Spanish counterparts than with their countrymen down on the plain. There are places in the Pyrenees where you will see twenty banks for a population of 2000 and be proudly told it was a necessary measure in view of all the money the village made from smuggling, and one can still meet nostalgic septuagenarians happy to entertain visitors with tales of their adolescent adventures as smugglers.

At the same time that smuggling was both engaging the Andorran population with the outside world and laying the seeds for future wealth, debates about whether the principality should profit from its privileged position by becoming a centre of **gambling** continued to disrupt the tranquility of local politics. The controversy may seem trivial, but gambling was a touchstone issue in the evolving political life of Andorra, aligning reformists against conservatives. There were frequent attempts to start casinos and it's from the first proposal in the 1830s' that Andorra's rigid, patriarchal society in which there was no room for dissent from the community, began to fray at the edges.

To the extent that Andorra did not become another Monte Carlo, the conservatives, supported by the Bishop, won, but only at a cost, first accepting partial reforms to the suffrage and increased representation on the administrative *Consell General*, second, so alienating a large portion of the population that the people were ripe for one of the principality's most extraordinary political upheavals, and surely one that would have been better known had Europe not been preoccupied at the time with its own, considerably more serious and sanguinary conflicts.

Once the second road was complete, Andorra was inevitably engaged with the wider world and though the rude life of the herdsman and the romantic life of the *paquetaire* were to continue, modernity was ready to make it's entry and deal the death blow to conformity, which it did in the shape of **Boris Skossyreff**, a White Russian adventurer who'd been knocking about Europe since fleeing the October revolution in his homeland. Boris was not a man of modest ambitions and, in 1934, came remarkably close to persuading both the *Consell* and ordinary Andorrans that there was no room for such an archaic residue of feudalism as a principality in the 'modern' world, that it was an outrageous anomaly in the 'modern' world, that this was an antiquated, outdated, outmoded, thoroughly obsolete way of running one's affairs in the 'modern' world, and that what they really needed in order to bring themselves into the 'modern' world, was to take matters into their own hands and seize the day and be masters of their own destiny, like all the really 'modern' states did, and put aside all this antediluvian feudalistic nonsense and declare their independence and choose a thoroughly up-to-date, state-of-the-art, go-ahead, forward-thinking and, er, 'modern' *king*. Like Boris, for instance. And to show that he was no slouch at this king business, Boris offered them a small token of his aptitude and declared war on the Bishop of Urgell! Reminiscent of an Ealing Comedy, this was in some ways the last flowering of the old Andorra, the landlocked, romantic, isolated state that went its own way because nobody much cared where it went. Except now somebody did care.

For nine days, Boris held court in the Hotel Valira des Escaldes, distributing sweets to the children, more potent stimulants to their parents, and issuing the odd 'modernizing' edict. Sadly, the co-princes didn't see the funny side of this. The Bishop wasn't in the least bit happy about being the object of a declaration of war and, in view of the general political climate in Europe, the French were understandably sensitive to any hint of autarchy, especially since Boris had also declared himself regent for the King of France. The Bishop sent in the *guardia civil*, the French sent in the *gendarmes* (an invasion greatly facilitated by the new roads) and the brief but glorious regal career of Boris I, 'By Grace of God Our Father, Supreme Sovereign Prince of Andorra, Lieutenant-General of its Armies, Baron of Skossyreff, Count of Orange and Defender of the Faith', came to an untimely end. Hustled off to Barcelona, he was tried and deported to Portugal, after which little is known of him. In 1937, he was arrested once again, this time in Aix-en-Provence. The French expelled him to Holland, the Dutch expelled him to England, and he was never heard from again. His legacy? It was suddenly decided that universal (rather than householder) male suffrage was essential if people weren't to express their frustrated political energies supporting another thoroughly modern, thoroughly foreign king.

In the sixteenth century, the Huguenots got cold-shouldered when they rolled up in Andorra hoping for a welcome, but three hundred years' later, the principality' neutrality had turned it into a haven for **refugees**. Perhaps encouraged by the fact that many of those fleeing the Carlist Wars came from Catalonia, with which it had many cultural affinities, Andorra became known as a place of escape, a reputation subsequently confirmed during the Spanish Civil War and World War II. In both conflicts, it sheltered fugitives of various political persuasions and, despite territorial incursions from both Spain and Occupied France, managed to avoid conflict and maintain its neutrality. Curiously enough though, at the same time as refugees were flooding into Andorra, there was an exodus of Andorran nationals, largely economic migrants, many of whom settled in the Perpignan region.

In a **postwar** Europe hungry for pleasure and pushing the boundaries of what consumer items were considered essential, the newly accessible, tax-free principality was finally swept into the modern world and, after centuries outside the capitalist loop, the Andorrans set about catching up with a vengeance, turning their tiny nation into a glittering shop window, enticing their war weary neighbours to Spend! Spend! Spend! Within the space of a single generation, a community of subsistence farmers, herdsmen and packmen was transformed by commerce, legal and otherwise, into one of the world's richest states, with a per capita income higher than Japan's. The **commercial boom** of the fifties was augmented by the growing popularity of skiing through the sixties and seventies, and has continued through the last thirty years, despite the superfluity of ski-stations in Europe and the increasing competitiveness of prices across the borders in Spain and France, thanks to the growth of alternative adventure sports and, above all, the rising number of very wealthy people in need of a tax-haven. It's now a purely capitalist country in the sense that virtually nothing is produced and the *legal* economy is based on services, principally tourist and financial.

What Boris would have made of all this is anybody's guess, but to acknowledge the principality' accession to that 'modern' world the would-be king held so dear, in 1993 a modern **parliamentary democracy** was finally established and the function of the co-princes in Andorran affairs reduced to a ceremonial role. To celebrate their accession to the modern world, the Andorran government paid their UN dues on time, in full, plus a little bit more - a sufficiently rare and quixotic gesture in the history of the United Nations as to suggest something of the old, romantic Andorra persists to this day.

The suspicion that old habits die hard is confirmed by an anecdote I read in a Catalan newspaper several years ago. The basic facts are true, though whether the anecdotal slant is anything other than apocryphal, I don't know - nor do I care, as it's too good a story to ignore. In view of its fiscal status, Andorra has become an extremely lucrative market for the international **tobacco** giants, so when the government suggested anyone wanting to sell cigarettes in the principality had to buy the country's tobacco crop (around 650 tons a year), the multinationals were only too ready to oblige. But once the crop was harvested, it was discovered that the dark Andorran tobacco (smokers not too concerned about the back of their heads can still buy Andorran cigars, largely made for local consumption) was not suitable for the more popular Virginia brands, and the companies had a lot of surplus tobacco on their hands. At which point the Andorrans stepped forward, murmuring commiseration and consolation, and pointed out that they just *happened* to have installed an incinerator down the road and for a small consideration… Whether the sequence of events transpired in precisely this way, I have no idea, but it's difficult to resist the conclusion that a people weaned on smuggling lore could overlook such a perfect scam. I suspect it's a denouement that would have gratified Boris.

Quo vadis? How the country is to develop in the future is not, at least to the casual visitor, at all evident. Judging by the queues of cars climbing to **Pas de la Casa** on a late summer's day, the shopping spree hasn't finished and somebody must be doing well out of the principality's fiscal status. Who, though, is open to question, as anecdotal evidence suggests a decline in conventional summer tourism is hurting hoteliers and restaurateurs, while the cheaper ski-resorts now being promoted in Eastern Europe are gradually leaching away the winter clientele that has been so important for the last three decades. Meanwhile, Andorra's other traditional activity has taken a darker turn.

Nowadays, Andorra imports around 3000 tons of loose tobacco and 2000 tons of ready made cigarettes every year, which (if my back-of-an-envelope calculations are to be trusted) works out at something in the order of a 20-a-day habit for every man, woman and child in the principality. Even allowing for legitimate exports and the duty-free allowance accorded to daytrippers, it's estimated that 60 million contraband cigarettes cross the borders every year. Sixty million cigarettes are not shifted by a handful of solitary backpackers wheezing their way over the mountains. Sad to say, like everything else, Andorran smuggling has become altogether too lucrative to be left to a few peasant-farmers and is now a more grimly professional business, moving Spanish and French customs officers to mutter darkly about *mafias* organizing the illicit trade. The fear for the Andorran government must be that the economy becomes totally addicted to tobacco, hence my qualification above concerning 'the *legal* economy'. As every smoker knows, an addiction to tobacco generally doesn't endear you to your neighbours, and the Spanish and French governments are already complaining about the enclave's anti-social habit. Add to that the inevitable decline in tobacco sales in the coming decades and the propensity of organized crime to diversify, and you have what seems, in potential at least, to be a rather alarming situation.

One would hope that the efforts made to promote alternative forms of adventure tourism will have some success and the tremendous work done already to make the country rambler-friendly will continue. But again a note of caution must be sounded. What visitors to Andorra complain about most frequently is the apparently anarchic building that has taken place. This anarchy was not merely apparent as until recently there were no building regulations at all in Andorra. You just applied for your permit and stuck up what you wanted. Currently there's a moratorium on new building while the government set up a conventional zoning system to be regulated by each town hall, but since everyone knew this was imminent, promoters provisioned themselves with enough permits to keep themselves busy for the next couple of years, and the building continues apace. Hopefully though, once the new planning departments are set up, the local authorities will be sufficiently mindful of what they have inherited in terms of natural beauty to avoid further blighting it with the frequently ugly blocks of stone-clad flats that have evolved from what was once a harmonious and coherent tradition of domestic architecture. Constructing countless apartments will serve no purpose whatsoever if the buildings spoil the beauty that attracts visitors in the first place and consequently remain empty.

The other common complaint concerns the concentration of cars. A good proportion of those 12 million visitors are bussed in, but enough drive to make traffic a major headache, notably at the points of entry and in **Andorra La Vella**. And even without the visitors, the locals own over 60,000 cars, virtually one for every man, woman and child in the principality. This is undoubtedly a problem that requires urgent attention, but one sometimes wonders just what sort of attention it's receiving. A recent and entirely laudable car-sharing scheme, was greeted with what appeared to be widespread if good-natured derision. Meanwhile, I have heard talk of plans to build a superhighway linking France and Spain via Andorra. If this is so and they opt for the costly solution of tunnels, it might well be the saving of the principality. If, on the other hand, as I have also heard suggested, they choose the mind-bendingly barmy option of building a surface motorway along one of the valleys, the consequences hardly bear thinking about. A large part of the principality would be reduced to a motorway service station - admittedly one in a superb location, but still a service-station rather than a country. Surely nobody could be *that* stupid?

What will come of all this is anybody's guess. The government seem to have good intentions for breaking a tobacco habit that has developed over the last 150 years and nurturing in its place a viable and sustainable service-based economy that doesn't require choking the valleys with tarmac and tower-blocks. Whether good intentions will be enough in the face of that most pernicious of drugs (I'm talking about money here) remains to be seen. In the meantime, all I can advise is, get those boots on and enjoy what is one of the world's great walking destinations.

WALKING IN ANDORRA

The present publication is based around half-day and day-long excursions, but the quality and number of **refuges** in the principality, nearly all of which are free, make longer walks very tempting indeed. There are 27 refuges equipped with steel bunks, tables and benches, a fireplace, basic medical kit, an outside spring and a supply of firewood. More importantly, they are regularly cleaned and have a helicopter rubbish collection, a great service if you've ever tried to exhume some of the Pyrenees other unmanned refuges from the mounds of litter in which they're interred. In most cases, there is a section reserved for shepherds, which is kept locked in their absence, but the public part is open all year round. To make use of this superb facility, I have included two overnight walks (see Walks 21 & 30), but for anyone with a little high mountain expertise, numerous other itineraries can be adapted into longer walks. If you remain resistant to the appeals of overnight walks, do not simply dismiss these itineraries as numerous classic linear ascents appear within the longer walks as short versions.

The other significant aspect of the walking infrastructure are the **paths**. This may seem blindingly obvious in a book about walking, but the range and quality of Andorran paths are quite exceptional. Trailblazed by herdsmen, smugglers, horses and cows, these paths are now clearly signposted and well waymarked, and are maintained not by the vagaries of passing walkers, but systematically by teams of school-children and students working under the supervision of a mountain guide during the holidays.

If you see a signposted itinerary not featured in this book, you can set off confident that it won't simply disappear in the mountains. Even more impressive, waymarks on routes subsequently considered too dangerous for the average leisure walker are effaced with grey paint, rather than simply left to fade of their own accord.

The third distinctive feature of walking in Andorra is **water**. The principality has 59 lakes ('the land of a thousand lakes' boast is poetic license (SP?), though the degree of license is very marginal since it's virtually impossible to walk in Andorra for more than an hour or two without stumbling across a lake), the largest being **Estany de Juclar** (21 hectares) (Walk 19), other notable lakes including the **Estanys de Tristaina** (Walk 1), **de les Truites** (Walk 7), **Forcats** (Walk 8), **Angonella** (Walk 10), **Esbalçat** (Walk 13), **Vall del Riu** (Walk 16), **Salamandres** (Walk 18), **Siscaró** (Walk 20), **Cabana Sorda** (Walk 21), **Pessons** (Walk 22), **Ensagents** (Walk 26), and **l'Illa** (Walk 30).

WHO'S IT FOR?

Inevitably, given the terrain, the majority of walkers attracted to Andorra will be experienced walkers accustomed to long-distance hiking, but this is by no means an exclusive profile.

Canillo cable car, Casamanya prominent

High mountains don't automatically call for high levels of testosterone, there are plenty of walks suitable for adventurous leisure walkers who don't necessarily gauge satisfaction by fatigue, cable-cars that operate during the summer (see Appendix D) give the opportunity of doing linear descents, and there are enough easy walks suitable for energetic families to make Andorra an ideal destination for walkers of all ages and capacities.

I have resisted the temptation to just keep on climbing and have included several short excursions suitable for non-walkers anxious to escape the tawdry mall-mentality of the major towns (see Walks 9, 23, 24 & 27), while nearly all the itineraries, however superficially long or demanding, feature strolls and/or short versions designed to maximize their utility. That said, beware of local publications that airily dismiss a 1300-metre climb as an 'easy, level walk' (sic). These are mountains. They do tend to go up.

WHEN TO GO

Despite falling within the climatic area loosely defined as 'Mediterranean', Andorra is obviously not the sort of place one visits with a view to wafting about on balmy palm-lined promenades. There are various formulas for quantifying the degree to which climate is modified by height, the most famous equating 150 metres altitude with a temperature drop of 1° or, alternatively, 100 metres up with 100 km north, which would pitch Andorra somewhere between Belgium and Greenland, a fact that's worth remembering when planning your trip. Whatever time of year you go, temperatures vary greatly according to altitude, a difference that is compounded at night. If you intend sleeping out, either bivouacking, camping or even staying in refuges, a good sleeping bag is essential (see Equipment and the section on Overnighters below).

Although there are walks that can be done in Andorra throughout the year (the first snowfall is generally in December though it can come as early as September), the rambling season is basically spring through to autumn, always bearing in mind that it can snow as late as May (which I'm also told is the rainiest month) and the high peaks can still be under snow in June. Daytime temperatures during summer average 23°C (75°F) night-time 15-20°C (59-68°F) - though obviously, temperatures will be less in the high mountains. June, early July and September are perhaps **the best months for walking**, if only because July and August are the Spanish and French holiday months (see note on arriving by car in the next section), when traffic into the principality can be very heavy. For flora, early to mid-summer is best. For photographers, I'd recommend September, when the crisp, autumnal light is quite exceptional.

GETTING THERE, GETTING ABOUT, GETTING A BED

Flights: given its geography, Andorra has no airport, though there is a project to develop one at **La Seu d'Urgell**, due to open in 2006. At present, Easyjet (www.easyjet.com) serves Barcelona, FLYbe (www.flybe.com) Toulouse, and Ryan Air (www.ryanair.com) Carcassone, Perpignan and Girona, all within ready striking distance of the principality. FLYbe have their own bus link with Andorra and some hotels (notably the **Alba** in **El Tarter** - see Appendix A) arrange their own pick-up service.

Train: again, a non-starter inside the principality. The nearest station on the Spanish side, is Puigcerda and on the French side La Tour de Carol. Both are connected to Andorra by a bus service.

Coaches: Eurolines (www.eurolines.com) run direct buses between London and **Andorra La Vella**.

Car: if you have the time, taking a ferry and driving is the most agreeable option. The main motorway routes **through France** are fairly obvious, but taking the national and departmental roads is infinitely more pleasurable and only marginally longer (2-3 days rather than 1-2). One attractive route might be to follow the national roads from Caen through Laval, Angers, and Poitiers to Angoulê then take the departmental roads cross country through Pé to Montauban, after which national roads lead round Toulouse and through Foix and Tarascon to **Pas de la Casa**. Going further east, from Carcassone there is a superb approach through impressive gorges via the D117/D118 and Mont-Louis (see note on maps in ' Stuff" below). Alternatively, there are frequently special deals on the ferry to Bilbao, from where one could cross the Basque country and Navarra via Pamplona, then pick up the N260 to reach Andorra via **La Seu d'Urgell**.

If you arrive by car, try and avoid driving into the principality at weekends or high days and holy days - notably The Assumption, when everyone else in France, not just the Virgin, seems to feel it's time to be ascending heavenward. Even on an ordinary weekday in Summer, cross the border early in the morning or late in the afternoon if you can. The spectacle of cars queuing to get in can be quite surreal at times, especially since once you're in the principality and up in the mountains, everyone seems to have disappeared, as if the place is a black hole swallowing up motorists. Once *in situ*, cross **Andorra La Vella** as infrequently as possible.

Hire cars: all the regular companies are represented at the main airports, though there is the slightly unusual option once in Andorra of hiring a 4WD vehicle, which is worth considering since normal cars are barred from most of the dirt tracks.

Local buses: there are eight bus lines. Those linking **Andorra la Vella with Escaldes-Engordany**, **Encamp**, **Canillo** and **La Massana**, offer a virtually continuous service from 7 a.m to 9 p.m.. Beyond **La Massana** the service is much more limited. If you're relying on the buses, most itineraries will have to be extended by one of the many signposted paths starting in the towns.

For up-to-date **information on transport** into and around the principality, see the transport section on www.turisme.ad.

Accommodation (also see Appendix A):

Choosing a base: as a first stop, I would recommend one of the western towns, particularly **Pal**, **Ordino**, **Llorts** or **El Serrat**. However, if you want to see every corner of the principality, you should consider moving around and having at least two different bases, as you won't want to be ploughing across **Andorra La Vella** to reach the start of a walk. For the **La Valira d'Orient** valley and the southern massif, **Canillo** is a suitable choice. **Arinsal**, **El Tarter** and **Soldeu** are towns where English tourists tend to congregate, and as such are to be sought out or avoided according to temperament. As for **Pas de la Casa**, what can one say? It's a very nice place for French shoppers. If you feel like passing yourself off as a French shopper, all well and good. Otherwise, the only classic rambling itinerary in the vicinity is **Pic Negre d'Envalira** and even that is marred by ski-pistes.

There are 30,000 **hotel** beds in Andorra, so you should be able to get something to suit your pocket. There is no problem finding accommodation on arrival.

Alternatively, **Aparthotels** are a good option, since they generally combine the virtues of affordable luxury with money-saving self-catering.

Campsites are plentiful. Those in the main valley are either costly or noisy or both, but once you branch off into the affluent valleys most are idyllic and reasonably priced.

There are twenty-six free **refuges** in Andorra, each within a day's walk of its neighbour, so anybody willing to carry a heavy pack can have a very cheap walking holiday indeed.

THE WALKS

We've aimed to provide a wide **range of walks** from short strolls suitable for visitors of all ages and aptitudes, to off-path high-mountain itineraries only recommended for experienced walkers. Within each regional section the first walk is a relatively easy outing suitable for the first day. The remaining itineraries are arranged according to a roughly geographical logic, not length or difficulty.

Timings are all 'pure' timings excluding snacking, snapping and simply standing still staring. It is highly unlikely you will complete any of these walks in exactly the time specified. Allow <u>at least</u> 15 minutes per walking hour for resting, pathfinding and enjoying the views. Any walk timed at 2h30+ implies taking food, rather than planning to knock it off in the morning then go to the restaurant. Before you tackle the longer routes, time yourself against one of our shorter itineraries, then curse me for a slowcoach or a racing maniac as seems appropriate. All global timings include the return unless otherwise specified.

Exertion ratings are generally high since that's the nature of the landscape, but there should be enough strolls and short versions to satisfy less energetic walkers.

Several classic routes have been incorporated into the **overnight itineraries** making use of Andorra's magnificent network of refuges and other overnight possibilities have been suggested in the text. Short versions suggest ways in which these longer itineraries can be broken up, but I recommend coming equipped for at least one night out in a refuge. Andorra's so steep that after a few days of walking one tends to feel a bit grand-old-duke-of-yorkish and begin wondering why you're marching up the hill and down again everyday. The refuges give you the opportunity to enjoy the fruits of your efforts at greater leisure.

As indicated above, the **paths** are clear or are regularly cleared, well signposted and excellently waymarked. Most **itineraries follow yellow dots** and arrows, though there are occasional old red waymarks, too. Where a local itinerary coincides with a long-distance path, waymarks for the latter generally take precedence.

There are four principal **long distance footpaths**: the **GR7** descends via Andorra to Southern Spain; the **GR11** runs the length of the Pyrenees from the Atlantic to the Mediterranean and suffers a serious identity crisis in Andorra, splintering into so many versions that, if it was a human being, it would be receiving psychiatric care for a multiple personality disorder; the **GRP** is a horseshoe tour of the principality; and the **HRP** (French) or **ARP** (Spanish) is a tough high mountain traverse crossing the major summits of the entire chain.

The **GRs are waymarked** red-and-white, the **GRP** red-and-yellow. The **HRP/GRP** is only intermittently waymarked (either blue or blue-and-white) and is frequently dangerous, requiring climbing experience and a good head for heights.

The **GR107**, a N-S traverse of the Pyrenees following a route used by Cathar refugees, dips into Andorra very briefly in the south-east near **Portella Blanca d'Andorra**. Old GR waymarks in the Juclar valley maybe left over from an abandoned variant, but new GR waymarks at the **Collada de Juclar** suggest this maybe a variant of the **GR10**, the French equivalent of the **GR11**.

See Appendix C for more **details on Long Distance Footpaths**.

A word about cows. Despite their herd mentality, cows are not the most regimented of animals, especially when left to wander at will in high mountains, where they have a tendency to trace out dozens of parallel paths and half-paths, not all of which lead anywhere. Ermintrude may take the high-path, but Daisy will follow the low path, until Daisy tires of the low path and abruptly joins the high path leaving the low path going nowhere. Many of the walks in this book make use of cow paths. Unless specified in the text, always follow the waymarked path, even if parallel paths appear clearer.

In the **descriptions** I've tried to give enough detail for those who need confirmation they're on the right path, but not so much as to irritate more confidant pathfinders with superfluity. Bear in mind that many of the more rigorous high mountain walks will have comparatively brief descriptions since man's impact on the summits has been minimal and I have no desire to bore you by repeating that we keep on following the same path, so look carefully at waypoint timings. One sentence in the high mountains may cover half-an-hour' walking whereas five minutes on land more set about by people might require an entire paragraph. Conversely, pathless routes in low mountains may give the impression I'm describing every rock, tree and blade of grass. In each case, I've tried to adapt the degree of detail to the particular pathfinding requirements.

For ease of reference, the place names mentioned in a walk are written in **bold** text. 'Inverted commas' indicate names on signposts. *Italics* are used for *discrete Catalán or Spanish words* or very occasionally for emphasis. Consistency rather than deficient vocabulary accounts for all **climbs** being 'gentle', 'steady', or 'steep'.

OVERNIGHTERS

I strongly recommend scheduling at least one 'overnighter' in your holiday. Although this calls for careful planning and means lugging a heavy pack, the rewards are correspondingly great. There's nothing quite like the pervasive sense of well being felt as you sit on the stoop of your refuge, a good fire blazing away within, a glass of whatever you require to hand, watching the darkness descend and knowing the mountain is yours for the night.

A brief glance at the **timings for 'overnighters'** may have you thinking, "The boy's a wimp, I can do that in a day". In some cases, that may well be true. However, that begs the questions of why and whether you would take any pleasure of it. It's worth repeating here that these are 'pure' walking times and, once you've done the walk, I don't think you'll feel you've been cheated by too short a day.

A basic checklist of what to take for overnight halts in a refuge:

- sleeping bag (a lightweight down bag is ample during the summer)
- self-inflating mattress (Thermarest or similar) or traditional camping mattress
- clean socks, pants, T-shirt, long trousers for the evening (the pants do not presuppose some embarrassing accident, but clean clothes after an evening bathe are a real luxury)
- woollen jumper or sweatshirt/fleece and windbreaker (rolled rather than folded to reduce space)
- waterproof cape
- towel (the travel-towels sold in sports shops and which resemble a rather sorry looking synthetic shammy, are ideal - lightweight and very absorbent)
- candle
- pen torch or ultra-lite walkers' head light
- lighter/matches
- camping gas & two lightweight pans (ideally ones that can double as lids for each other)
- Swiss army knife or similar
- cutlery - generally a spoon and knife will be sufficient
- plastic plates
- spare plastic bags (the helicopter rubbish collection is a superb service, but everything should be bagged before being put in the metal

- receptacle)
- tea-bags & sachets of instant coffee (count how many you'll need rather than taking the entire packet)
- soft drinks, either powdered or, if you feel up to carrying the extra weight, an energy drink like Aquarius or Gatorade
- food

Food obviously involves balancing weight against need/greed. As a general rule, tinned/jarred meals are too heavy, although a good *cassoulet* gets even better at altitude. Dried foods like pasta, rice, and lentils (the sort that don't require soaking!) are easier to carry, though beware of pasta if staying above 2000-metres where camping gas stoves tend to reduce it to an inedible chewy mush, an improbable accomplishment but distressingly real. Nuts, charcuterie and pâté are a godsend on arrival when all you want is to stuff something in your mouth as rapidly as possible without having to hang around for it to heat up. Powdered soups can seem pretty villainous down on the plains, but something hot however chemically compromised is extraordinarily restorative at altitude after a hard day's walking. Biscuits and dried fruit add the necessary sweetness, while a bottle of whatever you fancy maybe wholly unjustifiable in nutritional terms but is the crowning glory in psychological terms.

And don't forget breakfast! Butter's not practical, but a hard cheese goes well with your individual portions of jam, honey etc. Fresh fruit is heavy, but incomparably refreshing at the right moment. After you've carefully calculated precisely what you'll need, add another sachet of soup and some extra bread, just in case you find you have to spend another night in the refuge.

Finally, if you really want to push the boat out, remember that most refuges will have a fireplace and an old grill lurking about in the corner. You probably don't want to delve too deeply into the hygiene aspect of this, but a couple of chops or a tofu-burger can be very welcome.

After all the eating, you won't want to be left with a lot of greasy plates, so take a tiny amount of washing up liquid (the mini-shampoo bottles from hotel bedrooms are an ideal container).

Finally, rather than just bundling everything piecemeal into your rucksack, use stuff-bags (plastic bags will do), load heavier things on top, and adjust the shoulder-straps so you can make proper use of the hip-belt. And don't forget, however tired you may be, that the saw, dustpan and brush are not merely decorative. Leave the refuge and surrounding land as you would like to find it. Toilet paper should be burned or buried, depending on the terrain. And shut the refuge door! Cows can be remarkably inquisitive and all warm-blooded creatures like to get out of the rain. You'd be amazed how many people leave the door open, but browsing through the visitors' books, you soon get the picture. Some of the cleaning teams' comments are quite bitter.

EQUIPMENT & SAFETY

The poet, priest and walker Jacint Verdaguer visited Andorra in 1880 and is said to have climbed several high mountains wearing a cassock and carrying an umbrella and a suitcase. But then nineteenth century romantics did a lot of things that are no longer recommended. Walking in high mountains requires proper equipment. This does not necessarily mean you have to visit specialist shops and spend large sums of money on the latest fad or a lot of costly gear, though it must be said that there is generally a good reason beyond mere labelling why outdoor clothing is so pricey.

Walking is one of the world's most democratic leisure activities, so don't let anyone tell you can't walk without this, that or the other. Nonetheless, many of these walks cover rough, remote ground, where conditions can change rapidly. For most of the walks, good boots with rigid or semi-rigid soles and high ankle support are recommended. And no matter how fine the weather, you should always take a warm-top, some form of waterproof, and emergency rations. See Discovery Walking Guides' standard recommendations for equipment on Page 40.

Andorra has an excellent recorded **weather forecast** which should always be consulted before venturing into the more exposed heights. Unfortunately, it doesn't exist in English, so if you don't speak Spanish, French or Catalán, you will have to ask in the tourist office. Remember that the 5 p.m. storm is as much a ritual in the Pyrenees as a cup of tea in England. Andorra doesn't suffer as badly as elsewhere, but locals say late August is the most tempestuous period.

The **weather forecast numbers** are:
>French   848 853
>Spanish   848 852
>Catalán   858 851

Basic rules:

. always walk in company
. always tell someone where you're going
. assess walks according to what you know of your own capacities
. in deteriorating conditions, turn back sooner rather than later; this is walking for pleasure, you've got nothing to prove.
. aim to be off peaks and crests before 4 p.m., which is when storms tend to start brewing

Special circumstances:

If you happen to be walking on **snow** during the Summer, bear in mind that an ice-crusted surface which is merely wearisome on the way up, is absolutely lethal on the way down.

If not navigating with GPS, beware of pushing on to the end in **poor visibility**. Even the simplest paths can be confusing when walked in reverse, blinded by cloud or mist.

If you do get into difficulty try to reach shelter (don't forget the refuges and their medical kits) and keep warm.

Ideally (though rarely a practical proposition since most people walk in pairs), **in case of injury**, one person should stay with the injured party and two people should go for help. See Appendix A for **emergency telephone numbers**.

If trying to attract the attention of rescue service, the conventional **distress signs** are as follows:

- both arms raised to form a V - "Yes, I need help"
- left arm raised, right arm down to form a diagonal - "No, I don't need help"
- I've never quite understood what you're meant to do if you've broken your right arm, but those are the conventions

Legally though rarely in practice, walkers and climbers who get into difficulty may be liable for the **cost of being rescued** unless they belong to an outdoor organization that indemnifies members against such eventualities.

Bear in mind that, though temperatures may be relatively mild, **insolation** is high, so suncream, lip-salve and after-sun cream are essential.

Sunglasses are essential in high mountains during bright weather, but they do distort vision and are best removed during a difficult descent where you have to check every step you take.

Swimming in mountain torrents is irresistible, but must sometimes be resisted. Beware of slippery rocks, always test the current before plunging in, and never venture into a torrent after heavy rainfall.

Finally, don't come over all Promethean and start defying the presiding deities during **electrical storms**. Given the high iron content in these mountains, standing on a summit in a storm is tantamount to climbing a church steeple, wrapping yourself round the weather vane, and waving a lightning-rod at the skies, roundly declaring God's illegitimacy. Every year people are struck by lightning in the Pyrenees, even experienced mountain dwellers like shepherds, often fatally. If you happen to get caught in a bad electrical storm, lay flat and let it pass. Beware of sheltering in the lee of large, solitary rocks.

Breaking the rules: all of the above have to be pointed out in a responsible publication. But don't let yourself be paralyzed by alarm. These risks are on the whole potential and the mountains are generally benign. And to be honest, at one time or another for one reason or another, not always entirely credible or sensible, I've broken every rule in the book - and I'm still standing!

PROBLEMS

There are no particular man-made problems to trouble the walker in Andorra. Virtually all the pasture and woods are communal property so access is not a problem. Thieves are swiftly ejected and I haven't heard of anyone having their car broken into.

FLORA, FAUNA & THE ENVIRONMENT

Gentian

There are 1300 **plant species** in Andorra and, to be honest, they're so lovely taxonomy seems a tiresome waste of time, when all you want to do is sit back and marvel. Among the plants we spotted and felt confident enough to name without coming over like a mad-scientist with a Linnaeus-complex were anemones, iris, willowherb, mallow, orchids, cyclamen, harebell, clustered bellflowers, various types of saxifrage (including *saxifraga umbrosa*, which in French goes under the engaging name of Painters' Despair!), oregano, liquorice (the roots are remarkably tasty), eglantine, and rhododendron.

Anyone who feels an urge to go back to the days of hunter-gathering will be gladdened by the **wild fruit**, mainly raspberry and strawberry, but also elderberry, bilberry and redcurrant. As for **trees**, up to 1500 metres one finds poplar, hazelnut, oak, birch and beech. From 1500 to 1800 metres fir and scots pine, and beyond that pine and more pine and more pine.

Above the treeline, standard alpine shrubbery prevails, particularly myrtle and the ubiquitous rhododendron, plus the classic high-mountain flowers such as gentian, mountain tobacco, and poet's narcissus or pheasant's eye, which has been adopted as Andorra' national flower, the two colours standing for the co-princes, the six petals representing the principality' six original parishes (the seventh is a recent addition). The variety of grasses in the high pasture and alongside woodland paths simply beggars belief.

Birds are equally various, including dippers, warblers, White-Winged Sparrow, chaffinch, woodcock, woodpeckers, crossbills, rooks, cuckoos, partridge, capercailzie, ptarmigan, falcons, kites, Golden Eagles, and vultures, notably the Great Bearded Vulture or lammergeier (etymologically 'vultures' but more candidly described by the graphic Spanish name *quebrantahuesos* or 'bone-breakers'). We also saw a tame jay at the Ansalonga campsite and three magnificent pheasants at the Borda de la Coruvilla above Arinsal. Perhaps the most emblematic bird is the capercailzie (*gall* in Catalán, *urogallo* in Spanish, *grand tetras* in French), though it's highly unlikely you will see one.

Apart from the bubbling carpet of grasshoppers frequently encountered at altitude (their babies clinging to their backs in Autumn), the most remarkable **insects** in Andorra are the **butterflies**, which are abundant, brilliant and beautiful. Unfortunately, the multilingual guide the Andorran government produced to butterflies is now out of print and, so far as we were able to ascertain, unavailable, so amateur entomologists should see what general guides they can find in the UK bookshops.

As for **reptiles**, paths on the flanks of valleys are often alive with lizards, the rivers are chock-a-block with remarkably tame frogs, and there is one lake known for its salamander population (see Walk 18). I have seen one publication that reproduced a photo of a rather poorly looking viper, but apart from that, the nearest I came to a snake was a maybe-snake tail disappearing into the undergrowth.

Living in a culture where hunting is not so much a sport as a moral obligation (I know of one local man on the French side of the border who feels bound to take his dog and gun 'out for a walk' every weekend with no very great hope or apparent interest in killing anything), **mammals** tend to be rather discreet, but we saw plenty of traces of wild boar, several isard (the Pyrenean ibex), two marten (one at the head of the **Ransol Valley**, the other above the **Estanys de Tristaina**), half-a-dozen red squirrels, twice as many marmot, and a couple of exquisitely pretty deer (again in the **Ransol Valley** and on the climb from **Grau Roig** to **Circ del Pessons**). There are also said to be otters, doubtless having a whale of a time with all the trout the government kindly put in the rivers for the fee-paying fishermen.

It's worth noting here that the Andorran disregard for frontiers has found its latest articulation in **hunting**. Having shot most of their own isard, the Andorrans are now straying across the borders into Spain and France where quotas, reserves and voluntary abstention have saved isard from near extinction and in some places seen their numbers multiply by twenty in half as many years. The Andorrans were delighted! So delighted, the French and Spanish authorities have recently (September 2004) felt compelled to set up, with the express and sole intent of keeping Andorran hunters at home, a brigade of forest rangers, equipped with 4WD vehicles, helicopters and, apparently, bulletproof jackets! It would seem that one crosses an Andorran hunter at one's peril.

Two animals with which man has had an intimate relationship, the one a measure of manhood, the other a measure of wealth, have been apotheosized in folkloric dances. The ***Ball de l'Ossa*** or Bear's Dance is a ritual repeated in one form or another throughout the Pyrenees, where the bear, being the only other known plantigrade and a pretty powerful one at that, was regarded with considerable ambivalence. Taking the form of a sort of fancy-dress Feast of Fools, bear dances were a night of licensed mayhem in which the bear (played by one of the villages more high-spirited youths) functioned as a Lord of Misrule, fomenting all manner of thrilling mischief until he got his comeuppance, the hunters of the village rescuing a young maiden from his predatory-cum-amatory attentions - the sexual overtones are explicit in many Pyrenean myths. Similarly, the ***Contrapà de Bou*** celebrated tauromachy, once again featuring a bull that got ideas above its station and came to a sorry end as a result.

Despite the repopulation programme in France, I haven' heard of anyone seeing a bear in Andorra, but you will come across cattle and the odd bull, some of fearsome dimensions and lively temperament. Traditional anxieties about a rampant nature can be safely put to one side, but the usual precautions should be taken: avoid disturbing livestock and remember that, in a neat reversal of mankind's particular propensities, a solitary bull is more easily agitated, and therefore more dangerous, than one in a herd. You may also wish to avoid walking in the vicinity of **Fontargent**, **Envalira** and **Engolasters** on the night of San Juan, when witches are said to indulge in wild orgies and the devil pops up to whisk away solitary walkers to an unspecified but doubtless undesirable fate.

Putting aside the menace of things wild and woolly, it is mankind as usual that has had the most detrimental effect on his **environment**. The traditional tendency to cluster in mutually supporting hamlets and the inevitable crowding of modern housing into the valleys means that the effects of building, though often lamentable, are concentrated and have had little impact on the mountains themselves. Alas, the same cannot be said for sporting activity. Cable cars are occasionally a boon to the lazy walker, but by God, we pay for it with the scars of ski-pistes and chair-lifts scoured across the landscape, while the long-term costs of deforestation may prove even dearer. Indeed, some people have already come close to paying the ultimate price for Andorra's development.

In the early nineties, **Arinsal** was hit by an avalanche. The story goes that there had been a relatively light snowfall followed by high winds, a combination the warden of **Coma Pedrosa Refuge** recognized as potentially dangerous. Expressing her fears to the authorities, she was met with a large measure of inertia, which only turned to alarm when she demanded an affidavit admitting that her warning had been ignored. All of a sudden, it was "Hey-ho! Culpability looms?" and the powers-that-be promptly set about evacuating some 3000 people. An hour-and-a-half after the evacuation was complete, the avalanche struck. No one was injured.

Despite that alarming story, the aesthetic and physical damage is nothing like as bad as in some places, notably in Spain, where entire mountainsides have been stripped bare and reveal themselves in summer as a grey mess of gravel and rock. At least in Andorra grass has been sown to ameliorate the worst results of the winter season. And to be fair, I would guess that between fifty and seventy-five per cent of Andorra's mountains remain intact and untouched by anything more exploitative than the annual transhumance, so that the higher valleys, cirques, lakes and peaks make for a striking contrast with the towns and ski-resorts. Moreover, the Andorrans themselves have tired of looking at the bare shale and rock flanking some of their newly widened roads and have begun an extraordinary greening scheme in which helicopters blast bare mountainside with soil and seed, sometimes with a reasonably happy result.

EATING & DRINKING

Unless you fancy a tobacco stew or find yourself befriending someone with a smallholding, good fresh **vegetables** can be hard to come by in Andorra (except in September when delicious surplus garden produce is sold in local shops), though the tomatoes are excellent, as is the fruit, in particular the melons and peaches. Restaurants seem to manage though, as you will find if you order a macè as a starter or a 'salad' (half-a-dozen slices of *charcuterie* to every leaf of lettuce), a vegetable soup (*sopa de verduras*) or *escudella,* a good solid pottage of legumes that will set you back on your feet after a days' hiking. Solidity is, on the whole, a fundamental quality of Andorran cuisine, partly due to the dictates of climate and topography, partly thanks to the migrant workers - you could walk a long way on one of the oval loaves of **bread** baked for the Portuguese, though these aren't available when the migrant workers go home for the August holiday.

The local **beef** (*bou*) is a big, rich meat as befits something that spends the summer rambling round the mountains, and the imported **lamb** (generally chops, *costelles de xai*) is excellent. *El brou* is a **broth** of meat stock with potatoes, cauliflower and chick-peas. *Civets* are marinated **game stews**, generally wild boar, rabbit or venison, but sometimes hare, partridge or, apparently, squirrel. *Botifarra amb seques (*or *mongetas)*, **sausage and beans**, will alarm anybody used to tinned products masquerading under the same name, and delight everyone else. Otherwise, **meats** are mainly grilled, griddled or barbecued, either over an open fire (*a la brasa*) or on a slate (*llosa*, a word my Catalán dictionary translates as a gravestone!), restaurants specializing in this generally identifying themselves by the Spanish name, *parrilla* (lit. grill or gridiron). The French influence, meanwhile, is apparent in more up market restaurants and in some local dishes, such as **duck** (*pato*). **Trout** (*trucha*) is, inevitably, *the* local fish. **Flap mushrooms** (*cè, cep* or *seta*) are found throughout the Pyrenees and regularly appear on Andorran menus.

When it comes to **puddings**, the prospect is not as pleasing as in France nor so dire as in Spain. Unless you're eating in one of the finer restaurants like the **Borda del Horto** (where I know of at least one individual, a man of otherwise temperate habits, who felt compelled to order three distinct sweets in a single sitting), your best bet is the excellent Catalán take on *crème brûlé*, a *Crema Catalána*, always provided it's home-made (*de la casa*).

Obviously, there's enough reasonably priced **wine** to have the best of us meekly sliding under the table every night of the week, though I must say, it wasn't quite as cheap as I had hoped/feared. Naturally, there are no Andorran wines, but one of the best and less internationally known Spanish reds is a **Segre**, a denomination taken from the river that runs through **La Seu d'Urgell**.

There are plenty of **springs** in Andorra, most of excellent quality. *Agua no potable* doesn't necessarily mean undrinkable, but does imply be-it-on-your-head as does *aigua no tractada* - untreated water. Experience suggests the consequences aren't to be regretted. Very occasionally, an overnight stop in the mountains will mean there's no other source than the stream. This is best avoided, but is unlikely to result in anything more serious than a mild case of worms, easily treated with an over-the-counter purgative available at any chemist.

TOURIST STUFF: WHAT TO DO ON A DAY OFF

Ski-centres remain open through the summer and organize a variety of **adventure sports**, including mountain-biking (see Appendix E), climbing (see Appendix F), paragliding, kayaking, horse-riding, quad bikes (if you fancy a flat head), archery, bungee jumping and skydiving. If that sounds altogether too strenuous for a 'day-off', you may care to enquire after **helicopter rides** (see Appendix A), or pamper yourself with a soaking in the ultra-modern **thermal spa** in **Escaldes** (www.caldea.ad). Trout **fishing** provides a compromise between the active and the wholly sedentary, but since this means buying a licence (8 days minimum, ask in any tourist office or ski-resort), you may wish to schedule more than a single day for this. Forty-five of the principality's lakes are restocked with trout every year.

With fifty-five **Romanesque churches** to choose from, the lover of

Santa Coloma

architecture is in for a treat. The oldest, like **Santa Coloma** and **Sant Miquel d'Enclar** (**Andorra la Vella**), date back to the ninth century, but more come from the tenth century (**Sant Romà dels Villars** in **Escaldes-Engordany**, **Sant Cerni de Nagol**, **Sant Romà de Juberri**, and the **Capilla de Sant Mateu** in **Sant Julià de Lòria** while the greatest era was in the eleventh and twelfth centuries (**Sant Miquel d'Engolasters**, **Sant Romà de les Bons** in **Encamp**, **Sant Joan de Caselles** near **Canillo**, **Sant Climent de Pal**, and **Sant Vicenç d' Sant Joan de Caselles** is said to be the best conserved, but **Sant Martí de la Cortinada** retains some of its original frescoes. The other churches are generally decorated with replicas, the originals having been transferred to Barcelona or, in at least one case, Germany! The architectural achievement is all the more remarkable when one considers that at the time these churches were built, the population of Andorra barely exceeded two thousand. The modern age has been less happily productive, though the **Santuario de Meritxell** by Ricardo Bofill is worth a visit.

Museums (www.museus.ad) tend to be very special interest (anyone for Iron? Post? Tobacco? Badges?)* but the summer home of the Areny-Plandolit family in **Ordino** is worth a visit, if only for the garden, and the Escaldes-Engordany museum dedicated to the sculptor Josep Viladomat is also interesting. If you're not sick to death of internal combustion after a couple of trips across **Andorra La Vella**, there's an automobile museum in **Encamp**.

However, if you want something other than nature, your best bet is to combine the architectural visits with a little local history on one of the cultural itineraries detailed in pamphlets available at the tourist offices. As with walking pamphlets (see Bibliography), different places seem to be distributing different booklets with the same name. The best is the newer booklet by Albert Villaró featuring three 'Romanesque Routes', a 'Rural Habitat Route', and 'The Iron Route'.

Duty-free shopping isn't what it was, but alcohol, tobacco and electronic goods are still cheaper than elsewhere, so any topers with a taste for nicotine and gadgetry are in for a good time.

Beyond the borders of Andorra the potential for day-trips and overnight visits is almost infinite, but the following suggestions may help narrow your focus. The easiest and most obvious direction to go for seeing something outside the principality is south, to the historic city of **La Seu d'Urgell** (www.laseu.org/turisme/eng), seat of the episcopal co-prince. It's an attractive, lively city, very Catalán in appearance and temperament, a pleasant place for an afternoon stroll, and a good base for trips into the impressive pre-

---

*Dismissed with the complacence of complete ignorance - they may be a miracle of creative curatorship.

Pyrenean range of Sierra de Cadí.
(see www.spain.info/TourSpain/Destinos/Provincias/Barcelona and click on Parque Natural Cadi-Moixeró)

The road **north** from **Pas de la Casa** is less immediately rewarding, but there are some attractive backroads leading to little known valleys tucked into the mid-range mountains (e.g. the road between Tarascon and St.Girons via Massat). For exploring this corner of France by road, get a copy of the Blay-Foldex 1:500,000 roadmap; the standard Michelin 1:1,000,000 is hopelessly inadequate.

(For highlights of the region, see www.paysdetarascon.com and goeurope.about.com/cs/frame/a/ariege.htm.)

Perhaps the most rewarding direction for excursions out of Andorra is **east** through the Cerdagne (Spanish, Cerdanya) (see www.pyreneesguide.com and www.cerdagne.com), the Pyrenees longest tectonic depression and the sunniest place in France. Politically noteworthy is the Spanish enclave of Llívia, the result of dextrous verbal juggling when the Franco-Spanish border was settled. Sensualists should head for **Dorres** and the immaculately preserved Roman baths, particularly in winter, when the experience of stretching out in a steaming pool in the open air overlooking a snow bound valley is beyond compare. Alternatively, if you prefer a more spacious bathe, the Bains de St. Thomas (www.bains-saint-thomas.com) above **Fontpedrouse** (en route to Perpignan) have a pool of hot spring water large enough to swim in, plus a Jacuzzi corner, a hamam, and masseurs offering various massages, including one specifically designed for walkers. The water is said to be good for your skin; I can't pretend my own looks are any the less battered after the half-dozen visits I've paid over the years, but the experience has always been a great sensual pleasure. The classic Traine Jaune (www.ter-sncf/train-jaune/default.htm) descending the length of the **Têt** valley is popular with sightseers and walkers alike, and is a good basis for a day's outing combining a bit of walking with some culture.

Both **Mont-Louis** (www.mont-louis.net) and **Villefrance de Confluent** (www.villagesdefrance.free.fr/page_villefranche_de_confluent.htm) are attractive tourist destinations enriched by the work of the great French military architect, **Vauban**, a man with the prescience to design forts that would appeal to latter-day holidaymakers as much as they appalled contemporary opponents. And if you have a car, the drive from **Villefranche** to **Mentet** (one of the Pyrenees' great places) is an extraordinary outing in itself, made all the better by the prospect of a grand meal at Odile's **Auberge Bouf'tic** when you get there. Finally, a little way further down, on the edge of the Languedoc-Roussillon plain, is the small city of **Prades**, the heart of one of France's major fruit-producing regions and host to the annual (July-August) Pablo Casals chamber music festival (www.prades-festivals-casals.com).

There are no major roads directly to the **west**, though the drive across the border to **Os de Civís** is a pleasant excursion combined with a sidetrip to the **Santuari de Canòlich**. Otherwise, if you' passing that way, you should visit one of the Pyrenees most celebrated valleys, the **Val d'Aran** (www.aran.org), and/or take a trip on the **Río Noguera Pallaresa** (www.noguerapallaresa.com), where traditional techniques for riding timber downriver have been adapted for the modern sports of rafting (April-August) and the gloriously imbecilic hydrospeed - essentially rafting without the raft. Further west, a little to the north of Huesca, lies the **Sierra Guara**, (www.guara.org) one of the places that pioneered canyoning.

If arriving by plane, **Girona** (www.ajuntament.gi/turisme/index2.html), **Toulouse** (www.ot-toulouse.fr/English) **Carcassone** (www.carcassonne-tourisme.com) and **Perpignan** (www.perpignan-tourisme.com) merit an overnight stop, while **Barcelona** (www.bcn.es/english.htm) calls for a couple of months…or at the very least a long weekend. The fairytale confections of **Gaudi** and the slightly less hallucinatory works of the other great Catalán modernists, **Domènech i Montaner** and **Puig i Cadafalch**, are within comfortable walking distance of one another, while the Romanesque collection at the **Museu d'Art de Catalunya** is as much a miracle of installation as artistry. And, if Andorra proved too peaceable, the waterfront bars and clubs are among the trendiest nightspots in Europe. Finally, for a grand meal before you go, try the **Asador de Aranda** on **Avinguda Tibidabo** (www.asadordearanda.com), where they practice the delightfully deranged policy of charging a set price per head for wine and bread…then just carry on pouring.

If arriving by car, anyone who has the time really ought to do a tour of the **Costa Brava**, (www.costabrava.org) visiting the small resorts near **Palafrugell** (www.palafrugell.net), the **Dali** museum (www.salvador-dali.org/eng/teatre.htm) in **Figueres**, and his old stomping grounds on **Cap Creus** (lookingaround.free.fr/spain/catalunya and www.cbrava.com) where you discover his alleged surrealism was more closely modelled on reality than many a work by superficially more conventional artists. Motorists are also within striking distance of the great **Cathar** redoubts in the **Corbières** (www.languedoc-france.info), and of the French **Côte Vermeille**, notably **Collioure** (www.collioure.com) and the **fauvist** museum dedicated to **Matisse** and **Derain**.

LANGUAGE

Catalán is the official language used in government and by the broadcast media, but most people are trilingual with Spanish and French, and there are many English speakers, too. Spanish is the most widely spoken language and, on the whole, more appreciated, especially in service industries where most of the front line staff are of Spanish origin, but a few words of Catalán in the right place and at the right time, will have Andorran nationals swooning at your feet.

ACKNOWLEGEMENTS

Jeannette, for following me into places she felt she really ought not to; Antoine, for Beethoven's Fifth; Ros & David, for sustained faith and for letting me loose on the high mountains.

LOCATION MAPS

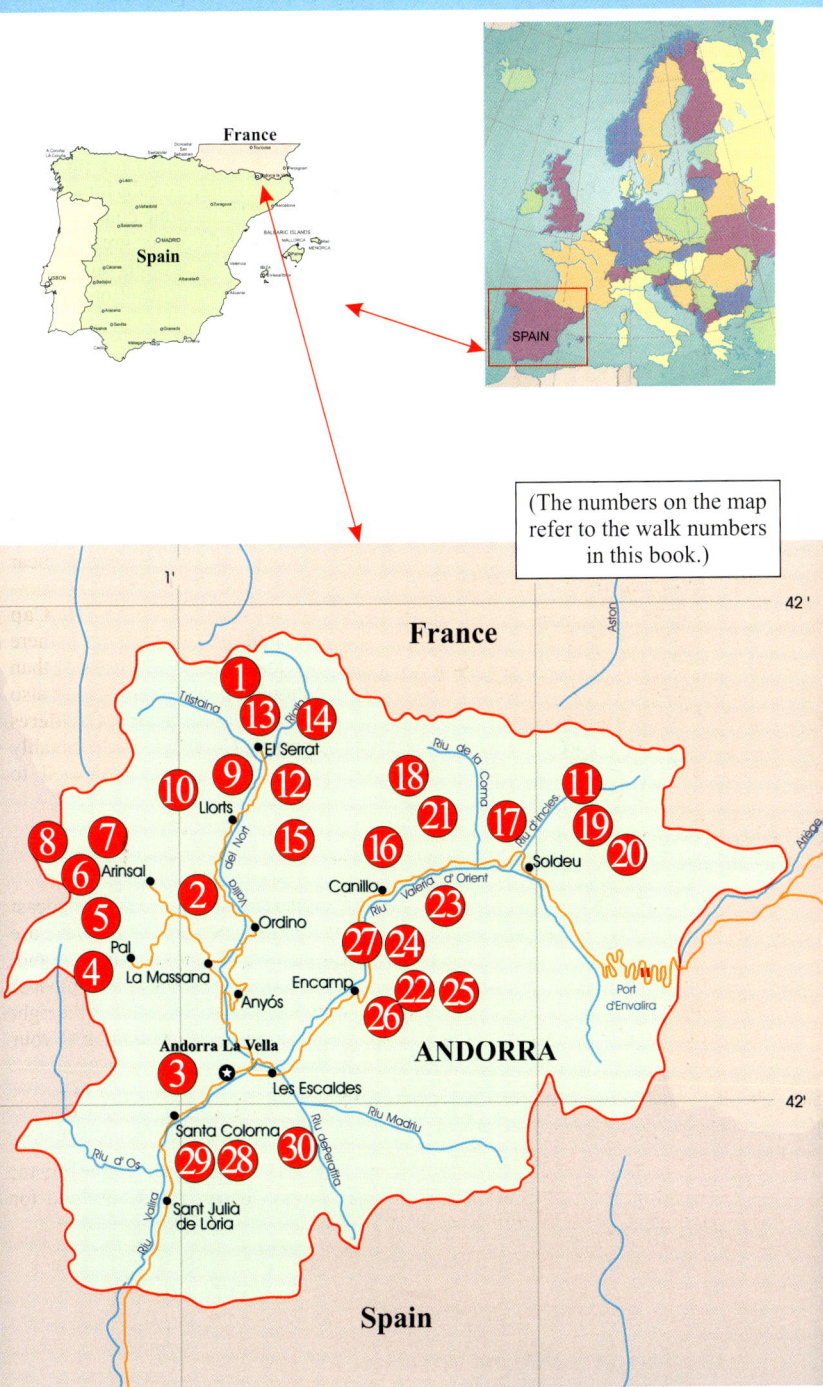

(The numbers on the map refer to the walk numbers in this book.)

Walk! Andorra 35

MAP NOTES

The map sections used to illustrate our walking routes in **Walk! Andorra** are licenced from the 1:25,000 scale maps published by Centro Nacional de Información Geográfica (CIGN) of Madrid, Spain. Each section is then re-scaled to our traditional 1:40,000 scale and the walking routes and waypoints added.

Eight CIGN 1:25,000 scale map sheets cover Andorra:-

182-II, 182-IV, 183-I, 183-II, 182-III, 183-IV, 216-I and 216-II

CIGN maps can be ordered direct from:-

> Centro Nacional de Información Geográfica
> General Ibáñez de Ibero, 3
> 28003 Madrid
> Spain/España

http://www.cnig.es website and email at consulta@cnig.es

Discovery Walking Guides Ltd expect to have copies of the CIGN maps used in our Walk! books available for direct purchase in UK, but at our publication date for **Walk! Andorra**, we are still negotiating our Distribution Agreement with CIGN. See our websites for current information:-

www.walking.demon.co.uk & www.dwgwalking.co.uk

MAPS

Original mapping reproduced under licence from:
The Instituto Geográfico Nacional
-
Centro Nacional de Información Geográfica

CARTOGRAFÍA ORIGINAL

INSTITUTO GEOGRÁFICO NACIONAL
-
CENTRO NACIONAL DE INFORMACIÓN GEOGRÁFICA

SYMBOLS RATING GUIDE

our rating for effort/exertion:-
1 very easy   **2** easy   **3** average
4 energetic   **5** strenuous

approximate **time** to complete a walk (compare your times against ours early in a walk) - does not include stopping time

approximate walking **distance** in kilometres

approximate **ascents/descents** in metres (N = negligible)

circular route

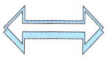

linear route

risk of **vertigo**

refreshments rating refers to the quality of refreshment opportunities, not the number of choices (may be at start or end of a route only)

Walk descriptions include:

- timing in minutes, shown as (40M)
- compass directions, shown as (NW)
- heights in metres, shown as (1355m)
- GPS waypoints, shown as (Wp.3)

Notes on the text

Place names are shown in **bold text**, except where we refer to a written sign, when any place names are enclosed in single quotation marks.

Please note that the spelling of place names used in the text can vary from that shown on the accompanying maps. There is often more than one accepted spelling in Andorra, and we have used those most commonly found on road signs etc., or used locally.

Catalán words are shown in *italics*, and if also in *purple*, will be included in the glossary (P.144).

Waymarked walking routes referred to in the text include:-

    Gran Recorridos   (GR) or long-distance footpaths.

Walk! Andorra   37

USING GPS ON ANDORRA

The GPS Waypoint lists provided in this **Walk! Andorra** guide book by Charles Davis are as recorded during his research of the 30 main walk descriptions contained in the book. In the interests of clarity, not all waypoints included in these lists are shown on the maps which accompany each detailed walk description. Where a Waypoint symbol is shown on a map it is numbered so that it can be directly identified against the walk description and waypoint list.

All the GPS Waypoints quoted in **Walk! Andorra** were recorded during the research of the walking routes, and are subject to the general considerations as to the accuracy of GPS units in the location concerned. After arriving in the Pyrenees, and Andorra in particular, you'll soon realise that these mountains make for potentially poor GPS reception at lower altitudes in comparison to the excellent reception on the mountain peaks and when walking the high ridges. When we do encounter poor GPS reception you should stay with the detailed walk description.

Despite the mountainous nature of Andorra's dramatic landscape, GPS reception is surprisingly good for the majority of our walking routes. Routes where some poor GPS reception was experienced are:-

Walk 2 (between Wps. 14 & 15)
Walk 3 (possible poor reception between Wps. 7 & 9)
Walk 8 (between Wps. 1 & 2, 4 & 5, 15 & 16 and 20 & 1 at start)
Walk 10 (between Wps. 1 & 2 and 5 & 6)
Walk 12 (unreliable reception between Wps. 4 & 5)
Walk 15 (poor reception after Wp. 27)
Walk 16 (between Wps. 3 & 4)
Walk 19 (between Wps. 3 & 4)
Walk 21 (between Wps. 3 & 4)
Walk 23 (a difficult valley route for GPS with poor reception between Wps. 4 & 5 and after waypoint 8)
Walk 28 (poor between Wps. 8 & 9 and Wp. 12 until Wp. 4)
Walk 29 (poor between Wps. 15 & 16 and Wps. 19 & 20).

Walk 30 'Tour of the South' is unfortunate in having sections of poor GPS reception. Originally Charles had included all waypoints recorded on the route but due to the poor reception on some sections we have deleted waypoints 4, 9, 10, 11, and 17 from the record of the route.

It is virtually impossible to reproduce the exact GPS Waypoint co-ordinates in practice when walking a route. While GPS Waypoints are quoted to 00.0001 minutes of arc, in practice you should expect 10 metres as an acceptable standard of accuracy when you have '3D navigation' (four or more satellites in view).

Signal Strength

Signal strength from sufficient satellites is crucial to obtaining an accurate location fix with your GPS unit. In open sky, ridge top, conditions you may have up to 11 satellites in view to give you a GPS location accuracy of 5 metres. Providing you have good batteries, and that you wait until your GPS has full 'satellite acquisition' before starting out, your GPS will perform well in Andorra for the majority of our walking routes.

To Input the Waypoints

GPS Waypoint co-ordinates are quoted for the WGS84 datum in degrees and minutes of Latitude and Longitude. To input the Waypoints into your GPS we suggest that you:-

- switch on your GPS and select 'simulator' mode.
- check that your GPS is set to the WGS84 datum (its default datum) and the 'location format' 'hddd° .mm.mmm'.
- input the GPS Waypoints into a 'route' file with the same number as the walking route number; then when you call up the 'route' on La Palma there will be no confusion as to which walking route it refers to. If your GPS will only accept three places of decimals then 'round off' the waypoints e.g. waypoint 7 in Walk 30 42 31.1994 N 1 35.7558 E would 'round off' to 42 31.199 N 1 35.756 E.
- repeat the inputting of routes until you have covered all the routes you plan to walk, or until you have used up the memory capacity of your GPS; even the most basic of GPS units will store up to 20 routes of up to 50 Waypoints for each route, and you can always re-programme your GPS while in Andorra.
- turn off your GPS. When you turn the GPS back on it should return to its normal navigation mode.

Note that GPS Waypoints complement the detailed walking route descriptions in **Walk Andorra,** and are not intended as an alternative to the detailed walking route description.

Personal Navigator Files (PNFs) CD version 2.01

Edited versions of the original GPS research tracks and waypoints are available as downloadable files on our PNFs CD. In addition to Andorra the CD contains **Tenerife**, **La Gomera**, **Lanzarote**, **La Palma**, **Mallorca**, **Menorca**, **Madeira**, **Axarquia**, **Aracena** and **Alpujarras**, plus **GPS Utility Special Edition** software and examples from our **Walk! UK** series of guidebooks. See DWG websites for more information:

www.walking.demon.co.uk & www.dwgwalking.co.uk

Confused by GPS?

If you are confused by talk of GPS, but are interested in how this modern navigational aid could enhance your walking enjoyment, then simply seek out a copy of **GPS The Easy Way**, the UK's best selling GPS manual. Written in an easy to read, lively, and lavishly illustrated, GPS The Easy Way takes you through all aspects of GPS usage from absolute basics up to GPS Expert and debunking the myths about GPS along the way; an essential purchase for anyone thinking of buying a GPS.

"A compass points north"
but
"A GPS tells you where you are, where you have been, and can show you where you want to go."

"Ask not 'What is GPS?' - ask 'What can GPS do for me?'"

GPS The Easy Way is available from bookshops, outdoor shops, over the internet, and post free from:
Discovery Walking Guides Ltd.
10 Tennyson Close
Northampton NN5 7HJ
www.walking.demon.co.uk & www.dwgwalking.co.uk

WALKING EQUIPMENT

See pages 24-26 for specific equipment advice for Andorra, particularly if you intend overnighting in a refuge, as in Walks 21 and 30.

From reading the postings on uk.rec.walking internet news group, it is obvious that walkers are very interested in the clothing and equipment used by other walkers. For some this interest borders on obsession, with heated debates over walking poles, boots versus sandals, GPS versus 'map and compass' navigation etc. etc. Walking magazines are packed with clothing and equipment reviews, opinions and adverts, but few walking guide books give more than a cursory mention to recommended clothing and equipment.

Having chosen Andorra for a walking vacation could mean that you are already an experienced walker with your own opinions of what is 'good gear'. At the risk of upsetting some walking fundamentalists, here is a brief rundown on our recommendations.

Backpack
A 25-30 litre day pack should easily cope with all the equipment you think you will need for a day's walking. A design with plenty of outside pockets to give easy access to frequently used items, such as ½ litre water bottles, is a good starting point. Well padded straps will spread the load and a waist strap will stop the pack moving about on the more adventurous routes. A ventilated back panel will help clear sweat on hot days and tough routes; a design with a stand-off frame is best for ventilation and worth the small increase in weight. Do spend time adjusting the straps so that you get the most comfortable fit.

As an alternative to traditional backpack designs, you might find the cyclist's packs produced by Nikko, and similar companies, a good compromise of stand-off frame, capacity, pockets and weight.

Footwear
Whether you choose boots, shoes or sandals they must be up to the task. You will need a hard sole with plenty of grip and a well padded foot-bed. Charles uses Bestard boots and I (David Brawn) can recommend the Bestard Race K shoes worn with thick mountain socks. Bestard boots and shoes are not widely available in UK, but if you happen to visit Mallorca, call in at their factory

shop in Lloseta.

Whichever footwear you choose, do make sure that you have covered plenty of kilometres in them before coming to Andorra.

Sun Protection
Be prepared for the sun at any time of year. Wear comfortable loose clothing and always carry a comfortable sun hat. Choose a design that gives you plenty of shade, is comfortable to wear, and stays on your head in windy conditions; our choice is the Rohan 'Legionnaire' style which protects neck and ears, while the author, Charles Davis, wears the famous Tilley endurable hat. You will be spending several hours a day outdoors and sunburnt ears (and neck) are both painful and embarrassing. Use a high-factor sun cream on all exposed skin.

We favour wrap-round sunglasses which, as well as reducing UV radiation, protect from getting grit in our eyes on windy days. When you do take a break always sit in the shade if any is available.

Water & Food
Dehydration is a real danger on the longer, more energetic routes. Always carry as much water as you think you might drink. A couple of ½ litre bottles, a few pence each from local shops, is the minimum, and add extra for longer routes. See the walk descriptions for information on potable water to be found on some routes.

Even on shorter routes, we would advise that you carry some survival rations. Chocolate bars and the like can provide welcome comfort when out in the wild.

Medical Kit
Antiseptic wipes, antiseptic cream, plasters and bandage are supplemented by lip salve. Also include tweezers and a small pair of scissors, and a whistle to attract attention if you get into difficulties.

Navigation
Do not compromise - buy the best guide book and the best map, and carry them with you. A compass is useful to orientate yourself at the start of a route and for general directions, but a GPS unit is far more useful - see Using GPS on page 38.

Clothing
Choose loose comfortable clothing and add a lightweight waterproof jacket to your back pack. Andorra promises everything from perfect blue skies with powerful sunlight, to grey rainy days and plummeting temperatures towards evening. Go prepared!

Other Equipment
You won't want to be carrying excess weight during your walking, especially on the longer routes with major ascents/descents. Digital cameras weigh less than their film equivalents, and a monocular is half the weight of a pair of binoculars. A mobile phone, and money (refreshments, taxis, public telephones, drinks machines etc.) are also recommended.

1 ESTANYS DE TRISTANIA

Easy access, sweeps of alpine roses, a baffling variety of orchids, picture postcard lakes, superb views, a perfect cirque and a perfect circuit make the **Estanys de Tristaina** essential walking for anyone not terminally soldered to the car-seat. Predictably, it's a popular itinerary and is often cited as a good high mountain route for families. I have seen young children doing the full walk, and it's true that it is very accessible, but crossing the **Costa Rodona** does involve rough, pathless walking and is mildly vertiginous in places, so it's not really suitable for everyone. The stroll and short version are recommended for all ages and capacities.

* given the sights to be seen and some rough terrain, allow at least 4 hours
** at the ski-station

Stroll
To the lakes and back - there's a path half way round the upper lake and an easy path/way circling the middle lake.

Short Version
To Wp.5, returning via the same way.

Alternative excursion
If you really don't feel like expending any energy at all but still want to see high mountain lakes, the **Creussans** ski-lift runs throughout the summer, offering either a simple trip to the crest (€5.30 one-way, €7 return) or a package-deal including lunch. The lift opens at 10 am.

Access: by car

The walk starts at the **Ordino-Arcalís** ski-station **Restaurant La Coma** at the end of the asphalted section of the CG3, not the signposted start 1km further down the road. From the **La Coma** driveway (Wp.1 0M), we climb behind the restaurant onto a clear path heading NE, passing under the **Creussans** ski-lift. Climbing steadily, we stick to the main path, soon crossing a rocky spur, bringing the middle and upper **Tristaina** lakes into view (Wp.2 15M).

Ignoring a waymarked branch to the left (our return route), we maintain our

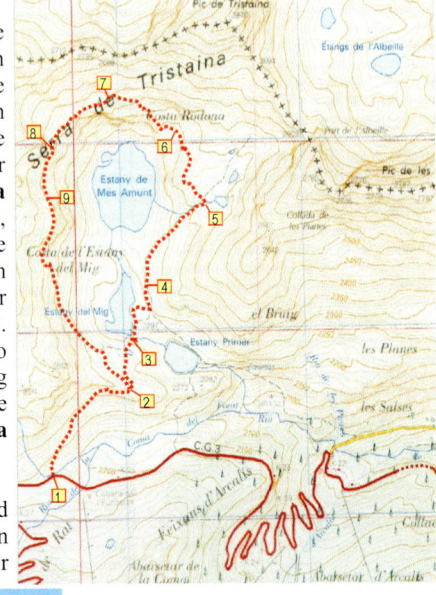

42 Walk! Andorra

north-easterly direction toward the nameless, but distinctively triangular 2644-metre peak. Although manifestly impossible from this perspective, the rest of the itinerary is visible from here and it's worth pausing as we descend toward the lakes to trace out the onward route.

Shortly after Wp.2

Crossing a small torrent linking the middle and lowest lakes (**Estany del Mig** and **Estany Primer** - the latter is not visited in this itinerary), we take the lower of the two paths below the triangular peak, then climb alongside the watershed to the east of the upper lake (**Estany de Més Amunt**). We then descend toward the north-eastern end of **Estany de Més Amunt** before climbing behind the cliffs defining it. This looks horrible, but is in fact a beautifully conceived, clearly waymarked route - whoever trail-blazed it deserves a medal.

Descending to the southern tip of **Estany del Mig** (Wp.3 20M), we cross the torrent and follow the lower of the two paths below the triangular peak, passing a rock with a large square of grey paint effacing an old waymark (Wp.4 30M), after which we find intermittent red and yellow waymarks. Our itinerary follows the yellow waymarks. The route, which is rough but clearly discernible, gradually bears away from **Estany de Més Amunt**, climbing steadily toward the flat lip defining the mini-lakes below **Port de l'Arbella** (also known as **l'Abeille**). Staying to the right of the watershed, which gradually swells to a small torrent, we climb steadily then steeply over the 'lip' into the mini-cirque defined by the **Pics de Tristaina** and **Arbella** (Wp.5 50M).

From here, the full circuit looks frankly suicidal, but bear with me: somebody has taken a lot of trouble to ensure it isn't! That said, if the slopes behind the upper lake are covered in snow (rather than just patched) turn back here.

Pic de Tristaina and the upper lake

Unmarked ways climb to the **Pic de Tristaina** (NNE) and **Port de Arbella** (NE), but we turn left (N), crossing the head of the watershed to follow a reasonably clear, cairn and waymarked path. After passing a chest high cairn, we descend behind the lake to a steeply sloping depression (Wp.6 65M) that may be covered with snow early in the season.

Once across the slope, the path climbs steeply behind the crags above the lake (the first slightly vertiginous section), passing occasional slightly obscure stretches where we have to look for the waymarks to avoid straying onto path-

The upper lake, from the north

like patches of erosion. After climbing alongside a boulder-chute, we cross rocks glazed with melt-off and climb onto a broad outcrop of granite mantled with iron deposits and mottled with pale green lichen (Wp.7 95M), where we can relax a little as the main climbing is over.

Cairns mark the descent on the far side of the outcrop, after which waymarks and more cairns guide us across a succession of shallow gullies, outcrops of rock and rockspills. Passing below a massive crag, we cross a comparably massive rockspill, on the far side of which (Wp.8 110M) we recover a clear dirt path that descends to a slightly vertiginous ledge. After crossing another large rockslide, we rejoin the dirt path (Wp.9 125M), which winds between the rocks and passes another chest-high cairn. We then descend through a slightly precipitous series of zigzags muddied by spring water, after which we have a clear descent back to Wp.2 (155M).

2 ROC DE CAUBA & COLL DE LES CASES

A straightforward but fairly strenuous climb up **La Massana**'s presiding bit of rock, a distinctive bald dome fringed with calcareous cliffs, with the option of a very strenuous loop via **Arinsal**. The views are fabulous and the forest is so full of fairytale echoes you'd be well advised to leave your riding hood at home. Thyme and oregano are particularly abundant alongside the path, and there are some delicious wild strawberries to be found in early autumn.

| 5 | 3½ H | 10.5 km | 850m / 850m | ↻ | 3* |

* in **Arinsal**

Access: by car and on foot from **Erts/Arinsal**

Short Version Roc de la Cauba

The walk starts in **Erts**, 150 metres east of the 'CG4/CS401' roundabout, on a signposted path next to the **Edifici Solar d'Erts**, in front of which there's ample parking in a broad lay-by. It's waymarked and very easy to follow, so description is largely for time-keeping and deciding if you want to do the full or short version.

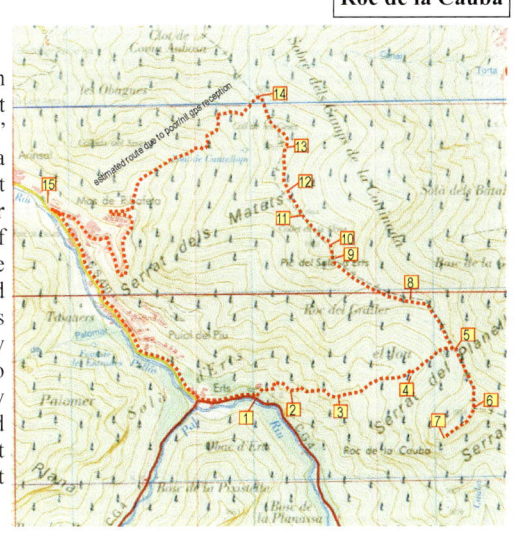

Despite being waymarked, the routes from **Coll de Jou** to **Coll de les Cases**, **Coll de Jou** to **Ansalonga** and **Coll de les Cases** to the north have never been mapped. We only had time to map the first. If you've got a GPS and time to explore the last two, we'd be glad to hear from you.

From the 'Camí del Jou - Roca de la Cauba' signpost at the entrance to **Edifici Solar d'Erts** (Wp.1 0M), we climb steeply on a narrow path lined with a sturdy wooden handrail, passing to the right of a second block of flats. The path then curves round to the right and traces a couple of long zigzags on an easier gradient, soon passing a broad grassy ledge from where we see **La Massana** for the first time (Wp.2 10M).

Continuing our climb through the woods, we cross a second, rockier ledge, within sight of the bluffs below **Roc de la Cauba**, after which we enter denser darker woodland of tall red pine. After a third open ledge overlooking **La**

Walk! Andorra 45

Massana (Wp.3 25M), the path levels off briefly before climbing gently then steadily through deep peaceful woodland. A little way beyond the massed banks of extensive raspberry bushes, we pass the overgrown ruins of an old farmhouse (Wp.4 40M). The path then climbs steadily to steeply toward the blue line of sky defining the ridge, where we reach a junction of waymarked routes at **Coll de Jou** (Wp.5 50M).

La Massana

Turning right, we stroll along the ridge, initially on the flat then through an increasingly steep climb to the subsidiary ridge behind **Roca de la Cauba**, once again overlooking **La Massana** (Wp.6 65M).

Roc de la Cauba

The path now veers right (SW) winding through the trees and crossing a couple of bare outcrops of rock - some care required here; they're not manifestly dangerous, but you wouldn't want to fall. A little over 200 metres later, we come to the final sloping rocks above the cliffs, which are manifestly dangerous, so I suggest staying some 50 metres from the end (Wp.7 70M); it's considerably safer and sacrifices nothing in views apart from the really toe-curling cliff top stuff. Having enjoyed the superb views (including **Pic de la Bassera**, **Pic Alt de la Capa**, **Prat Primer**, the **Perafita**, **Madriu** and **Agols** valleys, see Walks 4/5/29/28/30) we retrace our steps to **Coll de Jou**.

Whether you choose to do the loop is largely a matter of taste. It's an awful lot of effort for a handful of fine views, but if you're one of those ramblers who'd rather climb like crazy than return by the same path, then this is the route for you. For the full version, we climb along the ridge to the north west from **Coll de Jou**, enjoying fine views of **Pic de Casamanya** (Walk 15) before denser woodland closes around us again. After meandering along the ridge, we fork left at a Y-junction of waymarked paths (Wp.8 90M) - the branch on the right being another mystery enterprising GPS users might like to clear up.

After a very steep climb (which may well explain why it doesn't appear on anybody else's map, the lazy blighters), toward the end of which the path is little more than a waymarked animal trail, we come to a second Y-junction of faint ways (Wp.9 110M). Taking the fainter way to the right, confirmed a few metres later by a waymark, we climb north, rewarded for our admittedly very hard labour by brief but matchless views of **Casamanya**, after which the path levels out at a large pine with a distinctive waymark on the stump of a branch (Wp.10 115M), just west of **Pic del Solà d'Erts**.

46　Walk! Andorra

We then descend 50 metres (heartbreaking, I know, but so it goes) to the grassy **Collet de Llosa** (Wp.11 120M), a great favourite, if the traces of foraging are anything to go by, with the local wild boars.

The descent is promptly offset by a corresponding climb (and a bit more) passing an arrow painted on a tree, which appears to suggest we strike off path through the woods (Wp.12 125M). We don't. Sticking with the clear trodden way, we continue climbing, crossing another mini-coll before curving round to the north of the nameless, wood shrouded 2005-metre summit (Wp.13 135M).

Coll de les Cases, looking south

A steep, clear descent then brings us to the broad pasture at **Coll de les Cases**, where we join the GR11 at a junction of paths (Wp.14 145M), including yet another mysterious yellow-waymarked way heading north (perhaps a link with the GRP).

The GR11 descends on the right (NE) to **Arans**, but we turn left, toward the sharp peak of **Alt de la Capa**, and follow the south-western stretch of the GR11. After a first rapid descent (or, at least, as rapid as your knees allow), the path levels off briefly, heading south to cross a shallow watershed, then descends to a sharp right hand bend muddied by a meagre spring (155M). GPS receptions disappears completely after this, but it's of little matter as the path is clear and well-waymarked. Resuming our rapid (knees-permitting) descent, we wind back and forth through the woods, the gradient easing somewhat as we approach **Arinsal**. Emerging from the tree cover (170M), the path broadens to a trail, descending alongside a wide watershed to join the CS412 near its end in the **Mas de Ribafeta** residential area (175M). Turning right, we follow the road down to the CS401 in **Arinsal** (Wp.15 190M), 200 metres above the bus-stop, 1.5km from our starting point.

3 PIC D'ENCLAR & PIC DE CARROI

Glancing at this walk on the map, the first thing you notice is there's a lot of dirt track. If you like your walking a little on the wild side, don't be put off by this apparent domesticity. Wild we do - and then some. A Catalán mapmaking company (notorious for its 'creative' cartography) describes the route along the ridge as being molt aeri - 'very airy'. Given their customarily devil-may-care attitude to mountains, this delightful euphemism is not to be casually dismissed. It does not mean fluffing about in an indecisive way.

Definitely a dancing on knives job.

Although the route is never horrendously vertiginous, it is very, very 'airy', definitely a dancing on knives job, and no place to fall. It is only recommended for very experienced, very fit hikers totally at ease with off path antics. If you have to ask yourself, Can I do it?, the answer is probably no. But if you're up for it, the hour or so on the ridge is probably the most spectacular sixty minutes you'll experience in the principality. The Short Version offers some superb views, but is not a priority for a brief visit as the path itself is not particularly interesting. All the 'interest' is in the 'airy' bit.

The walk is not recommended at weekends, when you're liable to meet trail-bike enthusiasts on the **Camí de Collada de Montaner**, not to mention the dispiriting sight of a dozen 4WD vehicles at the hunters' cabin on the *collada* itself. The itinerary follows the GRP (yellow-and-red stripes) and yellow local path waymarks to **Collada de Montaner**, and nothing very much at all thereafter.

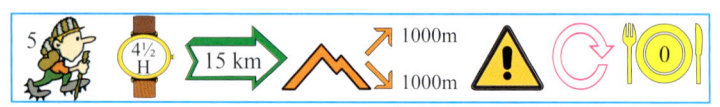

Access: by car or on foot from **Sispony**

Short Version
Pic d'Enclar from **Cortals de Sispony**, returning the same way.

To reach the start from the centre of **Sispony**, take the 'Els Cortals de Sispony' road (the CS320), setting the odometer at 0 at the end of the tarmac. The walk starts at a Y-junction (1.1kms on the odometer, officially km1.6) signposted 'Pic de Carroi' (L) and 'Cortals de Sispony' (R). There's generally room to park alongside the first 50 metres of the left hand branch. In the unlikely event of this being fully occupied, continue along the same track for 200 metres to the **Riu de Montaner** stream, where there are a couple more spaces.

From the Y-junction (Wp.1 0M), we follow the main 'Cortals de Sispony' track, ignoring a branch on the right 150-metres later (Wp.2). After climbing across attractive pasture, the CS320 track doubles back on itself, passing behind the **Bordes de Fenerols** (Wp.3 15M) before resuming its steady

48 Walk! Andorra

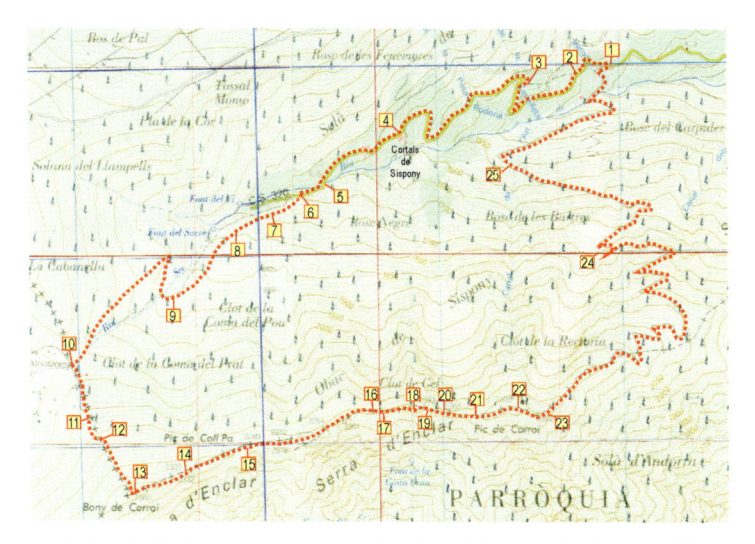

westerly climb. It then traverses the hamlet of **Cortals de Sispony** (Wp.4 30M) and curves round to ford **Riu de Montaner** (Wp.5 40M), dwindling to a much narrower stonier track. This is the starting point for the Short Version. There's room to park just beyond the stream. There are one or two rough stretches en route to Wp.5, but as long as you don't rev the motor and steer with a modicum of caution, nothing to cause any great grief to clutch or tyres.

Ignoring a fork on the right 150 metres later (Wp.6), we follow the narrow boulder strewn track to a second, signposted Y-junction (Wp.7 50M), where we again fork left, this time leaving the main track for a slightly narrower trail, the 'Camí de Collada de Montaner'. Climbing amid woods pungent with resin, we pass a junction with a parallel motorbike trail (Wp.8 55M) climbing from a little further along the main track. Sticking to the waymarked route, we climb steadily across a maze of interlooping motorbike trails, passing near though not within sight of two springs, the **Fonts del Vi** and **del Sucre**, respectively 'Wine'(no, I'm afraid not) and 'Sugar'.

The path levels off below a grassy clearing (Wp.9 70M) then curves north, crossing **Riu Sec** and bringing into view **Pic de Casamanya** (Walk 15), then the full span of the southern massif from **Pic Negre d'Envalira** above **Pas de la Casa** to the other **Pic Negre** above **La Rabassa**. We then veer back to the left (WSW), for a steady climb on a clear trail passing a muddy spring with a tin bath a little over 200 metres before reaching **Collada de Montaner** (Wp.10 95M). The GRP bears right here, crossing **Alt de Covil** before descending to **Coll de la Botella**. The grassy track to the west descends into Spain and **Os de Civís**. We turn left (S), without the benefit of waymarks, and follow the frontier for the final hard slog to the top.

Passing a tin hunters' cabin just above the *collada*, we climb a grassy slope to a rough way, largely defined by shallow erosion channels. After climbing steeply through the woods, we come to a clearing (Wp.11 105M) below the remaining scattered trees. Bearing slightly right, we follow the remaining traces of the way, climbing steadily until it veers east above the last mature trees and peters out in a grassy platform (Wp.12 110M). The rest of the climb

Walk! Andorra 49

is off-path, though the initial trajectory is defined by lines of exposed slate glinting in the sunlight. Bearing right (SSE), we climb straight up very steeply, initially along a rough way, then stepping between low but dense clumps of rhododendron, eventually emerging on the obvious but unmarked summit (Wp.13 135M) - and above the dramatic drop on the far side!

If you're doing the Short Version and don't fancy the head-on ascent as a descent, follow the main walk to Wp.14 then double back (NW), traversing the hillside to Wp.12.

We now follow the line of the ridge (E), still off-path but on relatively easy ground, toward the distinct, triangular summit of **Pic de Carroi** and the red-and-white antenna just beyond it. Sticking to the grassier stretches above the great sweep of rhododendron, we descend to a first saddle (Wp.14 140M), where we pick up a faint trodden way leading to a broader coll, **Coll Pa**, and what appears to be a salt-lick on a squat pile of flat stones buttressing a rusty tin tube (Wp.15 150M).

Off-path again, we continue along the line of the ridge, picking up a second faint trodden way after the next rise. Following the intermittently trodden way, we skirt to the left of a succession of small rises and rocky outcrops then pass above a small hanger, where we are forced onto our first narrow section, following the spine of the ridge itself (Wp.16 160M) - if you'd been thinking the Cataláns a bit precious with their 'very airy' (I confess, I had), this is where you begin to think again.

The natural 'menhir'

Carefully, very carefully, picking our way along the spine of the ridge, we recover a very faint trodden way 60 metres later (Wp.17), passing on our right a distinctive natural 'menhir'. We now pass a series of short jagged outcrops, following the very faint trodden way on the northern flank of the ridge - hands occasionally required for balance - until we come to a tiny grassy coll (Wp.18 175M), three summits from the end, though this is slightly difficult to call as the aerials behind **Carroi** are now out of sight.

The ridge from the west

Climbing straight back onto the rocky spine, we pick our way along the 2283-metre summit where, comfortingly, someone has constructed a small cairn (Wp.19 190M). From here, we can see our final way along the ridge. Don't relax yet, though! It's very, very 'airy'. Extreme care is still required.

From here, it's easier to follow the southern side of the ridge for another 80 metres till we come to a section flanked with twisted, tormented pine (Wp.20). We now stick to the central line of the ridge, only dipping down when overhanging boughs momentarily force us back onto the southern side, until we reach a couple of sturdy pine at the foot of **Pic de Carroi** (Wp.21 200M). A straightforward climb along the obvious line of rocks leads to the long summit of **Pic de Carroi** and its trig-point (Wp.22 210M).

From the trig point, we descend to the right of the antenna, where a gated path leads to the surfaced end of the **Carroi** track (Wp.23 215M). We now have a wonderfully dull descent (after all the 'interest' on the ridge, you'd probably be happy to walk on a motorway by this stage) following the track back to Wp.1. I say 'dull' for the surface, but the views are exceptional, the complete panorama of Andorra unfolded on all sides like a 3D relief map. There are no confusing branches, so we simply follow the track, drinking in the views, passing en route a barrier blocking access to unauthorized vehicles (Wp.24 240M) and the first of two minor branches on the left (Wp.25 255M) before re-crossing the **Riu de Montaner** and rejoining the CS320.

4 PIC DE LA BASSERA (PIC DELS LLACS)

The **Setúria** valley, one of Andorra's principal pastures, is generally seen either from the new road to **Port de Cabús** or from the **Coll de la Botella - Port Negre** cable-car. In this itinerary, we explore a slightly more eccentric outlook on the valley from the main summit at its head, generally mapped as **Pic de la Bassera** but known locally as **Pic dels Llacs** - a somewhat perverse piece of toponymy since the summit is virtually unique in Andorra in that there aren't any lakes in the immediate vicinity.

The maximum height - minimum fuss/maximum fuss - minimum height dichotomy depends on which route you take to the top. For the former, simply follow the yellow-waymarked ascent from the **Port Cabús** pass and return by the same path; for the latter, which is to my mind a lot more fun, there's the option of a splendid little scramble up the ridge dividing the valley from the **Torrent de la Font de l'Altar** in Spain. This pathless ascent is only partially marked with cairns, but is relatively easy to follow given the open, airy landscape. By the same token, it's all very exposed and is not recommended on a windy day. From **Port Cabús**, the mountain can look a little bleak and won't be to everybody's taste, but for those who favour the sort of wide open spaces that make you think if only your limbs were a little stronger and little longer you could probably take off and fly, it's a great walk. The views into Spain are superb.

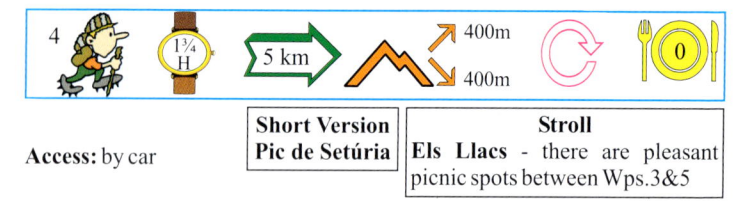

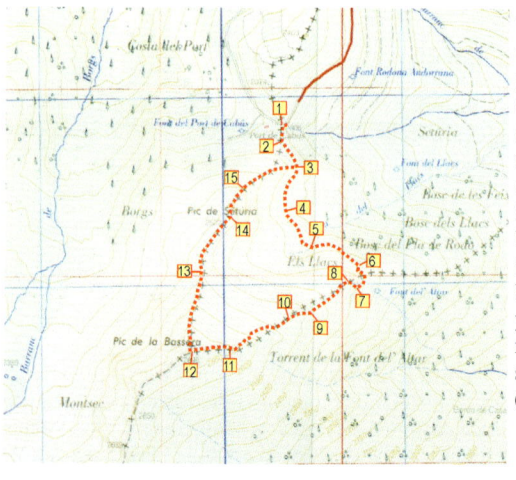

| 4 | 1¾ H | 5 km | 400m / 400m | ↻ | 0 |

Access: by car

| **Short Version** Pic de Setúria | **Stroll** Els Llacs - there are pleasant picnic spots between Wps.3 & 5 |

The walk starts at the **Port Cabús** pass, at the end of the tarmac road (CG4) and start of the dirt track descending into Spain, next to the blue 'Andorra' frontier signboard, below which a yellow-waymarked rock indicates the start of the itinerary (Wp.1 0M).

Setting off in a southerly direction, we climb across pathless pasture to join the waymarked tip of twin parallel cow paths 100 metres from the road (Wp.2). Following the cow-paths for a further 150 metres (SE), we cross a rise distinguished by a small double-headed arrow painted on a rock (Wp.3), at which point the alternative routes diverge. Maximum height/minimum fussers bear right here, leaving the clear path to follow the waymarked route up to and along the **Setúria** ridge.

Maximum fuss/minimum heighters continue along the cow path, descending into **Els Llacs**, a broad vale bisected by a central line of scattered rocks where the path peters out. Maintaining a southerly direction, we pass behind a wind-flattened pine (Wp.4 10M), 20 metres after which, we pick up a much rougher cow path climbing across a shrub-cloaked slope (SSE) before it in turn disappears in rough pasture patched with heather and small pine. We then descend into the dry, virtually indiscernible head of the **Riu dels Llacs**, where we pick up a third faint cow path just beyond a distinctively large boulder (Wp.5 15M).

We follow this faint path (ESE) through the scattered pine of the **Bosc del Pa de Rodo** for 275 metres, in the course of which it gradually dwindles away then disappears altogether in front of a large dead pine crowned by an arching bough (Wp.6 20M). A few metres before the dead pine, we bear right (SSE) on a broad shaly way marked with cairns leading us onto the tip of the ridge protruding from **Pic de la Bassera**. Following the cairns, we curve round the eastern tip of the ridge (SSW) on rough grass interleaved with fractured slate. Shortly before a long broad grassy depression, a small cairn (Wp.7) indicates where we turn sharp right, climbing NNW for 50 metres to a final cairn and the bleached skull of a cow (Wp.8 30M) - don't move it!

Looking south from here, we can see the **Bassera** summit-cairn. 100 metres to the southwest is a shallow outcrop of rocks and beyond that a thin post silhouetted against the skyline. We climb (SW), still off path, past the rocks to the grassy slope just below the post, a metal frontier-marker (Wp.9 38M).

Bearing right (W), we climb steadily up the grassy slope to a small *coll* (Wp.10 45M) overlooking **Port de Cabús** and **Els Llacs**, and readily identified by the scattered bones of a horse - apparently this pasture, much vaunted in local publications, isn't a particularly healthy place for ungulates. From the edge of the *coll*, we can also just see the tip of the snow-depth pole set in the summit cairn.

Port de Cabús from the crest

Bearing left (SW), we climb towards a craggy ridge, gradually curving west, before resuming our southwesterly direction for a final steep climb across a slope of loose slate (not recommended as a descent) onto the main crest (Wp.11 60M), which resembles the spine of an armour plated dinosaur. We now simply pick our way along the edge of the crest (W) to the summit cairn

(Wp.12 65M).

After enjoying a few moments sitting-on-top-of-the-world, we return via the obvious, waymarked route to the north.

The cairn-capped Pic de Setúria

Following a rough, intermittently trodden way (N), we descend steadily then steeply to another metal frontier-post (Wp.13 75M) directly above a *coll* on the neck of the ridge behind the small **Setúria** summit. An easy stroll along the ridge leads to the cairn-capped **Pic de Setúria** (Wp.14 80M).

Continuing along the tapering ridge on a gradually steepening descent (NE), we emerge below the rocks at the head of a sparsely vegetated mini-ridge defining the northern side of the **Els Llacs** vale (Wp.15 90M).

The ridge descent

If doing the maximum-height/minimum fuss option, this point can be identified by a slogan thinly painted on an overhanging rock declaring this a private mountain 'Propiedad de la Sociedad Ciudanos de Tor / Monte Particular'. A straightforward descent (E) along this ridge, initially on a clear path then on a broad shaly slope, soon brings us back to our outward route at Wp.3.

54 *Walk! Andorra*

5 STORM IN A TEACUP: PIC ALT DE LA CAPA

The vertiginous, pathless ascent of **Pic Alt de la Capa** from **Coll de Turer** certainly won't be everybody's cup of tea, but it's a sufficiently versatile itinerary to offer something for everyone: those wanting big vistas but no sweat can do the Stroll, picnickers should not miss Short Version A, walkers with a reasonable head for heights should opt for Short Version B, while adventurers and show-offs will be gladdened by the gruelling climb from the coll. The full walk is only recommended for experienced, sure-footed walkers with no fear of yawning empty spaces. The ascent is waymarked with yellow dots, the descent with yellow dots and red-and-yellow GRP waymarks. Do not do this walk when it's wet.

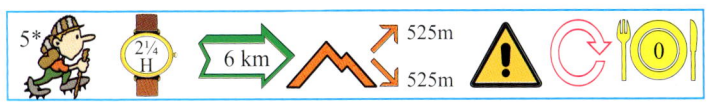

5* | 2¼ H | 6 km | 525m / 525m | ⚠ | ↻ | 0

* Note, this walk was done without the usual heavy pack and in rapidly deteriorating conditions that provided a keen incentive to get off the mountain as quickly as possible: timings may well be proportionately faster than usual!

Stroll	Short Versions
Take the **Coll de la Botella** cable-car (€8.50 return) and follow the ridge path to Wp.13	(a) to **Coll de Turer** - modest exertion for an excellent picnic spot; slight risk of vertigo (b) take the cable-car (€5.20 one-way) and descend via the GRP; slight risk of vertigo.

Access: by car

We start from the unmistakable **Storm In A Tea Cup** sculpture (Wp.1 0M), shortly after **Coll de la Botella** on the CG4 from **Pal** to **Port de Cabús**. Following a clear path climbing to the right of the sculpture, we fork right after 75 metres (Wp.2) on the yellow-waymarked **Camí del Coll Turer**, a rather optimistic name for what is essentially a very minor trodden 'way' following a contour round the foot of **Pic Alt de la Capa**.

Storm in a Teacup

The way, which is initially clear, winds between pine and a profusion of wild flowers, before crossing a small outcrop of rock (Wp.3 10M) and climbing steeply to pass behind a vertiginous crag. We then continue along a contour line traversing the precipitous slope, crossing two small watersheds (Wps.4&5 20M). The path then fractures and becomes less clearly defined, and we have to rely on the waymarks, repeatedly following short stretches of 'path' before climbing briefly to pick up the next waymarked stretch. After veering east, we recover a clear, trodden way descending slightly to the long grassy ridge between **Coll de Turer** (Wp.6 35M) and **Roca de Àliga**, a wonderful spot for a picnic and reputedly a good place for spotting izard.

Most people will want to turn back at this point, since this is where we begin the very steep, very pathless, and very precipitous climb up **Les Costes de l'Alt**. There are no sheer drops, but there's nothing much else either, as we climb up and up and up in a vast expanse of deepening emptiness. Climbing through the trees to the west, we pass a moribund, quadruple-trunked pine (Wp.7 40M) and cross an outcrop of rock onto a broad, grassy slope where there's an old, loosely planted waypost (Wp.8 50M), shortly after which a cone-like 'false-peak' comes into view.

After passing a second waypost (Wp.9 55M), we scramble over the false 'peak' (Wp.10 65M) and continue climbing steeply along the blade-like ridge running down from the summit. Passing fifty metres behind the pillar of what I fear must be a ski-hoist catering to hibernal suicides intent on hurling themselves down the **Costa de l'Alt de la Capa** (Wp.11 70M), we maintain a westerly direction along the ridge, climbing behind a high crag (Wp.12 80M). After the crag, a final, brief but steep scramble brings us onto **Pic Alt de la Capa** (Wp.13 85M), from where we have superb views of the great western summits.

The descent is considerably less precipitous, though some care is still required. N.B. If you've made the mistake of buying somebody else's map, ignore insane invitations to descend directly along the crest to the south. Maintaining direction (WNW), we descend to **Port Negre** (Wp.14 95M) and a small hut housing ski-lift machinery, midway along the ridge between **Pic Alt** and the cable-car station. Turning left through a gap in the fencing below the machinery hut, we follow the GRP waymarkings down to a faint cow path (Wp.15 100M). The path is narrow throughout, but its course across the lower slope is perfectly clear from above.

After a long SSW traverse across the **Costa de les Enles**, the path curves behind the first (Wp.16 110M) of two vertiginous outcrops of rock. Some may find the second outcrop particularly alarming, in which case climb onto the higher, unmarked cow path to put some distance between yourself and the drop. The main waymarked path then follows a contour line along **Costa de la Devesa** (SSE) before passing to the right of the central cable-car tower, where it runs into another slightly vertiginous path (Wp.17 120M), cutting back beneath the cables in an easterly direction. We now simply follow this path as it gradually levels out before rejoining our outward route just above the tea cup.

6 PIC DE SANFONS

If life has bamboozled you into a career in accountancy when you really wanted to walk the tightrope in a circus, this may be your big opportunity. Following the crest (and, incidentally, the frontier) behind the broad **Coma Pedrosa** *cirque*, we climb to the uncommonly long blade-like ridge that constitutes the summit of **Pic de Sanfons**. It's not dramatically vertiginous, but there's a distinct sense of dancing on knives as you approach the end. The views, notably of the **Estanys de Baiau**, **Coma Pedrosa**, **Pic de Medacorba** and the high summits of western **Catalonia**, are superb.

We had intended looking for a way down to join the GR11 at **Estany Negre**, returning to the **Collada de Sanfons** via the GRP, but unfortunately we were shooed off the mountain by an impending storm, so the full circuit will have to wait for a second edition. Happily, the linear route is spectacular enough to be worth doing both ways. Despite its relatively low exertion rating, the rough terrain and rather marginal nature of the path mean this itinerary is only recommended for experienced walkers.

N.B. The toponymy varies considerably between different maps, topographer A's **Port Negre de Pallars** being topographer B's **Port Vell**, while topographer B and topographer C's **Portella de Sanfons** is topographer A's **Port Vell** and is identified on the ground as **Collada de Sanfons**. Confused? Follow the map sections in this book!

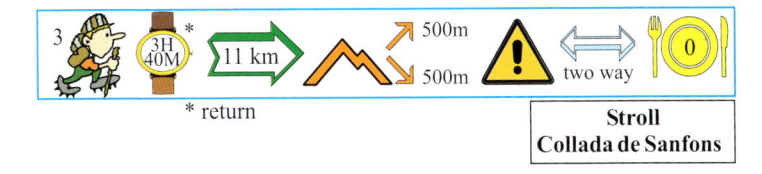

*return

Stroll
Collada de Sanfons

Access: by car & cable-car
The walk makes use of the **Coll de la Botella** cable-car, which operates between 10am and 6pm every day in July and August, and at weekends in June and September (until September 12th). The return journey costs €8.50, a one-way ascent €5.20. In the event of high winds (70km per hour) the cable-car will be closed. You wouldn't particularly want to be up here in a 70km per hour wind anyway, but if you are caught out, see Walk 5 for an alternative descent.

From the cable-car exit (Wp.1 0M), we bear left to find a clear path traversing the southern flank of **Pic de Port Negre**. Seventy-five metres later, we ignore a path descending on the left (Wp.2) toward **Coll Petit** and follow a contour line round to the west of the summit, descending briefly before curving NNE and climbing (the last hundred metres on a grassy, pathless slope) to the obvious coll at **Port Negre de Pallars** (Wp.3 10M) overlooking the **Arinsal** ski pistes.

Bearing left (NW), we join the red-and-yellow waymarked GRP on a clear path climbing steadily to 'Collada de Sanfons' (Wp.4 25M), waymarked on a large flat rock, from where we can see the crest stretching away to the long level top of **Sanfons**. The **Coma Pedrosa** summit and refuge are also visible

Walk! Andorra 57

to the north and north east. Seventy-five metres later (Wp.5), the GRP forks right, descending to **Estany de les Truites** and the refuge, but we stay on the crest, crossing a shallow depression full of fractured slate, soon after which we pass the first of the red waymarks (Wp.6 30M) that will accompany us to the summit.

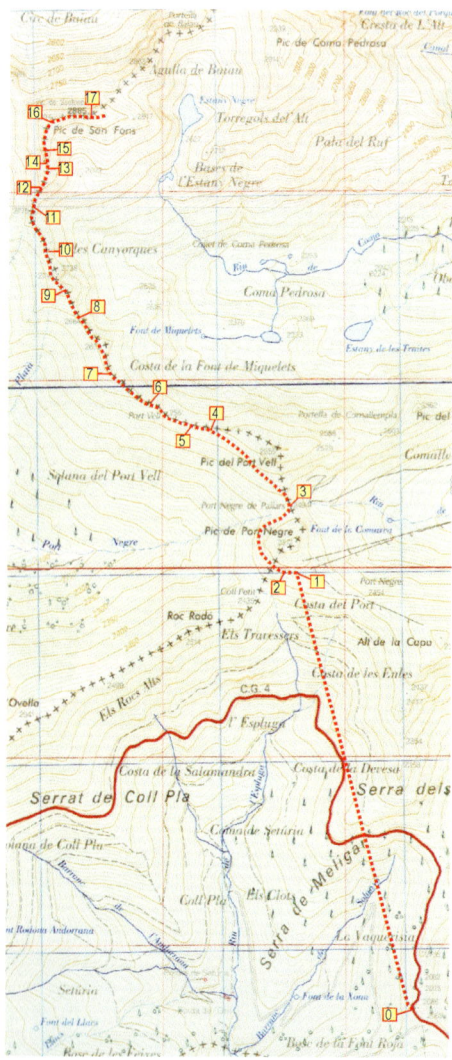

Estany de les Truites from the crest

The path more or less disappears here, but sticking to the crest and ignoring clearer cow paths following contour lines lower down, we climb to the first of three, craggy summits (Wp.7 40M), where there's a second red waymark. Following a flurry of waymarks, we skirt behind the second, cairn-capped summit, sticking to the western side of the crest and approaching a mini-coll immediately below the rise of the third and largest summit (Wp.8 50M), bringing back into view **Coma Pedrosa** and the GR11 below **Estany Negre**.

Following a reasonably clear way, we climb steeply straight up the rise to a tall cairn (Wp.9 60M) on the first really rough and slightly vertiginous stretch of the crest. Still favouring the western side of the crest, though now much nearer the spine, we pick our way round the rocks, passing occasional waymarks and going through a little rock 'gateway' (Wp.10 70M) directly in line with the

58 Walk! Andorra

refuge. Following a faint stretch of path, we descend briefly then climb across a broad coll, picking our way behind a succession of small crags until we reach the last coll before the final steep climb (Wp.11 80M), identifiable by a pile of stones that might once have made up a windbreak.

The ongoing way is initially clear, but soon deteriorates amid a chaos of sharp rocks, disappearing altogether below a small cairn (Wp.12 90M). We now follow the waymarks, straight up over the rocks (hands occasionally required for balancing), passing a second small cairn (Wp.13 100M). Forty metres later (Wp.14), a red arrow indicates where we cross very briefly back onto the western side of the crest before returning to the central spine at its narrowest point.

We eventually come to a small coll (Wp.15 105M) separated from the main crest/summit by two small outcrops of rock. Following the waymarks, we pass to the right of the first outcrop then immediately climb back onto the crest, passing the remains of an old signpost (Wp.16 109M), from where we have a fabulous view over the **Estanys de Baiau**. Its now simply a question of 'dancing' (I use the word advisedly) along the remainder of the crest to the trig point (Wp.17 115M) and the cairn on the summit just beyond it.

Estanys de Baiau

The return ... hopefully

We return by the same route, taking care after **Port Negre de Pallars** to follow the cairn-marked route over the rise to the cable-car, rather than the clearer cow-paths curving round to **Coll Petit**.

7 PIC DE COMA PEDROSA

Culminating points rarely make for the most interesting itineraries and **Coma Pedrosa** is no exception compared to some of the principality's other peaks. However, it does enjoy a certain rugged grandeur, the views are superb, and it is the highest peak in Andorra, therefore essential walking for many visitors. Don't undertake it lightly though: even with the cable-car cutting the climb, this is a tough walk and won't be suitable for everyone. If possible, arrange to be dropped off at the **Coll de la Botella** cable-car and descend to **Arinsal** via the GR11. If you're visiting after September 12th, when the cable-car closes, the peak can be climbed from **Arinsal** following the GR, which is straightforward and well waymarked.

For those doing the itinerary in reverse, Wps.19-23 include estimated distances from the preceding waypoint in the direction of the climb i.e. the distance after Wp.20 is from Wp.21.

5	*	12 km	**	one way	4 ***

*	**Port Negre** to **Pic de Coma Pedrosa**	2¼ hours
	Pic de Coma Pedrosa to **Port Negre**	1-2 hours (estimated)
	Pic de Coma Pedrosa to **Arinsal**	2¾ hours

**	Accumulated Ascent:	700 metres + 200 metres if returning via the cable-car
	Accumulated Descent:	900 metres if returning via the cable car, 1500 metres if descending to **Arinsal**

*** **Refuge de Coma Pedrosa**

NOTE: this itinerary was researched in foul weather with an evil wind sweeping across the crests and a malevolent looking storm working itself into a tizzy across the border; I've rounded intermittent timings up to compensate for the resulting haste, but don't be surprised if we seem to be going a little faster than usual!

> **Short Versions**
> (a) **Port Negre** to **Estany de les Truites** via the GRP, returning the same way
> (b) **Port Negre** to **Arinsal** via the **Refuge de Coma Pedrosa** (linear descent)
> (c) **Arinsal** to **Aigües Juntes** (confluence of the **Rius Areny** and **Coma Pedrosa**) via the GR11 (linear ascent)

Access: by car & cable-car (see Walk 6 for details)

We start by following Walk 6 to Wp.5, the Y-junction just after 'Collada de Sanfons' (Wp.5 25M). Forking right, we stay on the GRP (red and yellow stripes) as it descends across the shaly slope of **Costa de la Font de Miquelets**, gently at first then more steeply, gradually curving east onto a low rhododendron cloaked ridge at the head of the pasture behind **Estany de les Truites** and the **Refuge de Coma Pedrosa** (visible during the descent but now out of sight).

As the ridge tapers away into the pasture and the shrubs disappear (Wp.6 40M), you will see to your left a large outcrop of rock (the largest in the pasture) and, beyond that, a little over 100 metres from the GRP, a smaller outcrop with a cairn on top. Leaving the GRP, we cut across country (N), off path, traversing the marshy area of **Font de Miquelets** to the cairn-topped rock (Wp.7, from where we can see the main GR11/**Coma Pedrosa** path 300 metres ahead. Bearing slightly left (NNW), we pick our way through the debris and shrubs for 150 metres, still off-path, down to a wide rockslide (Wp.8), on the far side of which we join the main path (Wp.9 50M).

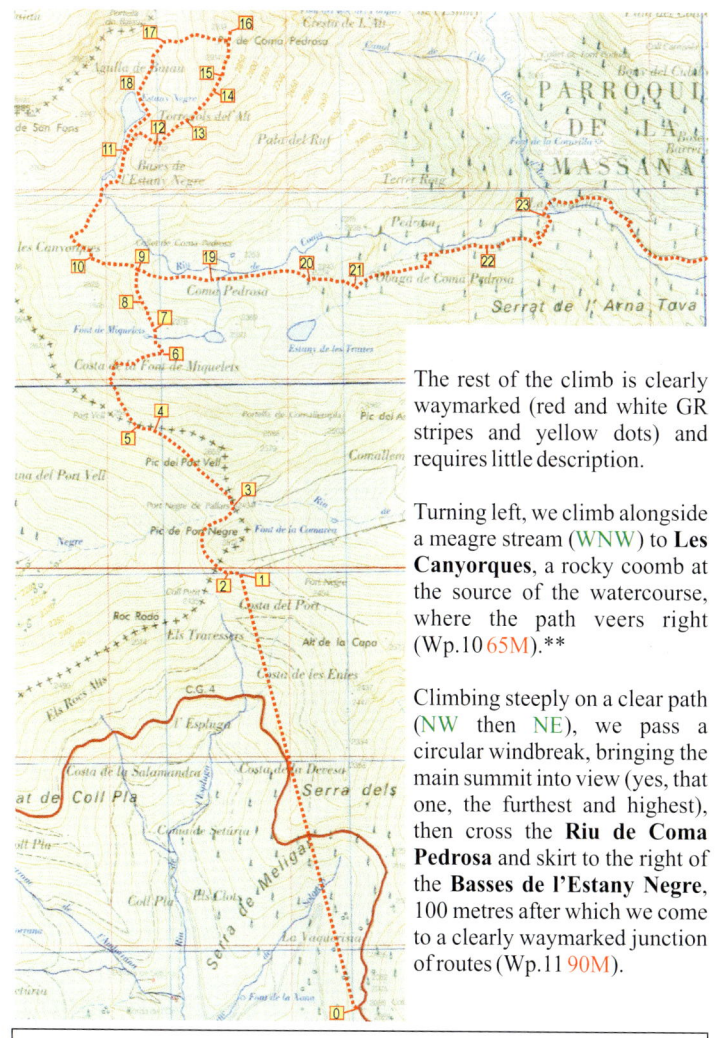

The rest of the climb is clearly waymarked (red and white GR stripes and yellow dots) and requires little description.

Turning left, we climb alongside a meagre stream (WNW) to **Les Canyorques**, a rocky coomb at the source of the watercourse, where the path veers right (Wp.10 65M).**

Climbing steeply on a clear path (NW then NE), we pass a circular windbreak, bringing the main summit into view (yes, that one, the furthest and highest), then cross the **Riu de Coma Pedrosa** and skirt to the right of the **Basses de l'Estany Negre**, 100 metres after which we come to a clearly waymarked junction of routes (Wp.11 90M).

Les Canyorques can also be reached by a faint, unpromising looking trodden way forking north as the **Costa de la Font de Miquelets** path steepens; the trodden way peters out after a while but the shortcut should pose no problems for GPS users or anyone with reasonable pathfinding skills.

Leaving the GR, we bear right for 'Pic de Coma Pedrosa', following a rough waymarked route (intermittently trodden but not really a path) climbing to a small coll (Wp.12 105M) from where we can see **Estany de les Truites** and, less happily, the heartbreaking row of mini-summits lining the ridge between us and the main peak. Don't spend too long contemplating this dismal spectacle, but concentrate on the fine views opening out on all sides, and on where you put your feet, as the final ascent is increasingly rough.

Following the cairns and waymarks, we cross the first line of mini-summits, the **Torregols del Alt** (Wp.13 115M) to a saddle below the first 'major mini-summit' (you'll see what I mean soon enough). After a brief scramble during which you may need to steady yourself with your hands, we pick our way along the south-eastern flank of the ridge onto a second 'major mini-summit' (Wp.14 120M) briefly bringing the peak back into view. After the third 'major mini' (Wp.15 125M), waymarks highlight the least difficult route along the ridge to a sandy-coloured coll, from where a final scramble brings us onto **Pic de Coma Pedrosa** (Wp.16 135M).

Descent to Estany Negre

To descend, return to the sandy-coloured coll and take the gritty yellow path (unmarked but obvious) snaking its way down to the west. This path is a gift to fans of rock-skiing (an unofficial 'sport' familiar to most walkers), but soon becomes very steep, so beware of building up too much speed as it's entirely possible you won't be able to stop. After a rapid, skittery descent, hopefully on your feet though this is by no means guaranteed, the path disappears in a sweep of debris, on the far side of which we rejoin the GR11 beside a waymarked rock set in a circle of stones, each painted with a white circle (Wp.17 155M).

Estany Negre at 165 minutes

After descending (SSW) to **Estany Negre** (Wp.18 165M), we follow the waymarks and trodden ways round the eastern side of the lake then pick our way across the debris at its southern end to rejoin our outward route at Wp.11 (175M) and retrace our steps to Wp.9 (200M 450 metres from Wp.19).

To descend to **Arinsal**, stay on the GR11 after Wp.9, following a clear, heavily waymarked path descending alongside the torrent towards the marshy pasture below the refuge, where we pass a signpost indicating a path climbing SE to the refuge (Wp.19 210M 500 metres from Wp.20). Sticking with the GR, we descend to a small flood plain where the torrent broadens to a stream, then climb briefly to the **Collet de Coma Pedrosa** (Wp.20 220M 300 metres), from where another signposted path climbs to the refuge, 150 metres to the south.

The descent from the collet to **Arinsal** follows an obvious, clearly waymarked trail with no junctions, so the remaining description is merely for the purposes of timekeeping. Following a rocky path, we descend steadily to cross a shallow stream, the **Estany de les Truites** watershed (Wp.21 230M 1km). A broad, stony path descends alongside the stream then winds across a small plateau before resuming its steady descent, initially alongside the **Riu de Coma Pedrosa**, then bearing away from the torrent on a contour, passing a rock waypainted 'La Font del Fenoll' (Wp.22 250M 500 metres).

After following the contour for another 200-metres, we descend steeply, gradually curving round to the north, winding through predominantly pine woods to a sturdy wooden bridge over the **Riu de Coma Pedrosa** (Wp.23 260M 500 metres).

Bridge over the Riu de Coma Pedrosa

100 metres later, we cross a similar bridge over the **Riu Areny**, after which we descend through the remaining woods before crossing a small sloping pasture to join the **Pista Pla de l'Estany** (270M Wp.2 of Walk 8). We now simply follow the dirt track down to the end of **Carreter Prats Sobrans** and the road into **Arinsal**.

8 ESTANY FORCATS

One of Andorra's great routes, and a good way to see the principality's highest mountain, **Coma Pedrosa**, without actually having to labour up to the top of the thing. The hermitic nature of **Estany Forcats**, is not so much a question of vocation as location. Tucked into a sombre cirque of grey schist, it's an austere place, isolated, utterly tranquil, and sober enough to make Andorra's other *estanys* look like frivolous youngsters whooping it up without a thought to the necessary gravitas of a truly venerable lake. The ascent is waymarked with red-and-white GR stripes, the loop via **Bordes de Percanela** with yellow and red GRP stripes and yellow dots.

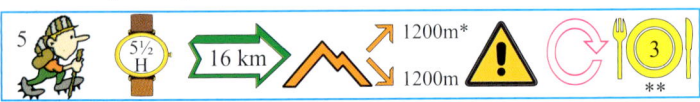

Short Version	* including the
Pla de l'Estany and Borda de Percanela	**Bordes de Percanela** loop
	** in **Arinsal**

Access: on foot from **Arinsal**

We start at the western end of **Arinsal** on the 'Camí de Coma Pedrosa i Pla de l'Estany', otherwise known as **Pista del Pla de la Estany**, which begins at the end of **Carreter Prats Sobrans**, the turning on the right immediately after the first tunnel above the village. There's generally room to park at the end of the tarmac.

From the end of the road (Wp.1 0M), we simply follow the **Pista del Pla de la Estany** dirt track (with the exception of a shortcut across the first bend) as it climbs steadily along the wooded **Coma Pedrosa** valley to a heavily signposted and waymarked junction, where the 'Coma Pedrosa' and 'Pla de l'Estany' itineraries diverge (Wp.2 25M).

The main lake from Wp.3

Staying on the main dirt track, the 'GR11.1A/GRP1', we climb (E) to the spring and farmhouse (currently being restored) at 'Borda de les Agunes', where the track swings back northwest. 200 metres later, at a clearly waymarked Y-junction (Wp.3 35M), we fork right on a path climbing to pass in front of the **Bordas de la Coruvilla**. Ignoring a yellow waymarked route to the right of the houses, we stay on the GR, rejoining the **Pista del Pla de la Estany** 50 metres west of the houses (Wp.4 45M).

After a steady climb between tempting raspberry bushes (amend timings to match your appetite), the track dips down briefly before climbing again and

64 Walk! Andorra

ending at the southern end of **Pla de l'Estany**, just west of a small cement cabin (Wp.5 60M).

A pleasant 150-metre stroll on a narrow but clear cow path across the **Pla de l'Estany** pasture brings us to a junction of routes (Wp.6), indicated by waymarked rocks and a couple of broken down signposts. The GRP bears right here for 'Les Fonts' and 'Camí de la Socarrada/Coll Carnisser', but we stay on the GR-variant to reach the superbly situated **Refuge del Pla de l'Estany** (Wp.7 75M).

The Refuge

From the refuge we head NE, crossing the **Riu d'Areny** then following a meandering route to the north before approaching the **Costa del Congost** crags on the eastern edge of the cirque, where there's a signposted junction of waymarked routes (Wp.8 95M). The 'Estanys de Montmantell' path climbs to the right, but we bear left on a faint but clearly waymarked route climbing steeply to the north.

Seventy-five metres after crossing an erosion channel near the head of the cirque, the path peters out (Wp.9 110M), but maintaining a northerly direction and continuing to climb steeply, we soon pick up another clear stretch leading to the broadest flow of a meagre waterfall on the **Riu del Port Dret**, which we approach via a slightly vertiginous ledge.

After crossing the **Riu del Port Dret** (Wp.10 120M), we pick our way across a short outcrop of rock to join another clear but narrow path climbing to the west - some care required here as the path traverses a steep slope. 350 metres

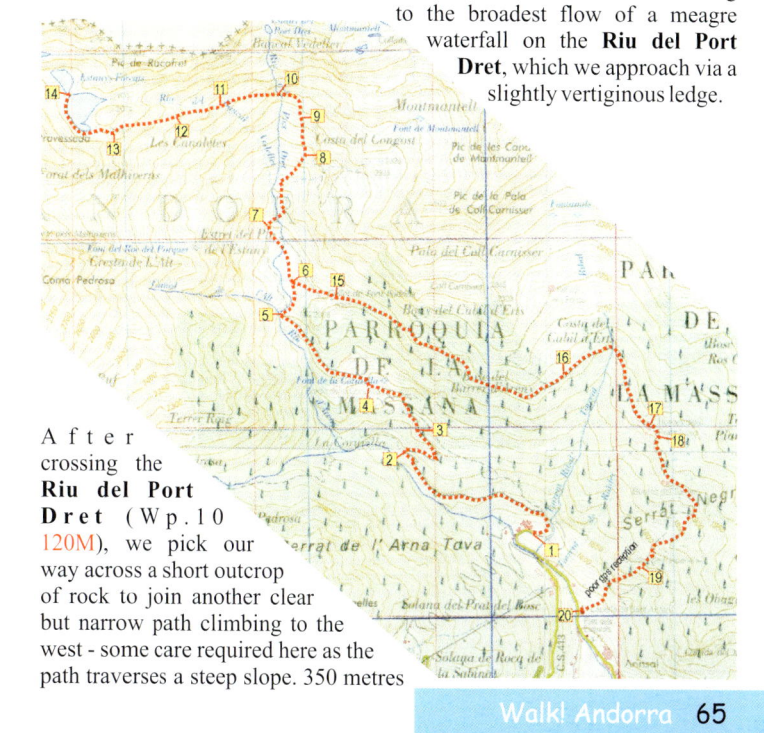

Walk! Andorra 65

later we cross the **Estany Forcats** watershed, the **Riu del Bancal Vedeller** (Wp.11), though you might not notice it as the water runs underground here, submerged in a rockslide, after which we climb along a rocky ridge into a grassy gully patched with debris (Wp.12 145M). Climbing through an increasingly rugged landscape of stratified rock resembling fossilized wood, we emerge at the top of the gully below a small tin hut (a hunters' refuge and adequate shelter in an emergency) (Wp.13 160M), 150 metres from the southern tip of **Estany Forcats**.

The GR curves round the sweep of debris to the south of the lake then climbs to the **Collada dels Estanys Forcats** and **Pic de Medacorba** (reputedly the trickiest walk-up in the principality), but to be perfectly honest, it's such a pills-aching business picking your way over the jagged schist, I really don't think it's worth it and would only recommend it to the sort of people who would disdain to read a book like this. However, it is worthwhile circling the edge of the main lake to the isthmus separating it from the second lake (Wp.14 170M). The clarity and quality of the water are quite extraordinary while the setting gives a strong sense of a distant, undisturbed past - you wouldn't be all that surprised if something primeval popped it's head out of the water! We return to **Pla de l'Estany** by the same path, taking particular care on the descent between the **Rius del Bancal Vedeller** and **del Port Dret**.

Most people simply return to **Arinsal** by the **Pista de Pla de l'Estany**, but I strongly recommend making the marginally greater effort of descending via the **Bordes de Percanela**, which is a far more attractive route. From Wp.6 (230M), we follow the waymarked route (E) across a grassy rise to the **Collet de Font Podrida** (Wp.15 235M), from where we can see **Arinsal**. The path levels off briefly, following a contour line before climbing again. 450 metres after the collet, the climbing ends and we embark on a delightful stroll, following a lovely path through the **Bosc del Barrer d'Areny**, winding along the mountainside amid generally healthy pine with fine views to the south-east. The path eventually curves NE into the **Ribal** valley, passing the signposted turning for 'Refugi de les Fonts' (Wp.16 265M).

Staying on the main path, we descend to cross the **Torrent de Ribal**, after which our route meanders across pasture to pass directly behind the **Bordes dels Prats Nou** (Wp.17 275M), where the GRP branches left, climbing **Serrat de la Burna**. We continue SE for another 50 metres to a junction of waymarked paths (Wp.18), where we turn right, descending (S) alongside the **Prats Nou** boundary wall. After passing above the abandoned **Bordes del Torner**, we curve round to descend across the **Percanela** pasture, soon passing the ruins of the same name. 125 metres after the **Percanela** ruins, we turn sharp right at a junction of waymarked routes (Wp.19 295M), following a waymarked path along the back of a short ridge. The path then winds down through woods before emerging in the open for a final steep descent alongside a meagre watercourse, eventually joining the main road between **Arinsal** village and the **Rocky Mountain Café**, beside a signpost for 'Camí de Percanela, Les Fonts' (Wp.20 315M). Turn right to return to the start of the walk, left for the village.

9 CAMINO REAL: EL SERRAT TO ARANS

Ludicrously easy (I've seen people doing it with a pushchair!), the old royal way (*camino real* or *camí ral*) along the **Riu Valira Nord** earns a discrete itinerary for wonderful flora (hazelnut, cherry, raspberries, oak, birch, and enough orchids and other wildflowers - notably vast iris - to fill a botanical sketch book), and by virtue of the fact that it can be adapted according to your needs, whether you're a dedicated walker determined to walk whatever the weather, a harassed parent hoping to sap the energies of a hyperactive child, a gourmand with a good meal in dire need of digesting, or simply a motorist suddenly seized by a desire to get out of the car.

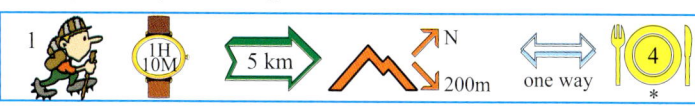

| 1 | 1H 10M | 5 km | ⋀⋁ | N 200m | one way | 4 * |

* **L'Era del Jaume** in **Llorts** is particularly recommended)

Access: by bus

The N°L7 bus leaves **Andorra La Vella** at 7.15am, 1pm & 8.30pm, and **El Serrat** at 7.45am, 1.45pm & 2.45pm, so for most people this will constitute an afternoon stroll. There are scheduled stops at **Escaldes-Engordany**, **La Massana**, **Ordino**, **Sornàs**, **Ansalonga**, **La Cortinada**, **Arans**, **Llorts** and **Les Salines**.

> **Extensions**
> The route can easily be extended south to **Ansalonga** or **Sornàs** and, if two cars are available, north west along the **Riu de Tristaina** or north east (see Walk 21) along the **Riu de Sorteny**.

From the **Hotel del Serrat** bus-stop (No. 364) (Wp.1 0M) at the southern end of **El Serrat**, we cross **Pont de la Farga**, the bridge directly behind the bus-stop, and bear left (SSW) on a broad drovers'trail running alongside a retaining wall.

At the end of the wall, the trail descends to the left, passing below a large farm building (Wp.2 5M), after which it broadens to a dirt track debouching on the **Les Salines** access road (Wp.3 10M). 100 metres along the road, we join the GRP (red-and-yellow waymarks) at a roundabout (Wp.4).

The trail descending from El Serrat

Bearing left, we pass a Romanesque bridge and follow the riverside road until it climbs to the right, at which point we continue along the riverbank on a gravelly dirt track (Wp.5 20M).

We now simply follow this track till it descends to the main road just south of **Aparthotel La Neu** (Wp.6 30M) on the northern fringe of **Llorts**. Turning left, we walk up the road for 100 metres to a track along the left bank of the river, where we pass the locked entrance to an old iron mine. After passing a

Walk! Andorra 67

The Riu Valira Nord below Llorts

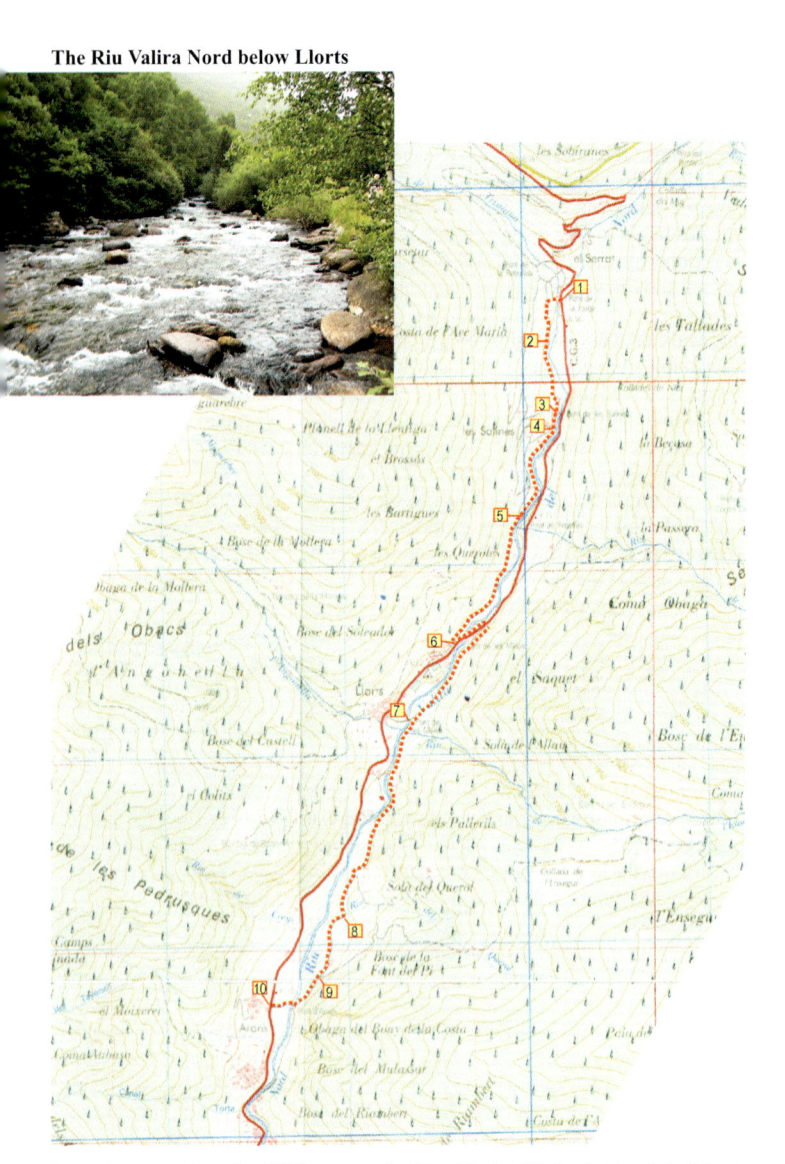

ferruginous spring, the GRP crosses the **Pont de les Moles** bridge into **Llorts** and we continue along the left bank of the river for 'Collada de L'Ensegur' (Wp.7 40M).

We now stroll downstream, passing another bridge over the river, a 'curly-wurly' crash-barrier, and a modern sculpture, after which the track bears away from the river and dwindles to a trail, curving behind hay fields and enclosed pasture. After a gentle climb, we cross a minor affluent and come to a crossroads (Wp.8 60M) where we turn right (WSW), descending to the junction with the **Bordes de l'Ensegur** track, signposted 'Pic de Casamanya' (Wp.9). Bearing right again, we descend to cross the bridge into **Arans**, taking a slip-road up to the CG3, emerging beside **Restaurant La Font d'Arans** and bus stop N°347 (Wp.10 70M).

10 ESTANYS DE L'ANGONELLA

One of those relentless walks that seem far more than their thousand metres but redeem the slog with their destination, in this instance a couple of quite exquisite lakes ringed by big mountains and a ribbon of blue sky. If your energies begin to flag, bear in mind that this is one of the walks said to have been done by the 19th century poet-priest, Jacint Verdaguer, wearing his cassock and carrying a suitcase and umbrella! Now that *is* hard.

The walk is very straightforward and can be done without a detailed description. All you need to know is that you stay on the main GRP-waymarked (red-and-yellow stripes) trail until the **Refuge de l'Angonella**, then follow the yellow waymarks up to the lakes. Vivid pink 'waymarks' in the woods are forestry workers' signs and do not indicate itineraries.

The walk might be extended into a leisurely overnighter or a strenuous day-walk by following the GRP over the **Serrat de la Burna** and descending to **Arinsal** via the **Bordes de Percanela** or **Pla de l'Estany**. There's usually room to park at the start of the walk in the centre of **Llorts**, but failing that, there's a second car-park 30 metres up the 'Casc Antic' road.

Short Versions	Stroll
(a) **Bordes de la Mollera** - attractive pasture and reasonably easy access to the torrent	**Bosc del Soleador** - there are plenty of fine picnic spots in the partially terraced woods and fields in the first 30 minutes.
(b) **Canya de la Sucarana** - pleasant pasture and grand views of **Pic de Casamanya**	

* in **Llorts**

Access: on foot from **Llorts**

From the centre of **Llorts** (Wp.1 0M), where there's a mapboard of both this itinerary and the route to **Arans** via **Sedornet**, we walk up the 'Casc Antic' tarmac road. When the road ends 75 metres later, we take an ancient trail climbing to the right of an old oven. Sticking to the main trail and ignoring minor paths branching off into roughly terraced pasture fringed with oak, beech, hazelnut and fern, we climb steeply, passing a pink waymarked foresters' path branching off to the left (Wp.2 15M) and the first of the water inspection hatches that line the path. Continuing our climb between birch and pine, we fork right 75 metres later at a major Y-junction (Wp.3), after which the gradient eases briefly before climbing again through the sombre pine of the **Bosc de Soleador**.

After the third inspection hatch, the waymarked route forks left at a Y-junction (Wp.4 25M) (the branch on the right climbs to the ruined farmhouses of **Bordes de Mollera**) passing a small *fuente*. We then climb through thinning woodland, crossing the course of a ferruginous spring before emerging in the open above the **Mollera** pasture, where we pass a dry-stone shepherd's cabin (Wp.5 40M). At the head of the pasture, we cross a log-choked affluent of the

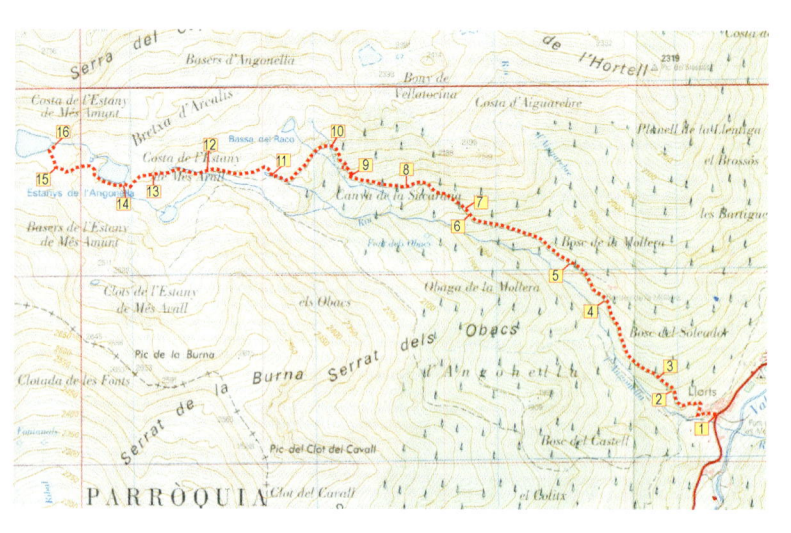

Riu de l'Angonella, the **Riu d'Aiguarebre,** and climb steadily amid the spooky-limbed pine of the **Bosc de la Mollera** - now's the time to start telling fairytales if you're walking with children! The climb goes on forever, passing a triple water inspection hatch (the sixth, but the first on this side of the valley with a tall red pole set in the ground) (Wp.6 70M), forty metres after which we ignore a minor branch on the left (Wp.7). Finally we climb past an impressive crag that looks like it's just pushed its way out of the ground, the remaining trees and shrubs clinging on by the grace of god. We get our own dab of god's grace behind the crag, where the path levels off (Wp.8 90M) at the foot of the **Canya de la Sucarana** pasture.

Climbing gently, we cross the pasture, not towards the obvious wooded gully descending from the lowest point on the ridge, but aiming about 400 metres to the right of the main watercourse, where a cairn (Wp.9 100M) marks the start of a steeper climb (NNW) along an affluent.

After a steady climb the path swings west, crossing the two watersheds feeding the affluent (Wp.10 115M) the first watershed), then follows a rough contour line curving round a rocky knoll (WSW) before a final brief climb leads to the **Pas de l'Angonella** (Wp.11 125M), fifty metres from the diminutive refuge - which allegedly sleeps six, but you'd need to be pretty matey.

Refuge de l'Angonella

The GRP forks left here, but we bear right, following the yellow waymarked route past the refuge and up the grassy rise of the **Costa de l'Estany Més Avall**. We then descend slightly on an initially clear path that peters out above the northern bank of the torrent (Wp.12 130M). Maintaining a westerly direction, we follow waymarks and cairns leading to another reasonably clear path fifty metres later, just beyond a meagre watershed. Following the path, which is sometimes faint but always discernible, we climb alongside the watershed then continue up the dry grassy swale at its head to a long level pass (Wp.13 145M) 175 metres from **Estany del Mig** (Wp.14).

Estany de Mes Amunt

Waymarks guide us round to the western end of the lake for our final 100 metre climb, following a waymarked route, initially on a rough path then directly up a grassy slope into a gully (Wp.15 165M), where we veer right (N) to reach the **Estany de Més Amunt** at its eastern tip (Wp.16 170M).

The waymarked route continues to the north up **Serra del Cap de la Coma**, crossing the **Bretxa d'Arcalis** onto the **Ordino-Arcalis** ski slopes, but we return via the same path.

11 PORT D'INCLES & ESTANYS DE FONTARGENT

This was once the classic legal (it did happen) trading route with France, commonly used up until the end of the 19th century by merchants, tradesman and travellers. All things told, it's not a bad little commuting route, and anyone obliged to fight their way into and out of some modern conurbation in order to do business may feel a little envious of men who's working day consisted of strolling across a mountain. Doubtless if you were hauling a couple of tons of pig-iron over the pass with a team of refractory mules, you wouldn't regard it with quite such starry-eyed romanticism, but even the most laborious haulage must have been meliorated by such a lovely landscape. The central section in particular is a delightful surprise since, from the road, there's no hint of the smoothly sculpted basin that cradles the small alpine pasture clumped about the banks of the **Riu del Manegor**.

All in all, it's the sort of landscape that is normally considerably further from any road, but here it's the merest stroll from your car and accessible to anybody able to walk up a steep English hill. As for the 'beach' at the end, that's simply the sort of place where you want to pitch tent and tell the world go hang. Maybe those old time muleteers didn't have such an easy time of it after all. They had to keep going. We have the luxury of whiling away the afternoon by the side of the lake. It's a memory that will sustain you through quite a few plane, train and car journeys during the rest of the year.

* at **Camping d'Incles**

Access: by car
The walk starts just before **Pont de Baladosa** at the end of **Vall d'Incles** on a waymarked trail signposted (slightly obscurely) 'Port d'Incles, Estany d'Anrodat, Estany de l'Isla, Pic de Anrodat, Cap d'Espones'. (N.B. Not the 'Camí de Port d'Incles' which begins 500 metres earlier). There's room for several cars to park at the start, otherwise there's a large parking area just after the bridge. References to 'left' and 'right' banks of the stream are based on the direction of flow and are therefore contrary to the direction climbed.

> **Stroll**
> **Riu del Manegor** - plenty of fine picnic spots beside the stream below Wp.3.

Setting off from the road (Wp.1 0M), we follow the yellow-waymarked trail (NE), crossing the **Riu del Manegor** a little under 100 metres later, where we pass the first GRP waymarks (red-and-yellow stripes) and start climbing up the left bank of the torrent. Climbing steadily along a rocky but easy path, we emerge on a grassy slope above a small waterfall (Wp.2 10M), where the gradient eases and the granitic massif of Anrodat comes into view. The slope soon levels out altogether and we stroll along beside the stream to a signposted junction (Wp.3 25M).

The GRP bears left here, fording the stream to cross the **Camí de Port Incles** and climb to **Cabana Sorda** (Walk 21), passing en route the path to **Estany de**

Looking back from below Wp.3

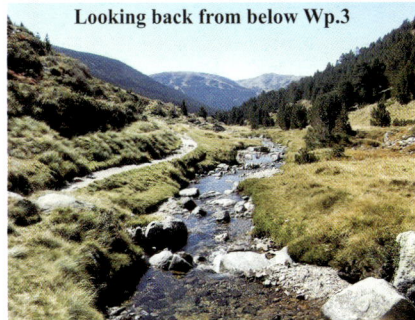

l'Isla and **Pic d'Anrodat**. All these paths are waymarked and are possible variations on the present itinerary. For the moment though, we continue (NE) on the left bank of the stream to the head of the pasture, where we are joined by the **Camí de Port d'Incles** (Wp.4 35M).

After a steady but straightforward climb, the clearer traces of path peter out temporarily and we cross onto the right bank of the torrent (Wp.5 45M), where we soon recover a clear trodden path. A gentler climb leads to a large waymarked rock (Wp.6 50M) beside a marshy patch of ground below the source of the **Manegor**, and the start of our final steady but brief climb to the gateway of large cairns marking the **Port d'Incles** (Wp.7 60M).

Descending into France on a clear path, we pass a small dry-stone shelter built into a slab of overhanging rock (Wp.8 65M). We then follow a cairn-marked route snaking through a sea of debris, the stone so heavily burnished by generations of hooves and boots, the cairns are largely superfluous, after which we descend to the grassy 'beach' on the southern side of the larger of the **Estanys de Fontargent** (Wp.9 75M). We return by the same route.

The descent into France

Walk! Andorra 73

12 REFUGE DE COMA OBAGA

The **Refuge de Coma Obaga** is not often visited, largely because it's not on any of the principal routes to major peaks or lakes, though it could be used as part of an unusual approach to **Estany de l'Estanyó** via the **Collada de Ferreroles**.

The refuge, and Vall d'Angonella

I'm tempted to say this lack of popularity is a pity, except that this state of neglect is part of its charm. The views of the **Angonella** valley are excellent, but for once it's not so much the situation as the refuge itself that's so appealing. In a country boasting some of the best unmanned refuges in Europe, this is among the prettiest, coziest, tidiest, best appointed and most evocative: tiny, isolated, its grassy roof festooned with wildflowers, it resembles a fairytale cottage, and you approach it with the growing suspicion that, any moment now, there's going to be a flurry of crumbs as the gingerbread men come tumbling out to greet you.

The ascent is strenuous but straightforward, comparatively easy and, once begun, well waymarked. The descent to **El Serrat** is something else. Excellent pathfinding skills are required, largely because there isn't any path, just a vaguely logical route picked out with yellow waymarks. Most maps don't even bother showing this way and those that do have clearly never surveyed it, as the route they depict bears scant relation to what actually happens on the ground. It's not for everyone and, I confess, I wouldn't have persisted had it not been waymarked. However, for walkers who are loopy about loops and happy with off-path scrambling on precipitous wooded slopes amid dense undergrowth, it makes for a very satisfying little circuit. There is no official indication at the start of the walk until the first yellow waymarks appear, 200 metres along the track climbing toward **Riu de Ferreroles**.

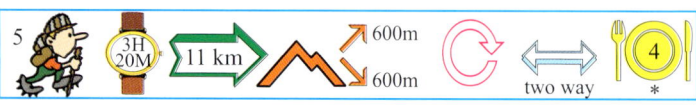

5 | 3H 20M | 11 km | 600m / 600m | ↻ | two way | 4 *

* in **El Serrat** & **Llorts**

Access: by car or bus or on foot from **Llorts**

We start opposite the **L'Era del Jaume Restaurant** at the bus-stop (N°353) (Wp.1 0M) in the centre of **Llorts**, where there are mapboards for the 'Bordes de l'Ensegur' (see Walk 15), 'Bordes de Sedornet', and 'Estanys de l'Angonella' (see Walk 10) itineraries. Taking the GRP (red-and-yellow) waymarked lane, we descend to cross **Pont de les Moles** and turn left following the **Camino Real/Camí Ral** (see Walk 9) upriver.

After passing a yellow waymarked branch climbing to the right (the 'Bordes de Ensegur' path), we rejoin the CG3 just north of **Pont de les Mines** (Wp.2 10M). The GRP doubles back on the left toward **Aparthotel La Neu**, but we turn right and walk up the road for 250-metres to tracks forking left and right. The track on the left descends to a 'new'(partially completed at the time of writing and not looking very dynamic) building, but we take the track on the right, which climbs (NE) dwindling to a path as it passes behind a couple of houses and crosses an iron bridge over the **Riu de Ferreroles** (Wp.3 25M).

One hundred metres after the bridge, we ignore an old waymark indicating a path to the left (Wp.4), and stay on the main trail, climbing steadily to steeply (SE then E) through the woods above the **Riu de Ferreroles**, an area known as **La Passera** or 'stepping stone', which tells you all you need to know really, as we toil up the sort of slope that would make a sprint up the pyramids look like child's play.

After fifteen minutes steady climbing we traverse more open woods, then cross a dry watershed (45M) before resuming our steep climb through densely forested land. We then enter an enclosed area (55M), where the woods become a little monotonous, tall, straggly pine rimed with desiccated lichen, looking like they want for nothing more than a good strong wind to come along and blow them all down to save them the strain of standing. Fortunately, we soon reach gentler slopes where the pine can grow out rather than merely up.

Approaching a muddy stretch, the path divides briefly (65M), the main, waymarked route on the right crossing the mud to curve behind a small pasture, the drier, steeper branch cutting directly across the pasture, so it's a question of different strokes for different folks, wet-&-wandering versus dry-&-steep. Either way, the two paths soon rejoin and we enter a second stretch of shabby woodland. After passing a second shortcut (ignore it, the main path is quite steep enough as it is), we finally emerge at the tip of a broad tongue of pasture descending from the heights of the **Solà de Coma Obaga**. Still climbing, we cross a couple of watersheds, 200 metres short of the **Refuge de Coma Obaga** (as yet invisible), which we reach a little over five minutes later (Wp.5 90M).

If you have any doubts at all about your pathfinding skills, turn back now. This is not the place to be practicing. You either need to be proficient with a GPS or have a lot experience reading the lie of the land. If you do the walk without a GPS, look back every twenty metres or so to check the waymarks, which are all placed for people coming the other way, in some ways a more logical approach, but more elitist in that it would effectively reduce this route to one suitable only for the sort of people who don't need a book to find their way in the first place. Given the terrain and lack of a trodden path, there are more waypoints than usual, and timings are more relative than ever. I therefore give distances rather than times between most waypoints. The distances are counted from the preceding waypoint and are not cumulative. Finally, beware of ankle-twisting rocks hidden in the grass.

Directly behind the refuge, you will find a very faint way heading north. The way divides after 15 metres and we take the lower fork, continuing to the north and passing behind the stumps of two dead pine, the second almost consumed by ants. Immediately after the second stump, 100 metres from the refuge, the way enters the woods where you will see, behind you, the first yellow waymark on this stretch (Wp.6).

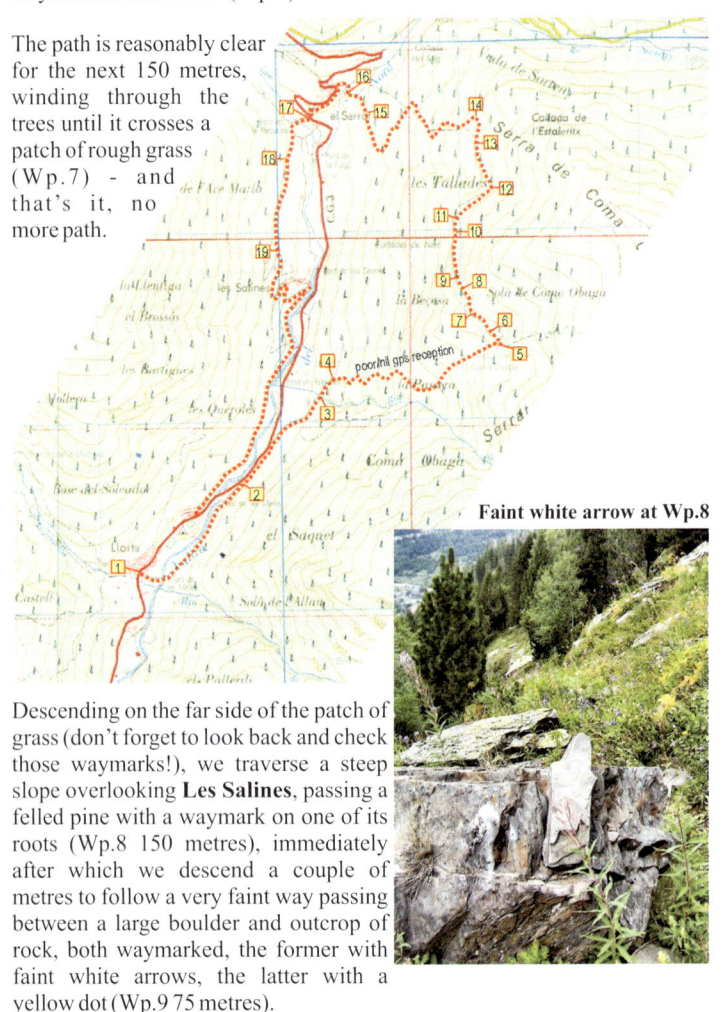

The path is reasonably clear for the next 150 metres, winding through the trees until it crosses a patch of rough grass (Wp.7) - and that's it, no more path.

Faint white arrow at Wp.8

Descending on the far side of the patch of grass (don't forget to look back and check those waymarks!), we traverse a steep slope overlooking **Les Salines**, passing a felled pine with a waymark on one of its roots (Wp.8 150 metres), immediately after which we descend a couple of metres to follow a very faint way passing between a large boulder and outcrop of rock, both waymarked, the former with faint white arrows, the latter with a yellow dot (Wp.9 75 metres).

Picking our way across an ancient rockslide, now largely covered with vegetation, we descend slightly towards **El Serrat** (NW).

After passing below a second large outcrop of rock with a yellow waymark, we climb past a curved, waymarked pine with a split in the base of its trunk, then follow a contour line, crossing a long rockslide from where **Llorts** is visible to the south (Wp.10 225 metres 110M). We then climb to a large triple-trunked pine, the trunks fused together at the base (Wp.11 50 metres), after which something that, with a large measure of optimism, might be construed as close kin to a path, follows a contour as best it can (NE) before dipping into **Les Tallades** (literally, The Cuts), a dry watershed overlooking the **Hotel El Serrat** (Wp.12 250 metres 120M).

Our way then descends (NW) through more open woodland to a patch of black mud marking a meagre spring (Wp.13 225 metres 125M). Clambering over several uprooted pine and birch, we cross both the muddy area and a second slightly marshy patch 50 metres later (where you'll find some of the tastiest raspberries in Andorra), after which we descend across a broad open slope densely carpeted with wildflowers and shrubs, to a tiny grassy platform behind a line of pine (Wp.14 200 metres 130M), at which point you can relax as the pathfinding problems are over.

At the far end of the grassy platform, we double back to the left (SW), and begin our descent, zigzagging down the mountainside on a clear route that is only a couple of hundred walkers away from being a bona fide path. After a long, steady descent, we cross another area muddied by a meagre spring before doubling back north-west for the final descent to **El Serrat**. Ignoring a minor branch climbing to the right (Wp.15), we descend to an access road beside a green-and-white barrier (Wp.16 155M). Turning right, we follow the access road up to join the CG3 at a U-bend round the **Hotel Tristaina**. We now follow the GRP back to **Llorts**.

Turning left, we descend past the **Hotel Bringué** then branch left at bus-stop N°367, following a cobbled lane through the old hamlet and cutting a long bend in the road. When the lane rejoins the CG3 (Wp.17 160M), we cross the road and take a grassy track leading to a bridge over the **Riu de Tristaina**, just above which there are some excellent bathing spots. The track then curves south to a Y-junction (Wp.18 165M), where we fork left on a cow path that eventually emerges below a U-bend on a dirt track above **Les Salines** (Wp.19 170M) (N.B. when the moratorium on new building is lifted, this will probably be asphalted).

Bearing left, we descend to the end of the current road, which we follow (GRP waymarked) down to the banks of the **Riu del Valira Nord**, where we double back to the south, joining Walk 9 at Wp.4 (185M). When the track emerges to the south of the **Aparthotel La Neu**, we can either turn left to rejoin our outward route, or right for the campsite.

13 PIC DE FONT BLANCA & ESTANY ESBALÇAT

Despite being one of Andorra's five highest summits, **Pic de Font Blanca** can look a little bland from below. Once you're on top though, it's anything but bland. On a clear day - and you wouldn't want to be up there on any other sort of day - the views are fabulous, stretching through 360º, including most of Andorra and a rare perspective on nearly every step of the 1000 metre climb. The impact may not wake the dead, but it should jolt all but the most jaded walker out of his ennui.

Estany Esbalçat tends to get neglected in the general glut of more celebrated lakes, which is a pity, as it's a lovely spot, nestling in its own isolated eyrie overlooking the **Valira del Nord**, and ideal for whiling away a long lazy afternoon - not that the approach is exactly lazy, but you get my drift.

Though the itinerary follows intermittently trodden ways and is waymarked throughout, the route is essentially off-path and you need to keep your eyes peeled to pick out the waymarks. There's a very slight risk of vertigo in the last 100 metres of the climb (exacerbated by the devil-may-care acrobatics of choughs and vultures swooping overhead) and on the approach to **Estany Esbalçat** (not desperately vertiginous, but very open).

5 | 5¼ H | 11 km | 1100m / 1100m | ⚠ | * | 0

* panhandle circular

Access: by car

Short Version Estany Esbalçat

The itinerary starts on the **Camí Vell de Tristaina**, the old road to **Tristaina** (now by-passed via the **Arcalis** tunnel), a right-hand turn located between two bridges shortly after km 20 of the CG3. We begin 150 metres from the CG3 (there's plenty of parking on the *Camí Vell*) immediately below the picturesque **Cabana de Castellar** refuge, where a mapboard outlines our itinerary and an alternative ascent via the **Portella de Rialb** (Wp.1 0M).

We take a broad trail to the east for 100 metres, then bear left (NE), following waymarks and cairns up a grassy slope to join a clear path winding through the **Castellar** woods. (N.B. If you find yourself climbing alongside the **Riu del Comís Vell**, either retrace your steps to pick up the woodland path or, when the torrent emerges from the tree cover, cut across the **Comís Vell** vale to join the described route between Wps.5&6.)

The path divides briefly after a little over ten minutes (Wp.2), but the two branches soon rejoin, skirting a small clearing a few minutes later, at the end of which, we bear left at a faint Y-junction (Wp.3 20M), maintaining direction (ENE) toward the V-shaped indentation of **Portella de Rialb**. Ignoring minor trodden ways to the left (Wp.4), we follow the increasingly faint, yellow-waymarked route into the **Comís Vell** vale, a broad grassy depression littered with debris. At a large waymarked rock (Wp.5 25M) just before the dry **Riu**

78 Walk! Andorra

de l'Estany Esbalçat, pale yellow waymarks indicate the 'Esbalçat' itinerary to the north (our return route), but we maintain an easterly direction, following slightly darker yellow waymarks.

Carefully following the waymarks, we wind across the pathless vale for a little over 200 metres, passing a rock indicating where the 'Portella de Rialb' route swings south (Wp.6). Maintaining direction (E), we climb along a slide of increasingly large and chaotic boulders, passing a couple of emergency 'burrow' shelters built under overhanging rocks (Wp.7 35M), immediately after which we cross the rockslide and climb steadily (ENE) to pass below bulbous crags (Wp.8 45M).

Climbing alongside the eastern flank of the crags, we join the **Riu de la Coma del Mig** (Wp.9 50M), which we follow for a steeper climb to a clear 'lip', where the watercourse more or less levels off and the broad curve of the **Coma del Mig** is visible to the north (Wp.10 60M). Following a faint trodden way for another 100-metres, we reach a junction of routes, just below the walls of several ruined cabins/windbreaks (Wp.11).

The 'Esbalçat' route heads west here, but we bear right, crossing the **Riu de la Coma del Mig** and climbing (N) along its left bank, initially on a faint path, then across carefully waymarked rocks, up to a prominent 8-inch wide waymark (Wp.12 75M) painted on a large brown boulder in a sweep of debris at the superficially dry head of the torrent. Cairns mark our continuing route across the final stretch of debris and over a second 'lip', bringing the full span of the Font Blanca crest into view. We then dip back into the grassy bed of the dry watercourse (Wp.13 80M) before climbing to a tiny, moss-blanketed pond at a confluence of watersheds (Wp.14 105M).

The way becomes more obscure here, but maintaining a northerly direction for another 15 metres, we cross the shallow watershed feeding the pond then bear right, crossing a grassy rise and approaching the edge of the coomb 100 metres to the east, where a couple of large cairns (Wp.15) frame a reasonably clear, waymarked path climbing SSE. This path soon disappears, but guided by well-spaced cairns, we climb an immense sweep of sparse grassland, gradually (very gradually, it's an awfully long half-hour) curving round ENE toward solitary crags, 100 metres before which we pass a large flat rock blackened by dry lichen and topped with a marble and granite cairn (Wp.16 120M).

Following the cairns, we climb behind the crags (NE) toward a broad stony *coll*, above which views open out to the east (Wp.17 145M), including **Estany Blau** and the **Rialb/Rabassa Valley** (see Walk 14), and the **Serrera** (Walk 17), **Estanyó**, and **Casamanya** (Walk 15) peaks.

A final steep, stony but clear climb (N) brings us to the summit of **Pic de Font Blanca** (Wp.18 170M).

Approaching the coll at Wp.17

Having drunk in the views, notably of the **Estanys Roig** and **Gnioure** to the north, we retrace our steps to Wp.11, taking particular care on the loose stones above the *coll*.

After all that climbing, even the idea of going upstairs to bed may seem a step too far, but I strongly recommend making the effort to do one more small ascent and visit **Estany Esbalçat**. From Wp.11 (235M), we take a narrow grassy path to the west, winding between rocks and rhododendron (NW) before climbing along a slide of massive boulders for 25 metres (Wps.19-20), at the head of which we pass two, tiny, dry *estanys* and emerge on a rise (Wp.21 245M) overlooking the southern tip of **Estany Esbalçat**. After a further, very brief climb (off-path but waymarked), we descend onto a partially tailored way across a rockslide, beyond which a narrow but clear path curves along a superb balcony high above **Comís Vell** before descending to cross the watershed at the southern tip of **Estany Esbalçat** (Wp.22 255M).

Estanys Roig and Gnioure

At the western end of the *estany*, 130 metres from the watershed and immediately after a corner-waymark (Wp.23), we fork left on a clearly trodden, waymarked route descending a grassy slope (S). (N.B. If you look back from this point you will see the nippled dome of **Pic de Font Blanca**, one of the few places on the itinerary from where the entire summit is visible.) We soon bear left (SE), heading toward **El Serrat** and what appears to be a sheer drop, shortly before which we veer west, bringing the starting point into view (Wp.24 265M). After a gentle westerly descent, the path doubles back toward **Comís Vell**, descending steeply then steadily through the woods (SE then E) to a waymarked Y-junction (Wp.25 280M). Ignoring the branch descending directly to the right, we fork left, passing under the contorted, octopus-like limbs of a toppled pine. Continuing in an easterly direction, we descend relatively gently but on rough ground until the path peters out next to a waymarked rock propped against the whorled stump of a dead pine (Wp.26 290M). (N.B. If you happen to see them, ignore old waymark arrows on the slope below the path 100 metres earlier.) Maintaining direction (ENE) for 75 metres, we come to the dry course of the **Esbalçat** watershed (Wp.27), from where we have a straightforward descent to rejoin our outward route at Wp.5 (295M).

14 PORT DE SIGUER & ESTANY BLAU

Admirable though modern Andorran path-making is, there's nothing quite like a time-honoured high mountain trail, and in this itinerary, we follow another of the traditional paths linking the principality with France. Given that Andorra is the 'land of a 1000 lakes', straying over the border to see a bit of water may appear perverse, but **Estany Blau** is one of the loveliest lakes in the region, and it seems fitting that we should acknowledge the trail-blazing exploits of the *paquetaires* by breaching the border ourselves once in a while. Moreover, the **Rialb** valley, formerly an important grazing area as evidenced by the large number of shepherds' huts, is an exquisite palette of water, grass, wildflowers and rock, that make the Stroll and Short Version particularly rewarding.

The walk is very easy, even when visibility is poor, and is waymarked with yellow dots. The picnic area at the start is a glorious spot in its own right, engulfed in lush vegetation and boasting countless plunge pools in the **Riu de Rialb**.

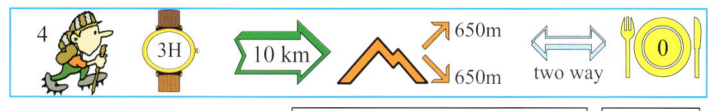

4	3H	10 km	650m / 650m	two way	0

Short Version	**Stroll**
Bear left at Wp.6 to explore the **Cirque de Rialb**.	**Refuge de Rialb**

Access: by car

We start from the **La Rabassa Visitors' Centre** car-park at the end of the asphalted section of the **CS370**, setting off on a broad trail (Wp.1 0M) behind a mapboard depicting the 'Port Vell / Portella de Rialb / Refuge de Besali / Port de Banyell' itineraries.

Climbing through La Rabassa woods

The trail climbs gently (N) through the **Aiguassos & Rabassa** picnic area, passing a small house before emerging from the woods and going through a gate into the **La Rabassa** pasture (Wp.2 15M).

Two hundred metres later, we pass a first metal bridge and a small picnic area, after which we stroll along the left bank of the stream before climbing to the **Font Freda** spring (Wp.3 30M). Following a clear, level path flanked by banks of rhododendron, bushy raspberry plants, and a bewildering variety of grasses and wildflowers, we pass above a second bridge and below the delightful **Refuge de Rialb** (Wp.4 40M). 250 metres later, we cross the third bridge (Wp.5) in the valley and follow the right bank of the stream for 150 metres before re-crossing via a fourth, storm-damaged bridge (Wp.6 50M) just below the **Cabanas de la Plata de les Romes** - for the Short Version, stay on the waymarked route along the right bank into the cirque; it eventually climbs to the **Portella de Rialb**.

A grassy path follows the watercourse (NW) for another 100 metres, before veering right and zigzagging up to pass some 100 metres southeast of the first **Cabana dels Planells de Rialb** (Wp.7 60M). Climbing steadily behind the cabin, we cross rough pasture riddled with watersheds. After fording a first distinct, running watershed (Wp.8 70M), we climb a stretch of slope striated by water erosion. We then ford a second watershed (Wp.9 85M), immediately after which a waymarked path branches off to the left (WNW) towards **Port Vell**. Continuing our steady climb (NNE), we pass the head of a third watershed (Wp.10 90M), after which a gentler climb traverses slightly marshy ground.

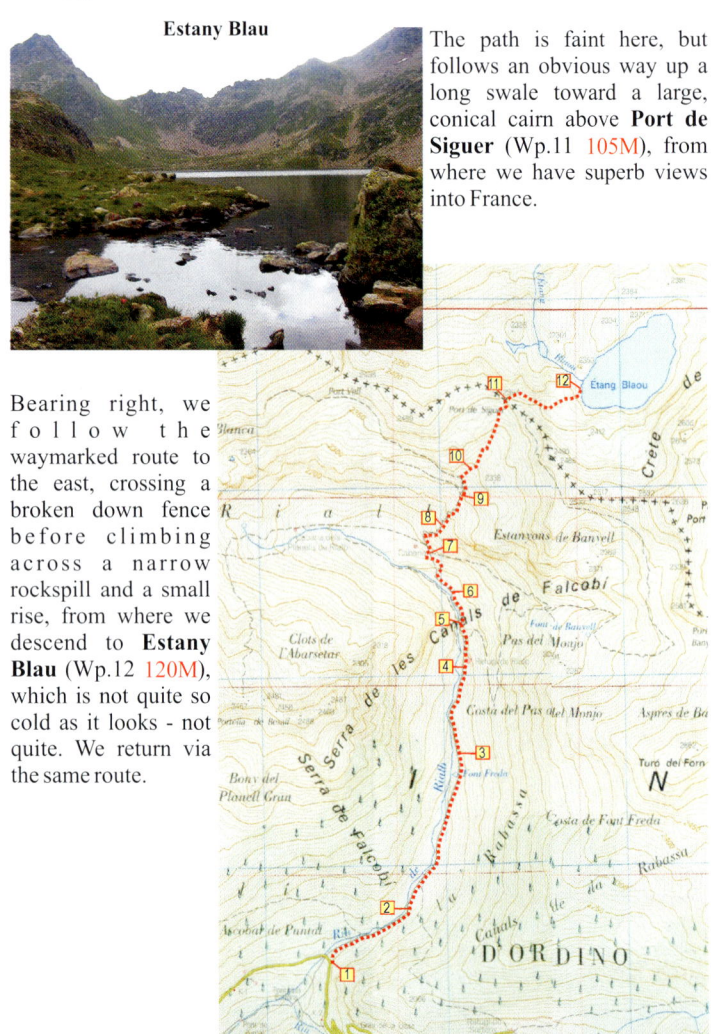

Estany Blau

The path is faint here, but follows an obvious way up a long swale toward a large, conical cairn above **Port de Siguer** (Wp.11 105M), from where we have superb views into France.

Bearing right, we follow the waymarked route to the east, crossing a broken down fence before climbing across a narrow rockspill and a small rise, from where we descend to **Estany Blau** (Wp.12 120M), which is not quite so cold as it looks - not quite. We return via the same route.

82 Walk! Andorra

15 PIC DE CASAMANYA + EXTENSION TO ARANS

Though not the highest or most spectacular summit in the principality, **Pic de Casamanya** earns its position as Andorra's emblematic mountain due to its central location and quite stunning views, encompassing virtually the entire ring of peaks defining the country. The path itself isn't terribly interesting, simply following a straight line directly up the mountain, but the constantly improving views amply compensate, and the sense of wilderness once you're on top is complete. A good first summit for getting the lie of the land and such a blindingly simple climb it should be suitable for a first experience of exploring high mountains. Bear in mind though that the straight-up-straight-ahead nature of the path means that it's more exhausting than the average 700 metre climb, and though it's never really vertiginous, the slope is very open and exposed, which can unnerve people not used to high mountains - that said, last time we were on top a three and a half year old girl was there with her parents, 'doing' her first 2700 metre summit!

While the main walk is suitable for most fit walkers, the extension involves an extremely rough and slippery descent through precipitous rocks, and a long stretch of easy but pathless walking with few way or landmarks. It is only recommended for very experienced walkers with excellent pathfinding skills and a head for heights. GPS navigation is very useful. The extension should not be undertaken alone. Given that it also requires being part of a two-car party or being dropped off at the **Coll d'Ordino**, you may wonder whether it's worth doing at all. The answer is a resounding yes. If you satisfy the above criteria, the full walk is one of the most spectacular and satisfying you're likely to have anywhere: breathtaking views, very varied landscape, extraordinary rock formations, a carefully waymarked but completely barmy descent through jagged rocks, total isolation, a floral fantasia, alpine meadows, torrents, forests … it's got it all!

Both itineraries follow yellow waymarks, though finding the waymark at Wp.21 calls for GPS or a large dose of serendipity.

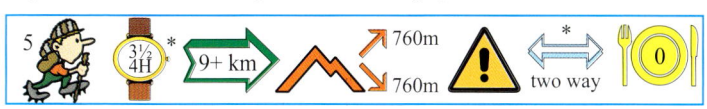

| 5 | 3½/4H * | 9+ km | 760m / 760m | ⚠ | * two way | 0 |

* allow 6-8 hours including stops for the full, one-way linear walk

Access: by car

Extension	Short Versions
Arans via **Coll d'Arenes** (3 hours 35 mins [from the southern peak] 1300 metre descent) - allow 6-8h including stops for the full, one-way linear walk. See text for full description.	**(a)** to Wp.5 - the views are already fabulous **(b) Bordes de l'Ensegur** (see Extension Wps.30-26 and the start of Walk 12; the waymarked itinerary from **Llorts** appears in '36 Interesting Itineraries on the Paths of the Vall d'Ordino & the Parish of La Massana' c.f. Appendix G)

The walk starts from **Coll d'Ordino** (Wp.1 0M) on the CS240 between **Ordino** and **Canillo**. Of the two paths leading out of the small parking area (get there early to be sure of an easy parking space), ours is the broader one climbing east. After running alongside the road for fifty metres, the path veers left to climb steeply then steadily through the woods. It's rather an abrupt start, but it's a lovely path set amid healthy pines and patches of flower-speckled pasture. At a Y-junction (Wp.2 10M) the waymarked route forks right, but either path is feasible, as they rejoin on the **Collada de les Vaques** ridge toward the end of the woods (Wp.3 15M) within sight of **Ordino**, the bare bulbous false-summit just below the southern peak of **Casamanya**, and the high peaks to the west.

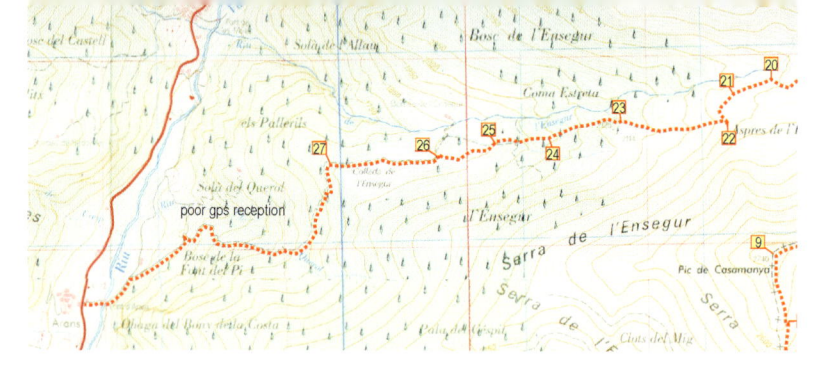

Walking on a carpet of flowers

The path climbs steeply again before levelling out in the final stretch of woodland, beyond which we re-emerge on the ridge with more superb views to the west (Wp.4 25M), in full view of the main climb up a broad swell of grassland, like an immensely bloated down. The way up is so obvious and so devoid of distinguishing landmarks, description is strictly redundant; it's simply a question of keeping on keeping on, straight ahead, straight up. It looks bare and bleak from below, but the views get better with every step (and there's a lot of steps), while a tremendous variety of tiny wildflowers make looking down to see where you're putting your feet, a constant pleasure.

For the purposes of pacing progress, the path skirts to the right of the first outcrop of rock above the last scattered stunted trees (Wp.5 45M), then zigzags up behind the second larger outcrop (Wp.6 55M). We then cross a small hump (Wp.7 80M) (not easily discernible from below), before the final climb over the bulbous swell of the false 'summit', where we cross a dry watershed (Wp.8 95M) before reaching the southern, 2740 metre **Pic de Casamanya** (Wp.9 110M), easily distinguished from the two preceding hummocks by a dais and stumpy flag pole. Remember, these are pure timings and unless you want your heart hammering away like a lively night down the disco, you'll need to stop for breathers/gaspers en route, so allow up to an hour on top of the above times. Most people will want to return by the same way, for which you should allow 1½ hours plus.

The far side of the summit overlooks the **Coma Estret**, which our extension follows for the descent to **Arans**. It's less than a kilometre away from the southern summit, but it's probably one of the most painstaking kilometres you'll ever 'walk' (if that's the appropriate term for progress that involves ample use of your bottom), so don't undertake it lightly or on a whim. Come prepared (extra clothing, plenty of food and water) and turn back if you have the slightest doubt about the weather or your own capacities. Otherwise…

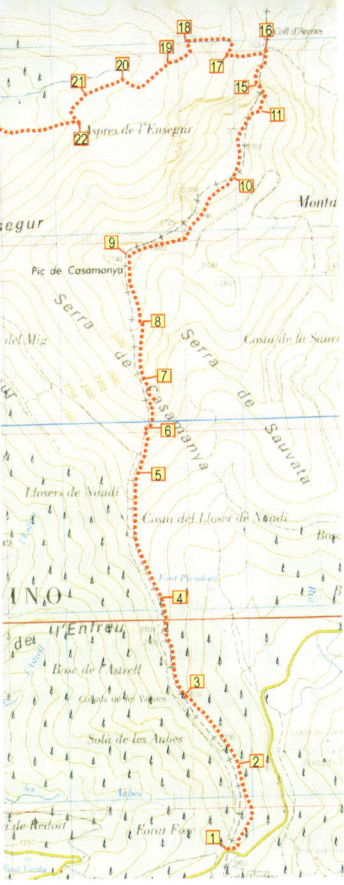

For the extension
We descend steeply along the slightly vertiginous crest toward the middle of the three **Casamanya** peaks, the 2725 metre **Pic del Mig** (ENE). At the breach between the southern and middle peaks, we take the highest of the narrow paths following a contour line below **Pic del Mig** and the 2752 metre peak. The path is very narrow and the slope very steep, so take it one step at a time, looking out for the occasional yellow waymarks and cairns on the more obscure stretches. As we skirt the 2752 metre peak, the way all but disappears, but maintaining a north-easterly direction, we climb onto a broad stony plateau immediately north of the summit. The way is pathless here, but in the middle of the plateau, two large yellow waymarks (Wp.10 20M [from Wp.9]) confirm we're on the right route.

We now begin our descent across a broad moonscape of rock dotted with tiny flowers, maintaining a northerly direction and keeping an eye open for yellow waymarks every fifty metres or so. Staying on the heights, we pass some remarkable rock formations, rows of fractured dorsal fins suggesting a dilapidated dinosaur cemetery. At the end of the gently sloping plateau, we reach the

… a dilapidated dinosaur cemetery

difficult bit, what appears to be an impassable rocky drop down to the **Coll d'Arenes**. Slightly to the right, you will find the waymarked start of the descent (Wp.11 30M) - do not attempt any descent that is not

Descending to the Coll d'Arenes

waymarked: even the official route is hair-raising, anything improvised is liable to result in total alopecia.

The following description is largely for GPS users. Otherwise the waymarks are infinitely more useful than words. Even more vital are hands and bottoms, as there are several sections where it's make-like-a-crab time. The timings in the next paragraph are ludicrously long for such a short descent, but the descent itself is ludicrous, probably the slowest I've ever done, and I prefer to give maximal times rather than underestimate the difficulty. In all probability, you'll do it quicker, but whatever you do, don't rush.

After the first steep descent, a relatively easy stretch leads to a second precipitous slope (Wp.12 40M) where it's possible to walk upright, but with due care. We then lever ourselves down a mini-chimney (Wp.13 43M), after which we descend to a very steep, slippery section (Wp.14 60M) where it's either a question of upright rock-skiing or doing the crab. At the end of this section (Wp.15 70M), we pass rapidly through several stages of evolution and resume our upright posture for a comparatively easy stroll down to the **Coll d'Arenes** (Wp.16 75M).

The main waymarked trail continues north, crossing the **Pic de l'Estanyó** before descending to the **Refuge de Sorteny**. Our itinerary however bears left at this point into the **Coma Estret**, a delightful descent, hard on the knees but gentled by spongy turf and a carpet of wildflowers so varied and vivid it would make the people of Axminster weep with envy. To begin with there are no waymarks and only a few knolls and very brief stretches of cow path by which to orient ourselves, so a GPS is particularly useful. Otherwise, some care is required as finding the first waymarks on the descent is not at all evident. The main thing to remember is that we stay on the left bank of the **Riu de l'Ensegur**, 100 to 200 metres from the watercourse, seeking the path of least resistance throughout!

Heading west, we descend to the first, obvious grassy knoll (Wp.17 80M), a good place for a break after the rigorous descent through the rocks. It is possible to descend to the left of the knoll, but easier on the right. We then follow a watershed leading to the main torrent before climbing slightly to pick up a short stretch of cow-path (Wp.18 90M) cutting across the face of the knoll (S) into a shallow pasture. Resuming our westerly direction, we cross the pasture, descending toward a large rock and, beyond it, a watershed (formed by melt-off from the **Casamanya** summit) and what appears to be a clear path. A second short stretch of cow path (Wp.19 95M) traverses a steep slope (SW) below the large rock. Passing to the left of a grassy hummock resembling a large burial-mound, we descend along the **Casamanya** watershed (NW) to the apparently clear path (Wp.20 100M) seen earlier. In fact, this path only lasts for twenty metres or so, but maintaining the direction it sets (W), we pick up a fourth stretch of path 100 metres later. We then cross a couple of small rises and (hopefully) find a knee high rock bearing our first waymark, a yellow arrow indicating a left hand turn (Wp.21 105M).

Descending into the shallow depression just beyond the arrow, we turn left and climb very briefly (back towards **Casamanya**) to join the head of a long, grassy gully, where there are two more waymarks (Wp.22 110M). The worst of the pathfinding problems are over, though some care is still required as there are stretches of cow path that appear to offer clear routes, but which in fact lead nowhere. Ignoring all such illusory promises, we stay off-path, following the course of the gully as it gradually broadens to a marshy, intermittently boggy valley. The marshy area then resolves itself into an affluent of the **Ensegur**, which we follow for about 100 metres (WNW), ignoring several minor cow paths, until we come to a dark grey muddy path (Wp.23 130M), clearly visible from above and identifiable by waymarks on a rock just before it curves away from the affluent.

After bearing away from the affluent, the path follows a contour line through the woods and becomes slightly grassier but still clearly discernible. Descending steadily then steeply, we come to a second, very narrow affluent (Wp.24 140M), which we follow for another steep descent. Fifty metres after a confluence of watercourses, we ignore a clear path crossing the stream and continue for another fifty metres to a slightly more obscure but waymarked crossing (Wp.25 145M). The path now curves round to cross a wall, visible though much of the descent alongside the second affluent, from where we can see the abandoned **Bordes de l'Ensegur** farmhouse on the far side of the main torrent. We continue descending alongside another wall on an increasingly faint way, which eventually disappears altogether. Ignoring two cow paths into the woods on our left, we follow the wall through a right angle, descending (NW) to a broad trail (Wp.26 155M), after which path-finding is child's play.

Turning left, we follow the trail (in places virtually a dirt track) (WSW), crossing a pasture with superb views up the **Valira Nord** valley and (mind boggling stuff!) back to the **Coll d'Arenes**, which appears to be situated halfway to the moon. The trail then follows the fringes of a pine forest, where we must look for a gap in the trees on the left and a waymarked rock indicating the turning for 'Arans' (Wp.27 165M). Twenty metres from the turning, we join another path which we follow down through the **Bosc de la Font del Pi** woods - take care, stretches of the route are steep and unstable, and it's at this stage of a walk that accidents tend to happen.

Sticking to the main traces at each apparent junction, we cross the **Riu del Querol** (180M) and ignore forks branching off to the left (190M). After skirting several meadows, the path passes under a chest high wire (thoughtfully strung with plastic bags to stop you garroting yourself) and joins the end of a dirt track below a tall stone reservoir (205M). This track descends directly to the **Pont d'Arans** where, ideally, you'll either have a car waiting for you or will have arranged for somebody to pick you up. Otherwise, walk up to the main road for the bus stop, bars, restaurants and hotels. The bus north from **Andorra La Vella** passes at *roughly* 1.30pm and 9pm, and south from **El Serrat** at *roughly* 2pm and 3pm. If you think you might need to spend the night in **Arans**, there are two hotels, **Hotel Arans** (Tel: 850 111) and **Cal Daina** (Tel: 850 988).

16 VALL DEL RIU & RIU DEL MONTAUP

The **Estanys de la Vall del Riu** ascent is ordinarily treated as a linear route starting in **Ransol**, which is puzzling as it can form part of a much more satisfying, indeed near perfect, circuit climbing from the CS240, crossing the **Serra dels Estanys** spur and descending via the **Riu del Montaup** valley. The only thing marring this perfection is 800 metres on the road at the end*, but even that cannot spoil what must be one of the most memorable day walks in Andorra. The **Vall del Riu** is famous for its wild beauty, the river itself deemed so definitive it's dubbed 'The River of the Valley of the River', the waters of **Estany Gran** are of a matchless clarity, the views throughout are nothing less than extraordinary, and the pathless descent from **Serra dels Estanys** is such a breezy, liberating experience, you're hard put not to start flapping your arms on the off chance that you might just be able to fly.

The climb to **Estany Gran de la Vall del Riu** and the descent along the **Riu del Montaup** are waymarked with yellow dots and arrows. The climb from **Estany Gran** to the crest has old red waymarks. Wps.15-20 are off-path and unmarked, but route-finding is simple enough on a clear day. Unless proficient with GPS, do not reverse the itinerary: the way between **Serra dels Estanys** and **Riu del Montaup**, obvious in descent, would be very obscure in ascent.

* If you want to get the road-walking out of the way in the morning, there's a small parking bay just west of Wp.23. We only started from the **Bordes de l'Armiana** track because I wasn't at all sure the loop over the top was possible.

	Strolls
	(a) Bordes de l'Armiana - fine views from the benches at the end of the dirt track
	(b) Riu de la Vall del Riu (Wp.3) - riverside picnic spots and plunge pools
	(c) Bordes de Montaup - in reverse from Wp.23 - riverside picnic spots and meadows full of wildflowers

Short Versions
(a) **Cabana de la Vall del Riu**
(b) **Riu de Montaup** - Wps. 23-20 in reverse

Access: by car or bus (see text)

The walk starts from the sharp left hand bend (dir. **Coll d'Ordino**) at km 3.8 of the CS240 on a broad dirt track signposted 'Vall del Riu / L'Armiana / Refuge / Estanys / Pic de l'Estanyó' (Wp.1 0M). There's plenty of parking space in the first 100 metres of the track or, if the entrance is chained off, alongside the retaining wall above the bend in the road. Slightly bland walking on the track is relieved by clumps of camomile, bunches of oregano (bring a plastic bag if you're self-catering), and a tremendous variety of butterflies. At the end of the track (Wp.2 15M), we pass behind the **Bordes de l'Armiana** ruins, where we're joined by a path climbing via **El Vilar** from the **Sant Joan de Caselles** chapel (km13 of the CG2, a potential access point for those without private transport, ending the walk by following the yellow

88 Walk! Andorra

waymarks from Wp.23 down to **Canillo**). A natural way across bare rock burnished by the hooves of livestock brings us into the **Vall del Riu** and onto a lovely, virtually level path, lined with heather, raspberries, rhododendron, broom, wild carrot, juniper and gramineae, and animated by the panicked scurrying of lizards. NOTE: the small cabin visible in the crux of the valley is not the refuge. After passing a very slightly vertiginous ledge, we snake along the flank of the valley to the banks of the **Riu de la Vall del Riu**, 100 metres along which we cross onto the left bank via a bridge (Wp.3 35M).

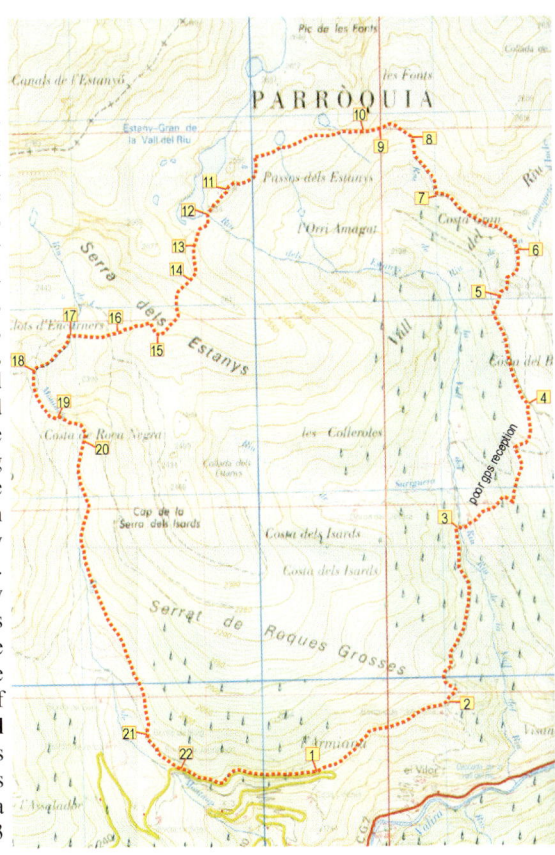

We now begin our steady climb (ENE), passing to the south of two ruins, at the first of which, we're joined by one of the 'Els Plans/Ransol' paths.

The well maintained *borda*

After following a clear, waymarked path winding through the woods (NNE), we cross the watercourse of a tiny spring (60M) and emerge above the main growth of trees at the foot of the **La Serreta** pasture, just below a well-maintained *borda* that doesn't appear on other maps.

Following the line of rubble-cum-wall defining the pasture round the *borda*, we climb to the east then, at a large waymarked rock 75 metres behind the building, resume our northerly ascent on an easier gradient, climbing to a clear path (Wp.4 80M) running NW/SE along a shallow trench (another 'Ransol' path, as indicated by a signpost 100 metres SE). Bearing left, we follow this level path to a Y-junction, where we fork right, crossing a tiny rise to the **Cabana de la Vall del Riu** refuge (Wp.5 90M).

We then take a pathless but signposted/waymarked route climbing (NNE) to join a clear path 75 metres behind the refuge. Bearing left, we follow the path to the north, crossing the meagre interlacing watercourses of the **Riu de la Comarqueta** (Wp.6 100M). The path then curves round to the west, climbing steadily for a couple of hundred metres before leveling out and following a contour line to a broad shoulder overlooking the central **Vall del Riu** torrent (Wp.7 115M). Bearing right, we climb along the shoulder (NW) toward the cirque below **Pic de la Cabaneta**, eventually crossing the swathe of rocks at the source of the central torrent (Wp.8 125M).

We now climb to the west alongside a long chute of sheared debris, initially on the southern side, then on the northern, passing a cairn in a patch of grass about two thirds of the way up (Wp.9 135M). At the head of the chute (Wp.10 140M), the way levels out in undulating grassy terrain fissured by outcrops of rock.

The first lake

Guided by waymarks, we cross a succession of small rises, passing to the south of the first two lakes. One hundred metres after crossing the watershed at the southern end of the second lake, we reach a junction indicated by a waymark painted on a rock, a double-headed arrow with the shafts connected at a right angle (Wp.11 155M). The clear path continuing west, curves round the head of **Estany Gran** to climb **Pic de l'Estanyó**; we however turn left, off-path but following a reasonably well waymarked route (S then SW).

After picking our way through a marshy area, we climb over the 2559 metre mini-plateau then descend to cross the watershed below the dam wall at the southern end of **Estany Gran** (Wp.12 170M).

The yellow waymarks end here, but old red waymarks indicate the way onto a clear path (Wp.13 175M) (visible since Wp.11) climbing steadily (SSW) to cross the **Serra dels Estanys** (Wp.14 185M), from where we have a quite stunning view of the **Casamanya** massif. A very faint path bears right here, climbing to the crest route on **Serra de l'Estanyó**, but we maintain our southerly direction (off-path and without waymarks), bringing into view the curve of **Coll d'Arenes** and, directly ahead, the grassy 2393 metre knoll (identifiable by a long stain of grey shale on its northern flank), between which we can see the **Clots d'Encarners** confluence of watercourses.

This confluence, which lies more or less south-west below **Casamanya**, is our next objective, but to avoid too steep a descent we aim (S) for the broad neck behind the 2393 metre knoll, an easy descent so long as the grass isn't wet. At the neck (Wp.15 200M) we turn right (N), following a very brief stretch of cow path for 50 metres into a swale, where we bear left to continue our steady descent towards **Casamanya** (W). Passing just below the western tip of the stain of grey shale, we <u>cross</u> the first of several cow paths (Wp.16 205M) that follow contour lines to the south.

Maintaining direction (W), we go through a shallow V-shaped indentation in the slope and descend to cross the **Riu de Montaup** (Wp.17 210M) about 75 metres below the green roof of a water inspection hatch that resembles a tiny cabin (a first hatch at the source of the stream was visible through much of the descent). We now simply follow the **Montaup** down to the confluence with the **Clots d'Encarners** watersheds (Wp.18 220M), which from above appeared to be the main watercourse.

One hundred metres downstream, a very brief stretch of cow path climbs onto the right bank, which we follow down to join the yellow-waymarked **Coll d'Arenes/Casamanya** path where it crosses onto the left bank below a large overhanging rock (Wp.19 225M). After a steep descent to another green inspection hatch (Wp.20 230M), we cross a marshy patch then begin our long, gentle descent on a narrow path down to the **Borda de Roig** at the end of the **Bordes de Montaup** dirt track (Wp.21 250M), one of the few places in Andorra you're likely to see a substantial flock of sheep. Continuing on a broad, grassy trail that dwindles to a path below the **Borda de Janramon**, we descend to the road (Wp.22 255M) (signposted 'Coll d'Arenes / Pic de Casamanya').

The yellow waymarked route crosses the road, cutting several loops in the descent to **Canillo**, but we follow the road back to the **Armiana** track. (N.B. A trail climbing to the left looks like a shortcut avoiding the road - it ain't!)

17 PIC DE LA SERRERA

Pic de la Serrera is one of The Big Six, Andorra's fourth highest peak (after **Coma Pedrosa**, **Estanyó** and **Medacorba**) and among the best natural *miradors* in the north. Relatively easy walking and good paths make it one of the most popular high peaks in the principality, and it's best avoided at weekends when the route can get quite crowded. It is, however, an essential summit for anyone who wants to make any claim to having done some serious hiking in Andorra. Best to check the weather forecast before you set off. There's a small cabin just below **Coll de la Mina**, but the top is very exposed and no place to be hopping about dodging the lightning during an electric storm.

*This walk was researched in two parts; the first, to the **Estanys de Ransol**, as a rapid filler on a stormy morning; the second, to the summit, during a heavily loaded two-day trek across the north (see Walk 21). Bear this in mind if you get the impression I've gone haring up to Wp.7 like Brer Rabbit with a pack of hounds nipping at his heels, only to suddenly start dragging along like a lame tortoise with a paper bag over its head. This also explains why the descent time has been estimated.

The entire route follows yellow waymarks. The section between the second **Estany de Ransol** and **Coll de la Mina** (also known as **Collada dels Meners**) is also indicated by the yellow-and-red waymarks of the GRP. If you're hot and bothered at the end of the day, there's a fine plunge pool beside a small reservoir 30 metres upstream from the footbridge at the end of the **Ransol** road.

| 5 | 4H 25M* | 12 km | 1000m / 1000m | two way | 0 |

* see note in introductory paragraph

Short Versions
(a) **Estanys de Ransol**
(b) **Refuge de Còms de Jan** (2 walker, 1½ hours, ascents & descents 200 metres)

Alternative Walk
Taxi to the start and follow Walk 21 from **Coll de la Mina** down to **El Serrat**

Access: by car

Our ascent starts from the end of the **Ransol Valley** road on a broad trail signposted 'Estany dels Meners 2h15 / Pic de la Serrera 3h15' (Wp.1 0M). After following the trail for 30 metres, we veer right (WNW) onto a narrow but clear path climbing alongside a wall, from the end of which we can see **Pic de la Serrera**. After a long, gentle climb across a grassy slope dotted with pine and rhododendron, we cross a shallow affluent (Wp.2 10M) then draw alongside the **Riu dels Meners**.

Climbing steadily along the right bank of the torrent, we bear left at its confluence with the **Estany Mort** watershed (Wp.3 25M), following the main watercourse (W) and passing to the south of a rocky knoll. Shortly after passing a snow-depth pole, we come to a waymarked junction, clearly identified by the words 'Refugi de Jan' painted on a flat rock in the path (Wp.4

Walk! Andorra

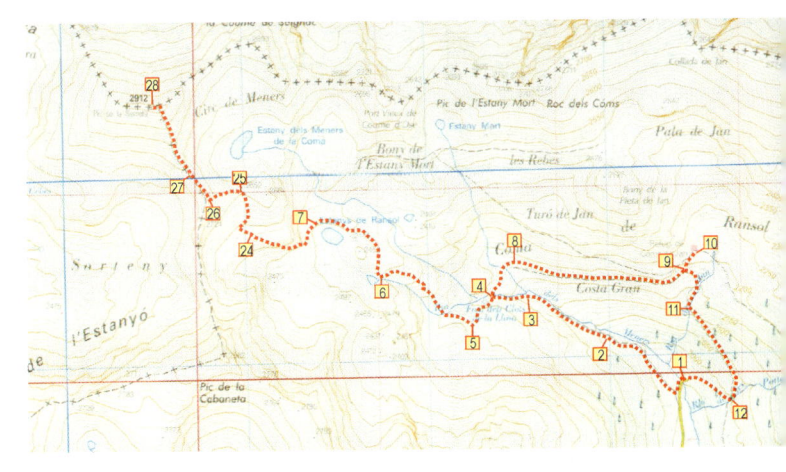

30M), where the main climb and Short Version (b) diverge.

For Short Version (a) and Pic de la Serrera
Take the left fork, climbing steadily behind the marshy area of **Font dels Clots de Llosa**, initially maintaining a westerly direction before gradually bearing southwest, following a broad watercourse. At its subterranean source in a rockslide (Wp.5 40M) we bear right (NW), crossing a branch of the **Ransol** watershed and approaching the foot of the main **Ransol** watershed.

We now have a long zigzagging ascent up to the lower, crystal clear **Estany de Ransol** (Wp.6 65M), from where we can just pick out the upright wooden poles of the old cow gate at **Coll de la Mina**. If you're doing Short Version (a), this is probably the place to stop, as the higher, larger lake isn't nearly so attractive. Beware of bathing; the water is heart-stoppingly cold.

Pic de l'Estanyó as seen from Coll de la Mina

Estany de Ransol

For the full ascent
We veer right, initially in a northeasterly direction but gradually bearing west as we cross two small rises, circling the higher, larger **Estany de Ransol**, behind which we join the GRP, clearly identified by a rock emblazoned with the slogan 'GRP-1 Coll de la Mina' (Wp.7 80M). We now follow Walk 21, Wps.24-28 to

Pic de la Serrera (145M), with the option of climbing directly from the mine cabin below **Coll de la Mina** to Wp.27. We return by the same route. Estimated descent time, 2 hours.

Short Version (b)
For a short walk to the **Refuge de Còms de Jan**, bear right at Wp.4 (30M), crossing the marshy area of **Font dels Clots de la Llosa** and fording the main torrent. There's no path as such, but following the waymarks (N) we traverse the neck of the rocky knoll mentioned above. We then cross the **Estany Mort** watershed and bear right (E) to cross the head of a subterranean spring (Wp.8 35M), after which we pick up a faint cow path. Note that there are several such paths traversing this slope, all tending in the same direction. For simplicity's sake, we follow the waymarked route passing a 4 metre high dead pine 200 metres after the spring. The cow path winds along the contour for a little over five minutes, then climbs very gently before curving round to the overgrown ruin of a shepherds' cabin (Wp.9 50M) just short of the refuge. Following the waymarks (there's no longer a path), we climb directly across a grassy, debris strewn spur to the refuge (Wp.10 55M).

To return to the road from the refuge
We retrace our steps to the ruin and bear left (SE) to pick up a waymarked path that has its origins slightly to the east of the refuge.

The path descends to the **Riu de Jan**, then follows the right bank of the torrent (SSW) before veering left and fording it below a superb plunge pool (Wp.11 65M). After crossing a second, meagre branch of the stream, we descend steadily through the woods (SE), away from the road, before doubling back to the right (WNW) at a second torrent, **Riu de les Portelles**, where we ignore a waymarked branch path to the south (Wp.12 80M). We now simply follow the main path back to the picnic area and the footbridge at the end of the road.

Riu de Jan

18 ESTANYS DE LES SALMANDRES & CAP DE TOSSA D'ENTOR

Entor is the long spur between **El Tarter** and **Pic de la Coma des Varilles**, and a significant strip of land as it helps define two of the most popular valleys in Andorra, **Ransol** and **Incles**. The climb to **Estanys de les Salamandres** is a delightful medium level mountain walk, ideal for a preliminary exploration or if you don't want to risk a long walk in unsettled weather. The names of mountain lakes are often interchangeable, the one being no more blue or trout-laden than the other, but in this instance the toponym is apposite. This is one of the few places in Andorra where, if you look closely, you will indeed see salamanders (*Emproctus Asper*) sloping about in the shallows of the lake, sifting through the silt and snapping the odd unwary insect from the surface. The climb at the start is relatively steep and, had it gone on any longer, might have merited a higher exertion rating; however, it didn't so it doesn't. Don't be discouraged if this is your first walk. The climb does ease off and this is, overall, an easy itinerary. The main walk is well signposted and waymarked (yellow dots); Extension (b) is not … see the text to decide if it's right for you or not.

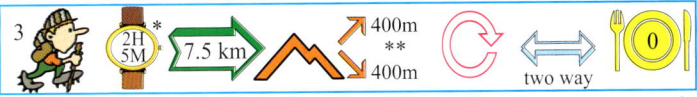

| 3 | 2H 5M* | 7.5 km | 400m ** 400m | two way | 0 |

* 2 hours 40 mins if including Extension (b)
** + 150 metres for Extension (b)

Extensions
(a) **Cabana Sorda** (see text)
(b) **Cap de Tossa d'Entor** (see text)

Stroll
Planells d'Entor - good place for a picnic, with fine views on either side

Short Version
Estany del Querol

Access: by car

The walk starts above the village of **Ransol** at the end of the CS262 on a path signposted 'Cap d'Entor 2h / Estany del Querol 1h30 / Estanys de les Salamandres 1h45 / Roca de l'Hom Dret 50' / Vall d'Incles 1h15' (Wp.1 0M). After climbing steeply for the first fifty metres, the path swings right on a gentler gradient leading to the woods, where it steepens again. Sticking to the main trail, we climb steadily (ENE) to a signposted junction (Wp.2 10M). The 'Camí de l'Hom Dret' continues to the east, but we turn left for 'Planells d'Entor / Estanys del Querol, de les Salamandres i dels Estanyons'.

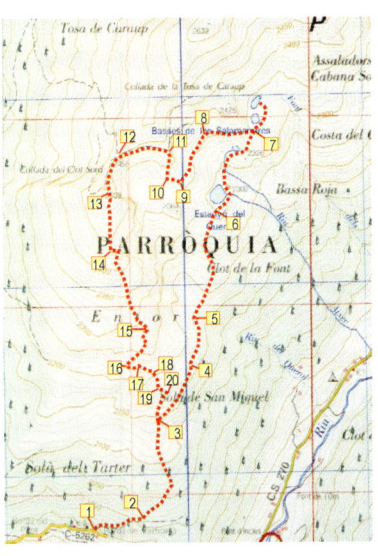

The junction at 30 minutes

Resuming our steady climb in a generally northerly direction, we make our way through the woods to the broad pasture of **Planells d'Entor**, on the far side of which is a second signposted junction (Wp.3 30M). Bearing right for the various *estanys*, we follow the waymarked route as it climbs gently, curving round the eastern flank of the **Entor** spur, bringing the **Vall d'Incles** into view.

After 100 metres on the level, we fork left at a Y-junction (Wp.4 40M) climbing a small rise before the way levels off again and crosses a dry watershed (Wp.5 45M) below a small, dry *estany*. The waymarked route forks left here, climbing a shallow grassy swale, but it's simpler to follow the obvious path curving round the eastern side of the swale and climbing steadily to a rise overlooking the **Estany del Querol** (Wp.6 65M).

Estany del Querol

Skirting to the right of the lake, we continue to the north, crossing a very meagre watershed and a marshy dell with aspirations to being a mini-*estany*, after which a final steady climb brings us across a second rise and down to the first of the **Estanys de les Salamandres** (Wp.7 80M), which isn't too cold and is a good spot for a first swim.

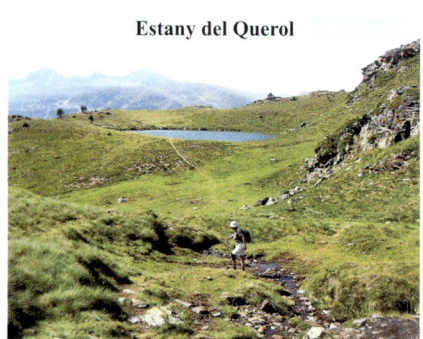

Extension (a)
The waymarked path to **Cabana Sorda** starts directly behind the second lake and joins Walk 21 at Wp.5. It's not a path I've walked, but I understand it is straightforward and easy to follow.

Most people will want to return by the same route (allow about 45 minutes), however there is an option for those hardened hikers who insist on a circuit and regard a linear return as an insult to ingenuity and/or energy. It's not difficult or dangerous, but does involve rough, off-path walking and calls for supernatural pathfinding skills on the descent through the woods. If you're experienced, totally at ease walking off-path, perfectly competent with GPS or possessed of the necessary occult powers, then Extension (b) may be for you. If in any doubt, return by the same path.

Extension (b)
From the rise just south of the **Estanys de les Salamandres**, a clear (initially unmarked) cow path curves WSW, generally following a contour but occasionally climbing briefly, crossing the head of the meagre watershed to the north of **Estany del Querol**, where we find the first of several old red waymarks (Wp.8 5 minutes from Wp.7). Sticking to the main cow path, we pass below a long line of craggy rocks and climb onto a grassy ridge directly behind **Estany del Querol**, where the path peters out in the grass (Wp.9

10M). N.B. The *estany* is invisible from this point, but we can see **Soldeu**.

To the west we can see the **Cap de Tossa d'Entor** crags, the natural pass at the **Collada del Clot Sord**, and a clear path running in from the north. Turning right, we trudge directly up the grassy slope (WNW) to a point overlooking the mini-cirque below the pass (Wp.10 13M). Turning right again, we continue climbing (N) to join the end of the clear path at the head of the long line of craggy rocks (Wp.11 16M).

We now follow the main path (WSW) (there's a second lower path that leads to the same point, but the higher path is broader) to the ridge just north of the *collada* (Wp.12 20M), from where we have superb views of the **Ransol Valley** and **Pic de la Serrera**. Bearing left, we pick our way along the ridge, slightly favouring its eastern flank, to climb a natural but unmarked way to the **Cap de Tossa d'Entor** summit (Wp.13 30M).

... superb views ... (from Wp.12)

This is quite an impressive little climb, and the gentle grassy slopes to the south suggest the difficulties are over. Unfortunately, gentle grassy slopes tend to be devoid of landmarks, and pathless woods are even harder to describe, so this is where, if you want for a GPS, the supernatural powers come in. Heading south towards the **Soldeu** ski pistes (slightly favouring the main track climbing on the right), we descend to a small rocky outcrop (Wp.14 35M), from where we can see the woods above **Planells d'Entor** and, to the left, the path we used in the approach to Wp.3. Descending to the left, passing the end of a short stretch of path, we pick our way down the long undulating grassy slope toward **Soldeu**, the woods and the outward path (SSE), winding back and forth to break the gradient. Descending into the hollow directly behind the highest stand of pine (Wp.15 50M), we lose sight of **Soldeu** and our outward path, and the really tricky bit begins, negotiating a way through the woods. Fortunately they're not dense and, though there are still no paths and no visible landmarks, there is a natural way down, following the grassy curves of the hillside between discrete stands of trees.

Bearing right, we head south-west for 100 metres, then swing left (SE), and begin winding back and forth down the smoothly sculpted curve of the hillside, till we find a very faint trodden way in the grass descending to a T-junction with a short stretch of path following a contour line (Wp.16 55M). Turning left, almost immediately off path again, we head east between a line of trees and a long wall of smooth, sloping rocks, passing the grassy depression of a dry pond (Wp.17, 75 metres from Wp.16). One hundred metres further east (Wp.18), we bear right to descend a fairly steep slope toward the distinct muddy scar of a dry spring (Wp.19). Following the tiny dry watercourse from the spring, we descend to a narrow but clear grassy path (Wp.20), a little under 200 metres north of Wp.5 (65M), from where we follow our outward route back to the start.

19 ESTANYS DE JUCLAR, & A NEAR NOAH EXPERIENCE

Despite being dammed and numbering among Andorra's most visited lakes, the **Estanys de Juclar** are a wonderfully wild little hideaway, and this may well be the itinerary where the sense of wilderness is most acute most rapidly. The lakes are backed by the summits of **Pic de Noé** and **Pic d'Escobes**, which feature in many Andorran legends, the former being one of the peaks on which Noah is meant to have landed and nailed his ring to the summit as a token of something or other, I've never quite understood what. Another ring-nailer said to have frequented these parts is Louis the Pious, like his father, Charlemagne, a regular actor in accounts of how the country came to be founded by the Carolingians. There's no more proof for this tale than any of the others, but at least there's a clearer symbolism to Louis' rings, said to represent the liberties conceded to the new marcher state.

Considerably less nebulous than such legends are the mountains themselves - you could see why a man might come up here if he had a ring to hide- a series of daunting pinnacles and crags which take the definitions of rambling to their very limit. 'Pic d'Escobes' is signposted from the **Vall d'Incles** and I've even seen people continue past the end of our walk onto the summit - I didn't see any of them come back, mind you. In any case, there *is* a 'way' onto the top and those with climbing experience may like to try it. I didn't. Hence our 'near Noah experience', climbing to an already precipitous pinnacle a little way short of the main peaks. Some maps indicate a loop descending via the **Clots de Estany Segon**. You can draw your own conclusions about that on the ground; suffice to say, some novels celebrate a cult of suicide, but it doesn't necessarily make it a very alluring idea.

If all this has you reaching for your heartburn tablets, rest assured, there is also easy rambling up here and anyone who calls it a day at either of the two *colls* is guaranteed a gratifying walk. The rest is strictly for the birds.

Until **Coll de l'Alba**, the walk follows reasonably clear paths and is well waymarked with yellow dots and, beyond the refuge, some puzzling GR waymarks (possibly a variant of the GR10). The final climb is decidedly off-path and indicated only by cairns. There's a large parking area immediately south of the start of the walk.

| 5H | 14 km | 850m / 850m | ⚠ | two way | 3** |

* 3 to the lakes, 4 to either *coll*, 5 to the pinnacle   ** at **Camping d'Incles**

Access: by car

| Stroll |
| Font del Travenc |

| Short Versions |
| (a) Estanys de Juclar |
| (b) Coll de Juclar |
| (c) Coll de l'Alba |

We start from **Pont de la Baladosa** (Wp.1 0M), shortly after km3 of the CS270 at the end of the **Vall d'Incles**, walking past the 'Camping d'Incles' and taking the rough rocky track that continues from the end of the tarmac road.

The footbridge

We follow this track, ignoring all turn-offs (notably the major, signposted trail to 'Siscaró', see Walk 20) (Wp.2), until it ends at a stone footbridge into the **Font del Travenc** picnic area (Wp.3 15M). Crossing the bridge, we continue on a broad trail which divides briefly before traversing a boulder slide.

The trail winds through the rocks, climbing steadily before levelling off alongside the **Riu de Juclar** torrent (Wp.4 30M). We now repeat this process, climbing across the successive 'steps' of a giant's stairway. Ascending a small gully, we climb onto the second, shallower 'step' (Wp.5 35M), where the torrent tumbles down a succession of noisy cataracts. Climbing through increasingly wild terrain, we cross a wooden footbridge above the principal cataract (Wp.6 45M).

After climbing steadily along the left bank of the torrent for 150 metres, the waymarked path veers right, away from the watercourse, climbing across the third and final 'step', where we pass faint sheep-paths branching off to the right (Wp.7 60M).

Bearing north round a knoll, we cross a flat patch of marshy pasture, either directly or skirting its western rim if it's water-logged, then traverse a sheet of rock crowned with a couple of large cairns, on the far side of which we re-cross the torrent by a tiny concrete slab bridge (Wp.8 65M). A pleasant stroll through a lovely wild rocky landscape bisected by the sparkling, rushing torrent leads to a small, solar-powered antenna near a ruin, immediately after which we cross a second concrete bridge below the tunnelled outlet from the dam.

The Refuge de Juclar

One hundred metres later, there's a Y-junction of waymarked routes (Wp.9 75M). The branch on the right climbs over a small rocky rise, the branch on the left remains more or less level until we have to scramble over the tip of the dam wall. In either case, they rejoin 100 metres later just above the dam, 50 metres after which a signpost points the way up to the **Refuge de Juclar** (Wp.10 85M).

Following the yellow-waymarked route, we wind through the rocks (ENE), briefly descending back toward **Estany Primer de Juclar** (at low water toward the end of summer stretches of the old path along the shoreline may reappear) before climbing onto a tortuous but well-waymarked route, bringing into sharp relief the rounded pinnacle of **Pic d'Escobes** and, just to its left, the pointed summit of **Pic de Noé** - anybody looking to land a boat up there was asking for trouble.

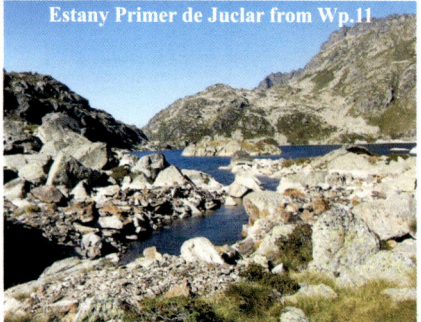

Estany Primer de Juclar from Wp.11

After passing low but rather vertiginous cliffs overlooking the lake, we come to a perfectly feasible rocky descent, touchingly equipped with a couple of loosely knotted rope handrails (Wp.11 100M).

Taking care not to tangle our feet in the dangling ends of the ropes (their most likely practical function), we descend onto a waymarked route across a boulder slide then follow a narrow path winding through the shrubbery before curving onto the isthmus separating the two lakes.

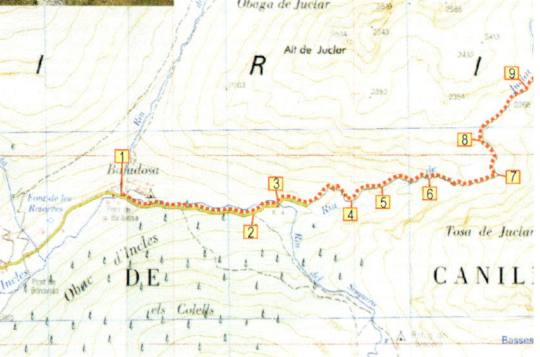

Following the waymarks, we pick up a clear path along the shoreline of **Estany Segon de Juclar,** soon crossing a bridge over the narrow channel linking the two lakes (Wp.12 115M).

From the northern end of the second lake, where the water-stain along the rocks is so regular it looks like a plimsoll-line, we climb to a rocky pass beside a small pond (Wp.13 125M). After following cairns guiding us across a sweep of thinly turfed debris, we recover a reasonably clear path, littered with shards of quartz glittering in the sun like broken glass, for the final climb to **Collada de Juclar** (Wp.14 140M), from where we have a fine view into France. Leaving the clear, recently GR-waymarked path descending into France, we turn right, following the yellow-waymarked route, initially on a faint trodden way then on a clear path climbing gently alongside a dry watershed to the **Coll de l'Alba** (Wp.15 155M), from where the views, notably over the summit and *estany* of the same name, are the best yet.

This is where life gets a little complicated. I suspect most people will be more than satisfied with what they've seen so far, but for those who always have to go just a little bit further ...

Turning right, we wind through the rocks, following a faint trodden way (SSE) that's initially unmarked, but soon passes a couple of cairns. The trodden way gradually disappears and we pick our way from cairn to cairn between great blocks of granite. Ignoring a thigh-high cairn on a ledge to the left overlooking **Estany de l'Alba** (Wp.16 160M), we follow the smaller cairns to the south, climbing towards the main rocky rise for another 75 metres, to a series of long, sharp, single stone cairns (Wp.17).

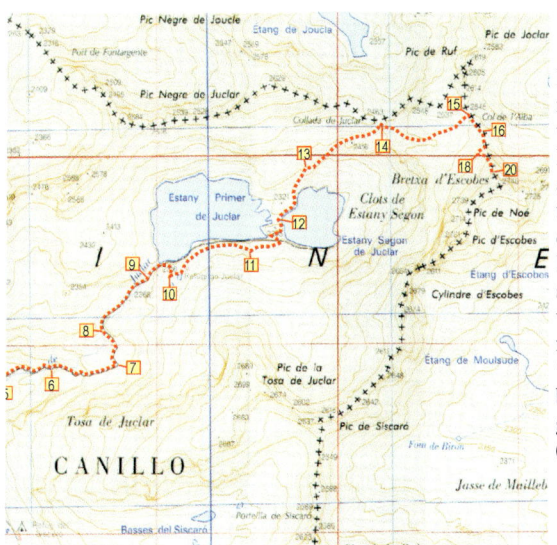

Bearing right (SW), now decidedly off-path, we head towards the **Estanys de Juclar** for another 75 metres until the natural way dips down (Wp.18) into a long rockslide above the second lake, and we veer left (E) for 50 metres, climbing a 'stairway' of rocks and boulders to a small grassy platform (Wp.19).

From here, we simply climb straight up (and I mean straight up) a steep rockslide toward a small sharp outcrop of rock pierced with an 'eyehole'. A final very steep grassy channel (hands required) brings us onto the mini-pinnacle supporting the 'eye' (Wp.20 180M) from where the views take whatever breath we have left. Anywhere beyond this, you're on your own! We return by the same route taking extreme care on the descent back to **Coll de l'Alba**.

20 ESTANYS DE SISCARÓ & CAP DEL PORT

The climb to the **Estanys de Siscaró**, named for the rush-like *siscall* that grow in and around the lakes, is one of the classic, easy walks from **Vall d'Incles**. In this itinerary, we take the usual walk one step further - well, quite a few steps further, actually - continuing up to the line of summits culminating in **Cap del Port**. It's a lovely walk, easily shortened to match flagging energies, but I strongly recommend taking that 'one-step' further as the views from the top are exceptional, and the silence and isolation on this little visited ridge total.

The full loop involves several long stretches off-path, but route-finding is never a problem, always supposing visibility is good - if it isn't, stick with one of the Short Versions. Take a towel: the temperature in **Estany de les Canals Roges** is such as to ensure bathing is generally a matter of leaping in, screaming, then leaping out, but by late afternoon on a sunny day, **Estany de Baix** is positively balmy. The walk follows the GRP (red-and-yellow waymarks) to **Estany de Baix**, yellow waymarks to **Estany de les Canals Roges**, old red waymarks for the final climb up **Tossa del Cap del Siscaró**, and nothing very much at all, apart from the occasional cairn, along the ridge.

5* | 4¼-5H | 13 km | 950m / 950m | ↻ | 3**

* 3 to the lakes ** at **Camping d'Incles**

Stroll	**Short Versions**
Along the dirt track to Wp.2 where two slip paths descend to the river	(all timings one-way, excluding the return) **(a) Refuge de Siscaró** refuge (50 minutes / 250 metres) **(b) Estany de Baix** (1¼ hours / 350 metres) **(c) Estany de les Canals Roges** (1½ hours / 450 metres) **(d) Tossa del Cap del Siscaró** (Wp.11) (1 hour 55 minutes / 550 metres)

Access: by car

We start as per Walk 19 from the **Pont de Baladosa** (Wp.1 0M), following the 'Font del Travenc' track for nearly 700 metres till we come to a signposted Y-junction (Wp.2 10M) where we fork right for the 'Basses i Estanys de Siscaró'.

A steady climb across grassy slopes mantled with shrubs leads to the **Riu de Siscaró** (Wp.3 25M). We now simply climb alongside the torrent amid great banks of rhododendron and wild carrot, either following the waymarks or the least muddy traces, until the gradient gradually eases and we emerge at the foot of the **Siscaró** plain beside an *estanys* signpost (Wp.4 45M) and within sight of the refuge (accessible via the bridge on the left).

Bearing right, we ignore a signposted branch for 'Planell Gran Soldeu' 125 metres later (Wp.5) and continue to the south, skirting a broad, marshy plain, bejewelled with orchids. On the far side of the plain, the path climbs gently then steadily, gradually veering west (Wp.6 60M) to traverse a small shoulder on the right of the **Estany de Baix** watershed (N.B. the GRP climbs directly up the watershed, but the main path over the shoulder is a gentler climb).

Estany de Baix

At a waymarked rock indicating another route to 'Soldeu' (Wp.7 67M), we bear left for the final gentle climb to the first lake, passing en route a tiny muddy pond and mini-*estany*. At a Y-junction 50 metres short of the main lake (Wp.8), we bear left then cross the head of the **Estany de Baix** watershed (Wp.9 75M).

The yellow-waymarked path climbs away from **Estany de Baix**, crossing a small rise, where we ignore a branch to the left (Wp.10 85M) and continue on the main path as it bears right, climbing between dense beds of rhododendron to the head of the **Estany de les Canals Roges** torrent (Wp.11 90M). If the shoreline is waterlogged, fork left immediately after crossing the torrent and traverse the rocky ridge before rejoining the main route at Wp.12. Otherwise, continue along the northern side of the lake then climb the watershed to the east, where you will find the first old, red waymarks. The rest of the climb is off path.

The watershed leads to a small valley (often frequented by izard) (Wp.12 105M), where we stroll alongside a shallow stream, guided by occasional cairns. After crossing a boggy area, we climb to a small rise at the head of the valley, just south of the source of the stream, where a large cairn and two clear waymarks indicate the start of the final steep climb (Wp.13 115M) up **Tossa del Cap de Siscaró**.

There's no path here, but the way is fairly obvious, winding back and forth along the path of least resistance (not that there's anywhere particularly lacking in resistance), generally following the watershed that starts below the

2766 metre *coll*, just south of the broad, smooth summit of the *tossa* itself.

Climbing towards the coll above the last lake

Following the intermittent stretches of trodden way, occasional cairns and red-waymarks, we climb steeply, initially in a southerly direction then ENE.

At the head of the discernible watershed, about 100 metres below the ridge, we come to a large flat rock with a red arrow indicating we turn right (Wp.14 140M), cutting across the flank of the slope (SSE) to join a clear, narrow path leading to the 2679 metre *coll* (Wp.15 145M), where great views open out over the broad sweep of **La Comarqueta** and the high peaks of the south.

The path climbs steeply to pass directly behind the 2747 metre summit, where it peters out on a level, grassy strip. Maintaining direction (SW), we come to a shallow hollow (Wp.16 160M) overlooking the 2652 metre *coll* directly behind **Estany de les Canals Roges**. After a straightforward grassy descent to the *coll* (Wp.17 170M), we follow a reasonably clear stony way for our final, 100 metre climb to the **Cap del Port** (Wp.18 185M), from where we have exceptional views, dominating the peaks defining the north-eastern frontier.

Continuing along the lunar-like crest, we head for a large cairn on the final 2691 metre summit, 30 metres before which, cairns on our left indicate a rough but gently sloping way descending across the southern flank of the summit to a depression in the ridge, from where we glimpse **Estany de Baix**. Maintaining direction (W) then bearing left (SW), we climb back onto the continuing line of the ridge, where there's a large cairn (Wp.19 200M), and we can see the natural pass at **Pas de les Vaques**. It should be possible to descend directly to **Pas de les Vaques**, always supposing you've got about six inches of rubber buttressing your knee-cartilage. Otherwise, continue along the ridge (SSW) toward **Port Dret**, following a narrow cairn-marked path running parallel to the distant line of the GRP, just visible down to the west on the slope of the **Costa de Port Dret**.

After the fourth cairn (approx. 350 metres from Wp.19), the path peters out. One could continue along the cairn-marked route to rejoin the GRP at **Port Dret**, but it's as easy and quicker to gradually bear right (SW then W then N), tracing a long curve across the **Costa de Port Dret** to rejoin the clear path just before the **Pas de les Vaques** (Wp.20 215M). We now have a straightforward but steep and slippery descent to rejoin our outward route at **Estany de Baix** (Wp.8 235M).

104 Walk! Andorra

21 NORTHEN TRAVERSE: INCLES TO EL SERRAT

A grand overnighter traversing the greater part of northern Andorra and encompassing everything that makes the Principality such an ideal walking destination: grandiose peaks, beautiful valleys, breathtaking views, crystal clear lakes, an embarrassment of wildflowers, cozy refuges, and the perfect peace of being all on your lonesome, a million miles from nowhere. The climb to **Cabana Sorda** follows a popular local path waymarked with yellow dots. Thereafter, we stick with the red-and-yellow GRP all the way to **El Serrat**. The climb between **Cabana Sorda** and the 2619 metre *coll* traverses precipitous, grassy slopes and is not recommended as a descent. The way down to the **Refuge de Còms de Jan** is rough and, from the perspective of the refuge, clearly impossible, but it's immaculately waymarked and poses no problems for experienced walkers. Thereafter, the route is straightforward, though don't underestimate the comparatively small but apparently endless climb on the second day. The extension to **Pic de la Serrera** (see text) is highly recommended, but demands a degree of fortitude after the slog up from the **Estanys de Ransol**. Take a break at **Coll de la Mina** first.

DAY ONE
VALL D'INCLES to REFUGE DE CÒMS DE JAN

5 | 3H 50M* | 8 km | 800m / 450m | one way | 0

*allow 5 to 6 hours

Stroll
Riu de Cabana Sorda - just above Wp.4 there's a lovely waterfall which would make an excellent picnic spot

Short Version

Estany de Cabana Sorda

Access: by taxi from **Soldeu** - if you're leaving a car at the start of the walk, there's plenty of parking space at Wp.1 so long as you arrive early

The walk starts from km 1.5 of the **Vall d'Incles** road, the CS270, on a trail signposted 'Estany de Cabana Sorda / Pic de la Coma de Varilles' (Wp.1 0M). At the end of a short stretch of track leading to fields, we bear right onto a waymarked path climbing alongside the **Font dels Comellassos** torrent, which we cross just below the treeline (Wp.2 15M).

The start

Climbing steadily through the woods, we cross two unnamed watersheds. After the second watershed (Wp.3 30M), the gradient eases briefly before steepening again on a clear path that eventually emerges from the tree cover at a Y-junction (Wp.4 60M) within sight of the **Cabana Sorda** cirque and alongside the torrent of the same name.

Walk! Andorra

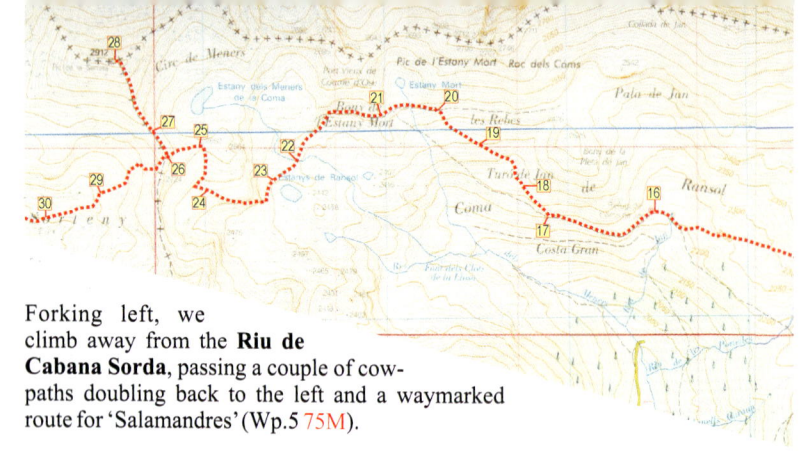

Forking left, we climb away from the **Riu de Cabana Sorda**, passing a couple of cow-paths doubling back to the left and a waymarked route for 'Salamandres' (Wp.5 75M).

One hundred metres later, we bear right at a Y-junction (Wp.6) and descend to cross the torrent below a lovely plunge pool, from where we climb to the **Refuge de Cabana Sorda** (Wp.7 85M) and the lake. This would make a perfectly satisfactory half-day walk in itself and you could do worse for a holiday experience than spending an afternoon lounging round the lake, watching the occasional trout surface. In fact, if you're doing the full walk, you may end up wishing you had spent the afternoon lounging round the lake, as we now begin the serious climbing.

The plunge pool at 85 minutes

On the far side of the mini-dam delineating the **Estany de Cabana Sorda** overspill, we pick up a narrow waymarked path climbing steeply (SW) across a precipitous slope. Taking care to follow the waymarks (horses have trodden several counter-trails across the slope), we cross two long rocky outcrops/shoulders, after which a slanting path traverses a steep slope to a third mini-shoulder overlooking the **Estanys de Salamandres** and the CS270/CG2 junction at **Port d'Incles** (Wp.8 120M).

Bearing right, we climb straight up a virtually pathless but waymarked slope (NNW) for 50 metres before veering left (NW) and following the waymarks traversing the broad curve of the **Pales de les Basses de les Salamandres** to a small, partially overgrown rockslide, after which an easy traverse following a contour leads to a sweep of debris and a waist-high, fin-like rock tipped with a waymark (Wp.9 135M). At the next rockslide just over 100 metres later (Wp.10), we bear right and climb very steeply (N) alongside the rockslide, to a *coll* (Wp.11 165M) just below the 2679 metre summit, from where we can see the **Ransol Valley** and (slightly to the right of the end of the road) the tiny grey roof of the **Còms de Jan** refuge.

Old waymarks along the crest toward **Pic de la Coma de Varilles** (identified in outdated publications as the GRP) have been effaced as the route was

The Estany de Cabana Sorda, from the HRP

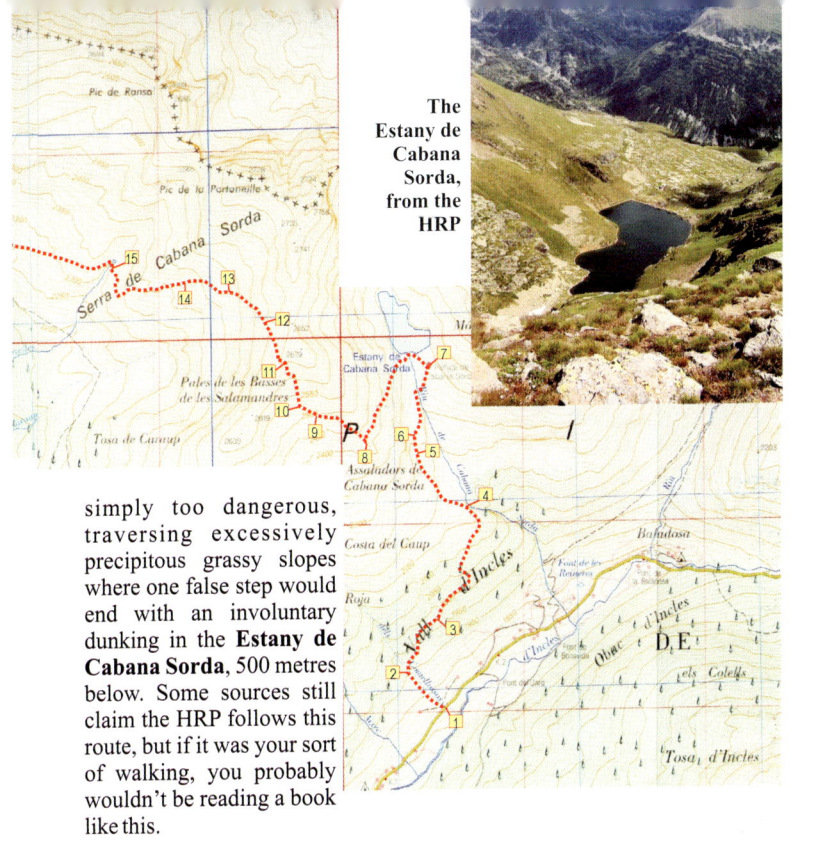

simply too dangerous, traversing excessively precipitous grassy slopes where one false step would end with an involuntary dunking in the **Estany de Cabana Sorda**, 500 metres below. Some sources still claim the HRP follows this route, but if it was your sort of walking, you probably wouldn't be reading a book like this.

For a safe glimpse of the **Estany de Cabana Sorda** from above, head north 150 metres to the first dip in the crest then return to the *coll*.

Following the new waymarks, we descend WNW towards the **Refuge de Còms de Jan** on a faint but discernible path traversing a broad shaly slope. After crossing a long, cone-shaped erosion trench (Wp.12 175M), we maintain direction (NW), descending steadily to a seasonal pond, generally a dark circle of dry mud by midsummer (Wp.13 190M).

Winding between scattered debris, we descend into a rough depression, passing a permanent spring (Wp.14 195M). Maintaining a westerly direction, we cross the stream below the spring and follow a faint, meandering cow path. Descending steadily, we curve round to cross the head of a second more substantial stream (Wp.15 210M). We then cross a small rise on a slightly clearer path, after which a final northwesterly traverse across undulating pasture strewn with large blocks of rock leads to the **Riu de Jan** and the **Refuge de Còms de Jan** (Wp.16 230M), from where we have a superb view down the lovely **Ransol Valley**, ideal matter for contemplation as dusk settles and the last cars of the day disappear into the gloaming. See Itinerary 17 for a short walk up to this privileged *mirador*.

DAY TWO
REFUGE DE CÒMS DE JAN to EL SERRAT

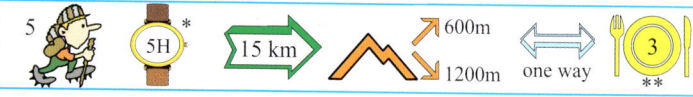

| 5 | 5H* | 15 km | 600m / 1200m | one way | 3** |

*but allow 8 hours   **in **El Serrat**

Short Versions
(a) **Riu de Sorteny - El Serrat** to Wp.36 in reverse. Can be extended by following the wayposted nature trails.
(b) **Refuge de la Serrera** - from Wp.36 in reverse

Stroll
The **Sorteny** meadows (Wps.36-34) for a stunning selection of wildflowers

Extensions
(a) **Pic de la Serrera** for the views
(b) **Llorts** for the campsite

Refuge de Còms de Jan

From the refuge, the waymarked route descends slightly to the southwest before curving west and climbing to a long rocky shoulder (Wp.17 15M). Veering right (N) we climb steeply along the line of rock before gradually bearing northwest as the gradient eases.

We then cross a small rockspill onto a flat sheet of rock (Wp.18 30M), after which we traverse the rough pasture of **Turó de Jan** and cross a dry watershed descending from the northern side of **Bony de la Pleta de Jan**. After another steady climb (NNW), a fifty metre level stretch leads to a large snout-like rock with curved arrow waymarks indicating that we bear right, resuming our northwesterly climb (Wp.19 45M) towards the head of a long, dark, shallow watershed. After a steady to steep climb, we cross a boulder slide and fork right at a Y-junction of cow paths (Wp.20 60M), crossing the watershed below **Estany Mort** a few minutes later.

We now have a gentle, level stroll to the west, crossing the **Bony de l'Estany Mort** spur (Wp.21 70M).

Following a narrow trodden way picked out with frequent

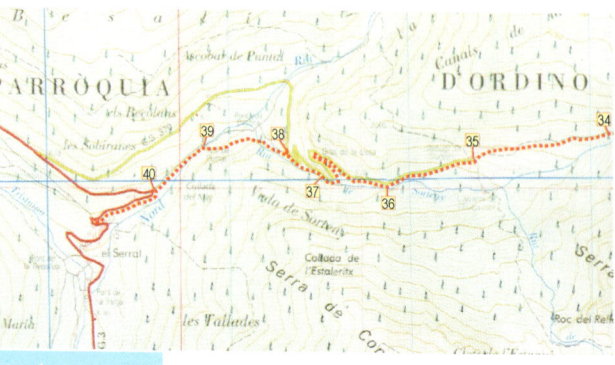

108 Walk! Andorra

waymarks, we curve round below the **Estany dels Meners de la Coma**, descending slightly to cross the **Meners** watershed (Wp.22 87M), shortly after which we join the main path climbing from the **Ransol** valley to **Pic de la Serrera** (see Walk 17) directly behind the largest of the **Estanys de Ransol** (Wp.23 90M).

The steady climb resumes, curving round the 2664 metre peak (NW) to cross a shallow erosion gully on a shaly slope sparsely populated with pale blue thistles (Wp.24 105M). Doubling back to the right (N), we climb onto gently sloping grassland defining the southern side of the **Estany dels Meners** (the lake itself is still invisible), where we swing left (Wp.25 120M) for our final climb past a small cabin and the remains of old iron quarries to 'Coll de la Mina' (Wp.26 130M).

Extension
The path up to **Pic de la Serrera** starts a few metres before the *coll* and is waymarked with old red and more recent yellow waymarks. After winding round the **Cap de la Serrera** crags, we descend very slightly to a mini-*coll* (Wp.27 5M) at the foot of **Pic de la Serrera**. N.B. this mini-*coll* can also be reached by a trodden 'way' climbing directly from the mine cabin.

Pic de l'Estanyo from Coll de la Mina

From here we have a straightforward ascent, zigzagging up the steep slope to the long, flat summit and the small trig point at its western end (Wp.28 25M), from where we have superb views through 360°. We return to **Coll de la Mina** by the same path (allow 15 minutes at a rapid pace).

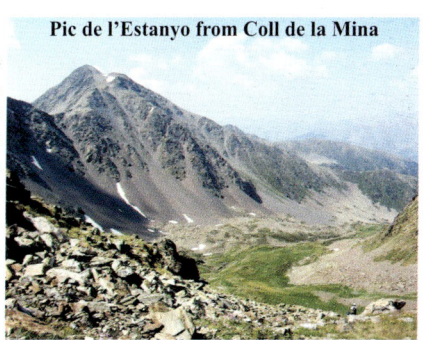

Continuation
The rest of the walk is on clear, well marked paths for which description is virtually superfluous. The remaining waypoints are therefore principally for the purpose of pacing progress.

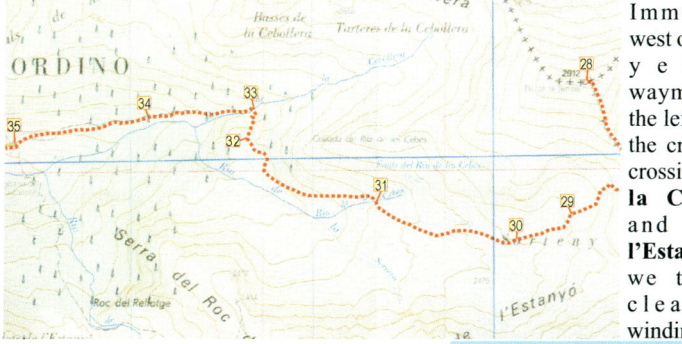

Immediately west of the *coll*, yellow waymarks on the left indicate the crest 'path' crossing **Pic de la Cabaneta** and **Pic de l'Estanyó**, but we take the clear path winding down

Walk! Andorra 109

into the high pasture of the **Clots de la Serrera**, passing the ruins of two shepherds cabins, the second of which (Wp.29 145M excluding the extension) retains just enough roof to provide very sketchy and very temporary shelter for two people in an emergency. After crossing one of the streams feeding the **Riu de la Serrera** (Wp.30 150M) and fording the flower swamped **Riu de les Cebes** (Wp.31 170M), we descend toward the diminutive and generally unmapped **Refuge de la Serrera** (visible for much of the descent between Wps.30 & 31).

The main path doesn't actually descend to the refuge (a good place for a break and a dip in the torrent), but curves round behind it (NNE), crossing a pass in a rocky ridge to the north (Wp.32 190M), from where it descends to a wooden footbridge (Wp.33 200M) over the **Riu de Cebollera** within sight of the **Refuge de Sorteny**. Bearing left, we descend alongside the **Cebollera** toward the woods above the refuge. After fording a small affluent stream (Wp.34 220M), we traverse a prairie veined with glistening springs and carpeted with more species of wildflower than I could count, let alone name. Emerging from the woods, we follow a long wall down to the **Refuge de Sorteny** (Wp.35 240M), which is spacious and well-appointed, but not particularly recommended during the summer holidays or at weekends, when its proximity to the road means it tends to get taken over by bibulous adolescents.

From the refuge, a broad trail descends to the end of the CS370 dirt track (Wp.36 250M) where, if you enjoy the luxury of belonging to a two car party, you will have a vehicle waiting for you. Otherwise, follow the dirt track down past the small botanical garden, ignoring the first two signposted shortcuts (part of the nature trails detailed in a mapboard at the **Sorteny Visitors' Centre**). The third shortcut (Wp.37 265M), following a tailored walkway along the right bank of the **Riu de Sorteny**, is worth taking unless it's very wet when it's easier to stay on the dirt track. In either case, 150 metres after the third shortcut rejoins the track, we leave the CS370 (Wp.38 270M), following the GRP down the old riverside path. Descending steadily through dense woodland, we now simply follow the course of the **Sorteny** crossing two bridges. After the second bridge, **Pont de Puntal** (Wp.39 285M), the path levels out and curves away from the river, passing a tiny hamlet and descending to the **CG3** just above **El Serrat** (Wp.40 290M). We now follow the road down into the village.

Unless you've taken the 'overnight' injunction literally and have walked right through the night or have spent an extra night out in the **Sorteny** or **Serrera** refuges, you won't be immediately catching the bus down to **Andorra La Vella** (dep. 7.45am, 1.45pm & 2.45pm), so it's now a question of checking into your (preferably) pre-booked hotel or, as we did, following Walks 12&9 down to the campsite at **Llorts**. I haven't stayed in the hotels in **El Serrat**, but both the **Hotel Tristaina** midway through the village (Tel: 850 081/Fax: 850 730) and **Hotel El Serrat** at the bottom of the village (Tel: 735 735 / Fax: 735 740 / elserrat@ahotels.com / www.ahotels.com) are friendly places, while the **Subirà** (Tel: 850 037) and **Bringué** (Tel: 850 300) look pleasant enough from the outside.

22 CIRC DELS PESSONS: ESTANY DE LES FONTS

This classic walk through Andorra's largest cirque is a good way to get into the wilds safely and easily, and is recommended for adventurous families or inexperienced walkers who want to experiment with something superficially off the beaten path - it isn't, but that's the impression you get. The massive granitic cirque is so chock-full of lakes, nobody can quite agree how many there are: some claim dozens, others cite sixteen, I counted eight major lakes, convention holds with seven, but whatever the case, there's certainly a lot of water. The numbers game is not particularly significant though, as there's so much to see you won't want to be wasting your time counting and defining what's a lake and what's not. Perhaps the only major drawback to this walk is that the location is so splendid and so popular it tends to induce Walkers' Snobbery, that sneaking resentment of other people cluttering up your own personal paradise; if you're prone to this unhappy malady and suspect you may want it all for yourself, go midweek and go early.

The walking researcher's lament: if you have any other publications about Andorra, you may encounter airy assertions that 'we start from the end of the dirt track'; and so we can, if we have a 4WD vehicle or take the official bus (which also calls at the **Restaurant Piolet**). This stricture does not stem from the track's impenetrability. So long as you're not fussed about the state of your tyres or longevity of your clutch, it can be driven in a normal car. But convention, confirmed by a polite notice, holds that it's only for 4WD vehicles. This insouciance regarding details is also reflected in other people's maps; to be honest though, maps are relatively redundant since, once you're on the GR, the route is almost excessively waymarked.

| 3* | 2¾ H ** | 9 km | 400m *** 400m | two way | 3 **** |

*   2 if you take the bus, 4 if you do the extension)
**   +40M return for the extension
*** +200 metres for the extension
**** at **Estany Primer**

Short Version
Take the bus to **Estany Primer** to avoid the initial climb

Extension
Estany del Cap des Pessons

Access: by car/bus
To reach the start, take the CS280 and fork right when you reach the immense esplanade between **Pizza Hut** and the **Grau Roig Hotel**; park 300 metres later in the **Edifici Cubil** car-park or 200 metres beyond that at the junction of the dirt tracks for 'Restaurant El Piolet' and 'Restaurant del Lac des Pessons'.

If you want to cut the initial climb, catch the bus to **Restaurant del Lac des Pessons**. The bus-stop is next to the barrier at the start of the dirt track. The trip costs €3 return, children under 10 go free.
Dep. times: 9.30 / 10.30 / 11.30 / 13.00 / 14.00 / 15.00 / 16.00 / 17.00
Dep. times from the restaurant: 10.00 / 11.00 / 12.30 / 13.30 / 14.30 / 15.30 / 16.30 / 17.30

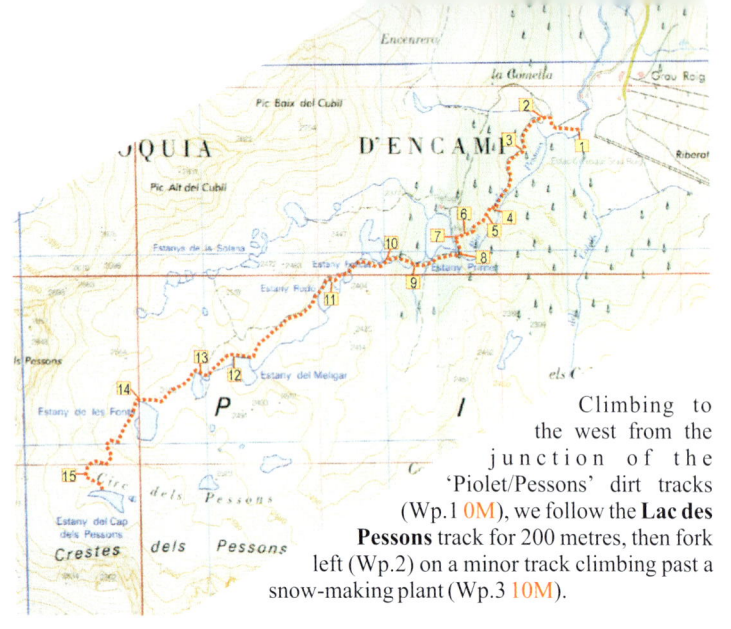

Climbing to the west from the junction of the 'Piolet/Pessons' dirt tracks (Wp.1 0M), we follow the **Lac des Pessons** track for 200 metres, then fork left (Wp.2) on a minor track climbing past a snow-making plant (Wp.3 10M).

The track, which is soon blocked to vehicles by a line of boulders, climbs steeply before levelling off and approaching the **Riu dels Pessons**, beyond which a firebreak climbs very steeply to the south. One hundred metres before the torrent (Wp.4 20M), a large stone arrow on the ground indicates a cairn-marked path into the woods on the right.

Estany Primer

Climbing steadily along this path (SW), we pass between two rocks with old black waymarks (Wp.5 25M) before reaching a Y-junction (Wp.6) (either branch will do, but we followed the clearer fork to the left), fifty metres short of the GRP (red-and-yellow waymarks) on the eastern side of **Estany Primer** (Wp.7 35M) - if you're doing the Short Version, this point is 100 metres south of the restaurant.

Bearing left, we follow the GRP for 75 metres to the junction with the GR7, just short of a sign detailing the various 'Montmalús' routes (Wp.8). Turning right, we cross a causeway and follow the GRP/GR7 round the southern side of the lake. We now simply stick to the GRP/GR7, following the red-and-white GR waymarks, all the way into the cirque, so if you don't care to be reading about what's manifestly all around you (and there's no good reason why you should), shut the book now. All you really need to know is that we pass to the south of the first two lakes and to the north of the rest - contrary to what some other maps suggest!

After winding round to the south of **Estany Primer**, we cross the main stream feeding it (Wp.9 45M) and climb the rocky ridge defining **Estany Forcats**, the second lake, re-crossing the stream just below the lake itself (Wp.10 55M).

As you circle **Estany Forcats**, you may encounter a very large, very immovable bull sprawled across the path; he's also very placid. Skirting him at a suitably respectful distance, we re-cross the stream and pass to the north of lakes Number Three (nameless) and Four (Wp.11 70M), **Estany Rodó**.

A gentle climb on a clear path leads us into the higher reaches of the cirque and a massive boulder chute on the northern side of **Estany del Meligar** (Wp.12 85M), harbinger of the chaos of granite that awaits you at the head of the cirque if you do the extension.

Estany de les Fonts

After lake Number Six (Wp.13 95M), again nameless, we wind between the rocks, as much on the level as one can be on such rough terrain, to the northern tip of **Estany de les Fonts** (Wp.14 105M), which is where most people will probably want to call it a day, as the rewards of visiting the highest lake aren't really commensurate with the extra effort.

Extension
If you're determined to see all the lakes or are set on an overnight walk, continue along the GR as it climbs steadily to steeply through a chaos of boulders threaded with silvery watersheds, until you come to a mini-plateau overlooking **Estany del Cap dels Pessons** (Wp.15 130M), a little over 100 metres to the southeast and easily accessible by a pathless, unmarked, but natural and obvious way.

From Wp.15 more ambitious walkers who wish to do an overnight walk have the option of continuing on the GR7/GRP via the **Collada**, **Pic** and **Portella dels Pessons** to **Refuge de l'Illa**, from where numerous long distance routes are possible, following the GR7 down the **Madriu** valley (see Walk 30), continuing along the GRP to the west, or following the GR11 into Spain before returning to **Grau Roig** via **Collada de Montmalús**. The way out of **Circ dels Pessons** is straightforward, climbing steadily to a small, boulder-lined snow-pit from where the zigzagging path up to the *collada* is obvious. Otherwise, return by the same route.

23 CAMÍ DE GALL: CANILLO TO SOLDEU

Don't be put off by the valley-hugging, road-shadowing simulacrum of this walk on the map. It's a lovely little trail, ideal for acclimatizing on the first day or for when the higher mountains are seasonally or atmospherically inclement. In the contents list I describe the itinerary as being suitable for 'virtually all the family', and so it is; I can well imagine it delighting adventurous eight year olds and not disappointing the sort of fit eighty year olds who've hung up their crampons but haven't quite given up on having a good time in the mountains! However, that 'virtually' should not be ignored as there are several slightly precipitous stretches that might discourage novices, sufferers from vertigo, or the parents of very young children. The only other drawback is the more or less constant hum of the traffic, but the proximity of the road does mean the walk has numerous alternative access/escape points en route. Several stretches of the path are lined with wild raspberries which, in late summer, will doubtless add another hour to the itinerary. The walk is well signposted and waymarked (with the itinerary symbol, the red silhouette of a capercailzie or *gall*), and there is only one point where the onward route is in doubt (see Wp.5). You'll see from the signboards en route that we do the itinerary in reverse. This is not mere perversity on my part, but an acknowledgement of the simple fact that the one thing you don't lack in Andorra is climbs; the opportunity to do a descent, should be grabbed with both boots.

There are several botanical information boards en route cataloguing notable flora, but only in Catalán. Among the trees, shrubs and flowers listed are: *beç*, birch / *escobes*, broom / *falguera*, fern / *freixera*, ash / *gabernera*, a cognate of downy rose and sweet briar / *gerds*, raspberry / *ginebre*, juniper / *maduixa*, strawberry / *molsa*, moss / *panical blau*, blue thistle / *tora blava*, monkshood / *pi negre*, black pine / *pi roig*, scots pine / and *saüc*, elder.

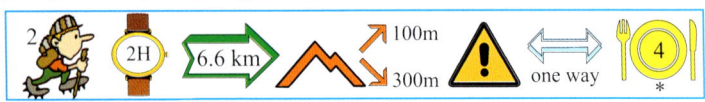

* in **Canillo**

Access: by bus

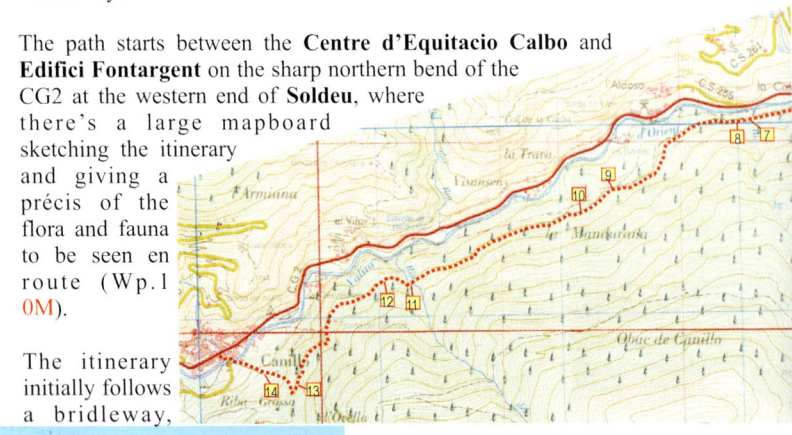

The path starts between the **Centre d'Equitacio Calbo** and **Edifici Fontargent** on the sharp northern bend of the CG2 at the western end of **Soldeu**, where there's a large mapboard sketching the itinerary and giving a précis of the flora and fauna to be seen en route (Wp.1 0M).

The itinerary initially follows a bridleway,

soon passing signboard No.IX 'El Palenquero' (Wp.2 5M) and a second sign for the 'Grau del Palenquero'. The literal meaning of *grau* in Catalán is 'grade, stage or degree', but it's commonly used for a cliff or crag, frequently one blessed with a terrifying combination of frayed ropes and rickety ladders for ramblers who like hanging about in the middle of nowhere; in this instance the *grau* appears to be a simple sheet of sloping rock. After crossing the *grau* and passing the **El Tarter** access, we descend to cross the **Pont de Collart** bridge (Wp.3 10M) over the **Riu Valira d'Orient**.

We now climb into the woods on a footpath running parallel to the muddy bridleway, which we rejoin at a drier stretch higher up. Climbing gently, we cross in rapid succession the **Riu de Collart,** 'Bosc de Beços' (birch wood), and **Riu L'Avetar** (*avet* = fir), and pass the **Collart** *mirador* and location board, immediately after which, we cross a dirt track climbing from **El Tarter** (Wp.4 20M). We continue on a narrow footpath, climbing slightly then following a contour winding through lush woodland before crossing the **El Tarter** ski-pistes and emerging on the edge of a steep dirt track (Wp.5 30M). At the time of writing, canalization work has disrupted the trail here and there are no waymarks. In theory, we continue through the woods alongside the track. In practice, we walk <u>down</u> the track for 150 metres toward the dismal skiers' car-park, above which we rejoin the signposted path.

The 'trampoline' bridge

The main road and path converge as we approach the booze-and-memento emporiums near the **Presa de Ransol** (Wp.6 40M), beyond which the path shadows the road, passing within sight of the excellent **Borda del Horto** restaurant before crossing a tailored waterchute via a suspension bridge that makes a very creditable attempt at passing itself off as a trampoline (Wp.7 50M). Anyone accompanying lively children with an animated sense of life's possibilities (especially those hitherto exposed to the dangerous precedent of Bouncy Castles) take a firm hold NOW! If you don't fancy bounding about like Tigger on Benzedrine and the chute happens to be dry, waymarks indicate an alternative crossing just to the left of the bridge. Seventy five metres later, we pass access path No.4 (Wp.8), worth mentioning as it joins the road a little way south of the **Bordes del Horto Restaurant**.

Plenty of flora along the trail

Continuing on the main path, we pass three more flora/location signboards. *Obac* or *obaga* is a very common word in local toponymy and designates the shady as opposed to the sunny (*solana*) flank of a valley. *Marrades* means detours or roundabout ways! The trail continues through the woods, now thankfully shielded from the road by the trees.

Ignoring a waymarked branch climbing to the left, the 'Camí de Ribaescorjada' (Wp.9 65M), which leads to the **Canillo** ski-pistes, we continue into the area known as **La Mandurana**. At the next Y-junction (Wp.10 70M), the branch on the left is a variant crossing the **Mandurana** woods, but we fork right, descending on the main trail across a slope awash with wild raspberries, before entering a lugubrious pine wood.

Some may prefer the lugubrious bits, because it is now, in the open stretches between more densely wooded sections, that we encounter the first slightly vertiginous slopes, some of the later ones with steel cables set into the rock as handrails. After passing a pronounced overhanging rock (*balma* = grotto), welcome shelter if you're caught by a shower, we enjoy fine views over the climbing wall on the main road and the **Cascada de la Vall de Riu**. After a brief, steep descent, we cross the canalized **Riu del Seig** (Wp.11 90M) and climb a tailored way across rocks to recover our occasionally vertiginous path (it's here that the steel cables start).

After the **Devesassa** *mirador*, the variant rejoins the main route (Wp.12) and we continue straight ahead, bringing into view the northern tip of **Canillo**, still way below us.

Tunnel and Urogallo symbol

We then go through a short tunnel in the rock and cross a sturdy wooden bridge over a waterchute. One hundred metres from the **Canillo** cable-car lines, we fork right (Wp.13 105M), descending steeply to the mouth of the cable-car station, where we join the road running along its southern side (Wp.14 110M).

Descending into town, we cross the river and take the **Pista de Petanca** pedestrian alley up to the high street, bus-stop and restaurants. The pizzas in **Restaurant Lulu** at the southern end of town are good.

24 THE LAZY MAN'S MOUNTAIN: SENDER DE LES TRES VALLS

Having invested rather heavily in cable cars and ski-piste restaurants, it's understandable that the business community in **Soldeu**, **Canillo** and **Encamp** is keen not to leave a lot of costly infrastructure lying idle for six months of the year, and have therefore developed the Grand Valira Campbase network of hiking trails to encourage walkers to use the facilities from spring through to autumn. It's a bit of a Catch-22, since that very infrastructure inevitably means the region is not going to please those seeking a pristine wilderness and is certainly not a priority on a short visit. However, there's enough pleasant walking with excellent views to merit at least one excursion on a longer visit or if you don't feel up to tackling the more rigorous ascents in the west and north. In this itinerary, we cater to the less energetic end of the spectrum, with an easy stroll traversing the three valleys formed by the **Rius Bor**, **Seig** and **Forn**.

There's a fixed charge for the cable car of €10, for which you can ascend and descend by any of the three cable cars. The area is also suitable for mountain-biking, the charge for one person and a bike being €18. There's also a service of free-guided walks plus various paying 'adventure' activities, including Frisbee Golf (sic) and something called 'Arapahoe', which as far as I can work out involves clinging to a scooter being towed by huskies! See www.grandvalira.com for full details or enquire in any of the cable-car stations.

Access: by cable car (**Soldeu-Espiolets**)

Extension
See text, and Walk 25

From the **Espiolets** cable-car station (Wp.1 0M), we follow the main dirt track to the west, ignoring branches to left and right.

... distracted by views of Casamanya ahead ...

It's a dull start, but already we're distracted by splendid views of the northern crest and, directly ahead, the triple peaks of **Casamanya**. The track descends (W), fine views opening out up the **Vall d'Incles**, and we pass our first signpost, at a sharp right hand bend (Wp.2 20M) where the 'Tres Valls' itinerary intersects with the 'Tossa d'Espiolets' path.

Descending into the **Riba Escorxada** ski-station, we pass under a chair-lift then leave the main track (which continues down to **El Tarter**), turning left (Wp.3 27M) then left again 250 metres later (Wp.4) just short of the **Snack**

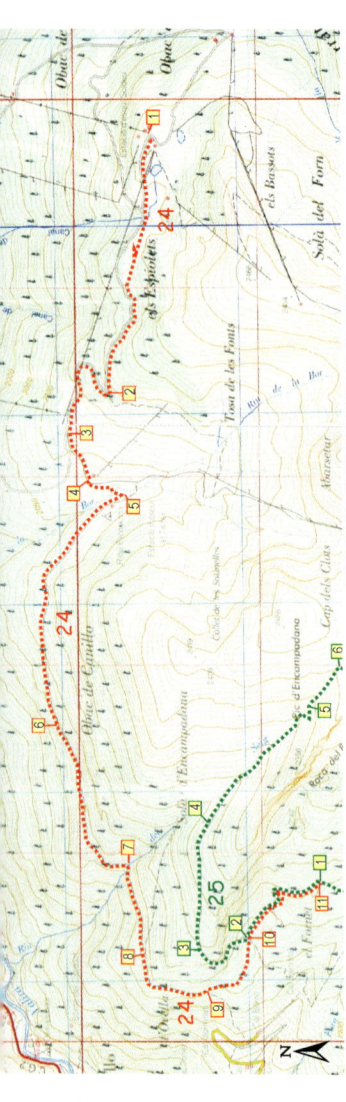

Bar Els Planells. After following a minor track/ski-piste for a further 200 metres, we turn right, passing in front of the **Refuge de Riba Escorjada (**Wp.5 35M), an attractive little refuge somewhat overwhelmed by the ski-pistes, eateries and chair-lifts; hard to believe such a muddle of stuff is required to slide down a mountain on a plank, but so it goes.

Refuge de Riba Escorjada

We now follow an agreeable, grassy track with fine views up the **Ransol Valley**, and pass the first reliable waymarks (yellow) and wayposts (red). The track follows a contour-line, curving southwest and gradually dwindling to a grassy path, passing a signposted fork on the right descending to 'Canillo per Aina i Les Bordes' (Wp.6 55M). After a brief but steep descent, the path levels out, curving round to cross the dry **Riu del Seig** (Wp.7 65M), and climb through mixed woodland, ash and birch mingling with the pine. Two red poles on the left (Wp.8 70M) indicate a way climbing to the **Solà** and **Pic de Encampanada** (see Walk 25), but we continue on the main path (W then SSW), coming into sight of the **Canillo** cable-car.

At the end of a sturdy timber barrier, we ignore a waymarked branch on the right which descends to the CS251, and fork left (Wp.9 80M), following a contour before passing under the cable-car and climbing (E) to a signposted junction just short of a dirt track (Wp.10 90M). If you want maximum walking for your €10, turn left here and follow Walk 25 from Wp.2. Otherwise, follow the track till it ends in a gravelly trail leading to a major dirt track just below the **El Forn** cable-car station (Wp.11 100M).

118 Walk! Andorra

25 PIC DE MAIANS

This won't meet with everyone's approval and, I confess, it elicits lingering hints of the puritan in myself. A rather bland, grassy ascent to a summit spoiled by a chair-lift followed by a descent on a cross-country ski trail, is not, after all, precisely pushing the boundaries of the wilderness experience. However, one shouldn't be too sniffy, because what you get instead is easy walking that lets you concentrate on the views, and what views they are, ranging from **Juclar** in the north through the great western peaks all the way round to the grand summits defining the **Madriu** valley. In sum, not a priority for the dedicated hiker, but a pleasant excursion for the less ambitious leisure walker. The climb is largely off-path, but is very well waypassed. The descent follows a clear trail. N.B. **Pic de Maians** is the name on most maps; the Grand Valira Campbase sketch map has re-christened it **Pic de la Portella**.

| 4 | 2H 25M | 8.5 km | 500m / 500m | ⚠ | ↻ | 3 |

Access: by cable car (**Canillo-El Forn**) or (+ 100 metre climb from the end of the CS251), by car

From the **El Forn** cable-car station (Wp.1 0M), we take the dirt track descending alongside the cables for 100 metres until it doubles back underneath the cables, at which point we follow red-and-blue waypasts onto a gravel path that soon runs into a dirt track. We then descend along the track to a signposted junction (Wp.2 10M), where we bear right (N), following the blue waypasts, for 'Pic d'Encampadana'. A steep climb (NNW) on a shaly trail intermittently waymarked with yellow dots leads to a broad but slightly vertiginous ledge which we follow to the west for 50 metres before bearing right on a rough way curving north and climbing steadily into the upper reaches of the pine wood.

The trail curves NE and the trodden way virtually disappears (Wp.3 20M), but frequent blue waypasts lead us along a very faint way climbing steadily between bushy pine, gradually bringing into view the bare, stone-capped ridge above **Solà de Encampanada**, and superb views across the broad sweep of the northern peaks from **Casamanya** in the west to **Juclar** in the east. We now follow a broad alleyway between the trees (E), passing waypasts every 75 metres or so. The alleyway gradually levels off and we bear right, passing a black-and-yellow snow depth post (Wp.4 35M) as we curve into the grassy valley at the head of the **Riu del Seig**.

... the broad sweep of the northern peaks ...

A little over 100 metres after the snow depth post, we see the red waypasts of the **Pic de Encampanada** itinerary climbing from the **Sender de les Tres**

Walk! Andorra

Valls (see Walk 24 Wp.8) before veering ENE up the **Solà de Encampanada**. We however stick to the blue wayposted route, climbing steadily (SE) along the flank of the **Seig** valley and then alongside a meagre watercourse below what appears to be the head of the valley. It's an easy climb, but a tad unremitting and made no easier by the fact that the apparent 'head of the valley' (Wp.5 60M) is actually some way below the twin reservoirs at **La Portella**.

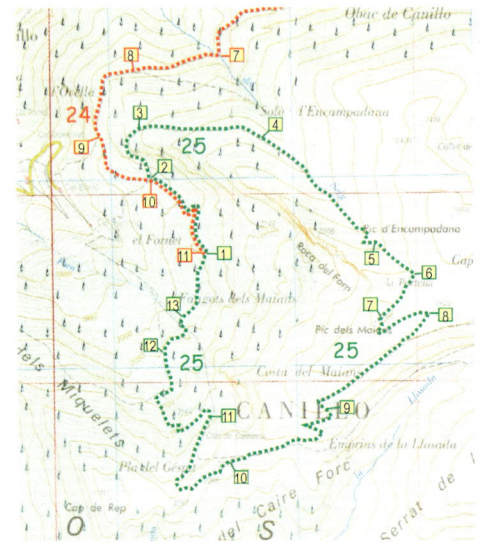

One hundred metres before the embankment round the reservoirs (Wp.6), we veer right for the final, gentle climb (SW) to the chair-lift hut (out of service during the summer) on **Pic de Maians** (Wp.7 75M). The summit itself has been beggared up by the chair-lift installations and, perhaps not incidentally, a large heap of dung, but the views, which stretch through 270°, are beyond contamination and are a constant pleasure throughout the descent.

Taking the dirt track on the southern side of the chair-lift, we follow it through a sharp left hand bend, descending (ENE) towards the **Portella** reservoirs, just before which there's a long fence, stretching (E) toward the **Collada del Cap dels Clot**. Seventy five metres along the fence, we double back to the southwest on a cross-country ski-trail (Wp.8 85M), which we follow, with one brief interruption, virtually all the way back to the cable-car (N.B. this trail can be reached more directly but less clearly by leaving the track halfway to the reservoirs).

The trail crosses the **Costa de Maians**, briefly converging with then bearing away from a ski-piste that doubles as a dirt track during the summer (Wp.9 95M). The second time our trail joins the ski-piste (Wp.10 105M), we ignore signs indicating 'El Forn' via the piste, and stick with the trail (SW), continuing along the **Cap de Rep** ridge for 250 metres before zigzagging down through the woods. We then shadow the piste for 150 metres before recovering the sinuous trail (Wp.11 120M).

At the next junction with the piste (Wp.12 135M), the wayposted itinerary descends to the artificial **Lac del Forn**, a rather redundant descent given Andorra's general abundance of lakes fashioned with considerably greater art by nature. I therefore recommend crossing the piste and continuing on the cross-country ski trail, rejoining the piste (Wp.13 140M) on the far side of the lake, five minutes from the cable-car station.

26 REFUGE & ESTANYS D'ENSAGENTS

An easy walk of consistent beauty and exceptional contrasts, including alpine pasture, idyllic woodland, a near perfect refuge, and two lakes set in an austere cirque of granite where the silence is so total it would make a Trappist monk sound chatty. A must for anyone who has ever had misgivings about pine forests, and I count myself among them, claiming they're monotonous, lugubrious and so forth; the woods between Wps.8&11 give the lie to such prejudices, being all light and variety. They're also a good place for mushrooms if you know what you're about.

| 3 | 3½H | 10.5 km | 550m / 550m | two way | 0 |

Access: by car

Stroll
Bosc de Campeà

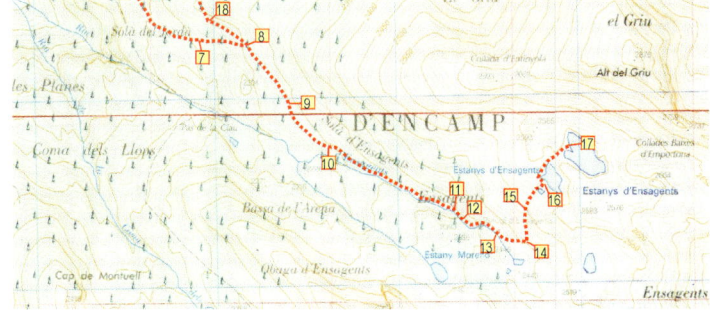

The walk starts near km6 of the CS220, on a dirt track branching right (Wp.1 0M), 50 metres after the signposted turning to 'Bordes de Rigoder'. The official start is a little lower down the road and is neither signposted nor waymarked at present, but this is a slightly easier beginning and there's more room for parking alongside the road. We follow the track for 50 metres until it curves round to the left in front a small shed housing rubbish bins (Wp.2), from where it climbs (E) behind a long straggling picnic area to the start of waymarked itineraries to 'Estanys de Enradort' and 'Pic Alt de Cubil'. We, however, go to the right of the rubbish shed, climbing past new picnic tables from where a narrow path runs along a walled pasture (SW) to join the waymarked trail (Wp.3 5M).

Ignoring faint traces forking left immediately after the junction and another branch on the left 150 metres later (Wp.4), we follow the main trail, climbing steadily (S) to a signposted junction with the **'Camí del Bosc del Campeà'**

Walk! Andorra 121

(Wp.5 15M). We stick with the yellow-waymarked route, which continues climbing to the south before levelling out and bearing SE. After passing behind a walled pasture, a brief climb brings us to a signposted junction, where the right hand fork climbs the 'Coma dels Llops' (Wp.6 25M).

The Solà del Jordà pasture

We bear left, following the 'Camí d'Ensagents', climbing steadily along a stony path into pleasant peaceful woodland where the stones give way to a tangled network of exposed roots. The path eventually emerges at the foot of the **Solà del Jordà** pasture (Wp.7 40M), 275 metres from a signposted junction of itineraries (Wp.8).

A non-waymarked route climbs ENE from here for 'Les Pedrusques, Pic de l'Aspra, Collada d'Entinyola, Alt del Griu'.

For the stroll
We double back to the left (NW) on another unmarked path that re-enters the woods 250 metres later (Wp.18). It then climbs very briefly before descending through sunny open woodland to rejoin our outward route at Wp.5.

For the full walk
We bear right, in the direction of 'Refuge d'Ensagents'. The path meanders through the woods, climbing gently at first then levelling off and crossing a tiny rivulet (Wp.9 55M). Delightful strolling through intermittently denser woodland, brings the dramatic **Coma dels Llops** crest into view. After picking our way along a narrow but not vertiginous ledge (Wp.10 60M), we climb gently alongside the **Riu d'Ensagents**, through an utterly idyllic landscape of spacious pine and varied undergrowth threaded with a myriad of springs.

Approaching a low rocky ridge topped with pine, the path, now little more than a muddy way, but still clear and well waymarked, briefly curves round to the left (E), to an apparent Y-junction of dry but obscure 'ways' just below the rocks (Wp.11 85M). A little over 50 metres to your right, toward the southern end of the ridge, you'll see a solitary pine with a clear yellow waymark on the trunk.

Bearing right, we climb across a rockspill frosted with raspberry bushes (a possible impediment to progress - the raspberries, not the rocks) to the solitary pine (Wp.12). After following a faint way skirting a raspberry-free rockslide, we pick up a narrow but clear path climbing steadily to the superbly situated **Refuge d'Ensagents** (Wp.13 100M).

A signboard just beyond the refuge indicates a number of unmarked ways to 'Pic dels Pessons, Pic dels Ensagents (both 1 hour 45 mins), Estany Moreno' and, our route, 'Estany Primer, Estany Segon, Collada d'Entinyola, Pic Alt del Griu (1 hour 30 mins)'. The arrow on the signboard seems to suggest we climb directly to the north, but in fact we maintain direction (ESE) for another 150 metres before bearing north (Wp.14) on a faint cow path marked with cairns.

Winding amid a chaos of rocks, the cow path crosses a meagre watercourse (Wp.15 110M) before climbing past a small pond to **Estany Primer** (Wp.16 115M). To reach the second lake, we follow a faint trodden way winding round the eastern side of Estany Primer then climb across a low rise onto a spit extending into **Estany Segon** (Wp.17 120M).

Estany Primer

Alt des Griu is the great builders' yard of higgledy-piggledy pillars and ragged blocks of granite to the north of the lake. **Collada d'Entinyola** is the grassy saddle to the northwest, directly in line with the spit protruding into the lake. There's no path as such to the top, but there are intermittent cairns. However, given the sheer beauty of the **Ensagents** ascent, I suggest returning the same way, with the exception of taking the **Camí del Bosc del Campeà** stroll option via Wp.18.

27 CAMÍ DE LA CANAL

An attractive short walk following the canalization pipe bringing water from **Ransol** to **Engolasters**. These linear contour-line paths like **Camí de Gall** (Walk 23), **Camí de les Pardines** (Walk 30), and the **Recs de Obac** and **Sola** flanking **Andorra la Vella**, are easily dismissed when you look at the map, where they appear to be nothing more than an inconsequential straight line to nowhere. In fact, they are frequently lovely little walks, ideal for a family stroll or stretching your legs during a 'day-off' after one of the more strenuous high-mountain itineraries.

Moreover, in this instance, the various waymarked ways we cross en route give ample opportunity for further exploration. After **Torrent Prego** we pass two not enormously informative nature itinerary sign boards, cataloging features of the surrounding landscape, including bearberry, birch, black pine, box, briar, hazel, juniper, moss, strawberry tree, and slate.

The walk starts on a sharp right hand bend at km3.2 of the CS220. There's room to park on the rough ground inside the bend. There are a couple of stretches en route where there's a very slight risk of vertigo. The extension to **Canillo** is not waymarked and passes quite close to a couple of private houses, so I suggest you avoid doing this descent during the weekend, when the houses are more likely to be occupied.

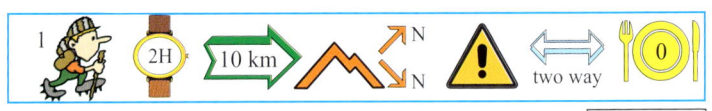

Access: by car

Extension Canillo

Overlooking Encamp on the route

From the bend on the CS220 (Wp.1 0M), we set off on a dirt track (chained against traffic), which passes a bench after 150 metres and dwindles to a path, descending slightly to cross a steep, waymarked route, 'Camí del Bosc des Llaus' (Wp.2 5M), which begins lower down the CS220 and climbs on our right to 'Cadira dels Dimonis'.

Twin footbridges take us over the **Riu dels Cortals**, 50 metres after which we cross a second, tailored path (Wp.3), this time following the **Funicamp** cable-car, and pass in front of a small ruin, where a slightly confusing signpost seems to indicate that the path climbs to the right. It doesn't. Staying on the level, we cross an unusual rock slide formed by massive blocks of slate. Trees then close in and the path dips up and down before crossing a third, waymarked itinerary climbing from the west, the 'Camí de Solans' (Wp.4 20M).

It then tunnels its way through dense woodland before fine views open out of **Pic de Casamanya**. After traversing a broad rock ledge, a slightly more substantial descent is followed by a corresponding climb back into dense woodland. We then cross the **Torrent Prego** (Wp.5 30M), the parochial limit of **Canillo** and **Encamp**, where the **Camí de la Llebre** (The Hare's Path) from **Meritxell** does an about turn.

The woodland become lighter, brighter and more varied after this point, and we pass the first of three location boards. After the second location board, which overlooks the **Santuari de Meritxell**, the **Vall del Riu** (Walk 16) comes into view, and we go through a short tunnel in the rock (Wp.6 50M).

Some 150 metres after the third location board, we come to a pleasant pasture (Wp.7 55M) (watch out for the strand of wire defining its boundary) which is an ideal spot for a picnic. Since most people will have to return to their car at Wp.1, this is a logical stopping point, but if any of your party wishes to continue and be picked up later, there are at least two possible extensions, though I've only explored one of them.

Extension
Crossing the pasture to a small stand of pine 150 metres from the boundary wall, we ignore a broad trail climbing to the right (E) (Wp.8), and stay on the path traversing the field (NE), descending through a second stand of pine to the **Riu del Forn**, a narrow but noisy torrent lined with poplar. Forty metres after the torrent, the path divides (Wp.9 60M), both branches following 'Camí de la Llebre' waymarks. The branch descending to the left leads to **Meritxell**, a route I've not explored, but which should be well waymarked.

The branch on the right climbs 50 metres to a fourth location board identifying, among others, **Roc del Forn**, **Pic de la Portella**, and **Pic dels Maians** (Wp.10). The 'Camí de la Llebre' curves back toward the torrent after this, but immediately <u>before</u> the location board, we turn left on a faint path following a grassy embankment between sloping terraces.

The path then dips into a dense dark alley of pine and descends to a dirt track above the picturesque **Borda del Pugicernal** farmhouse. Bearing right, we follow the track up to join the CS251 at a U-bend 150 metres later.

The Borda del Pugicernal farmhouse

From a wooden rubbish-bin shed on the northern side of the U-bend (left) (Wp.11 70M), a steep roughly concreted canalization path descends past a small house tucked away in the trees. Two hundred and fifty metres later, we recross the road (Wp.12) to join a tarmac lane descending past an attractive new house, where the lane becomes a broad grassy trail.

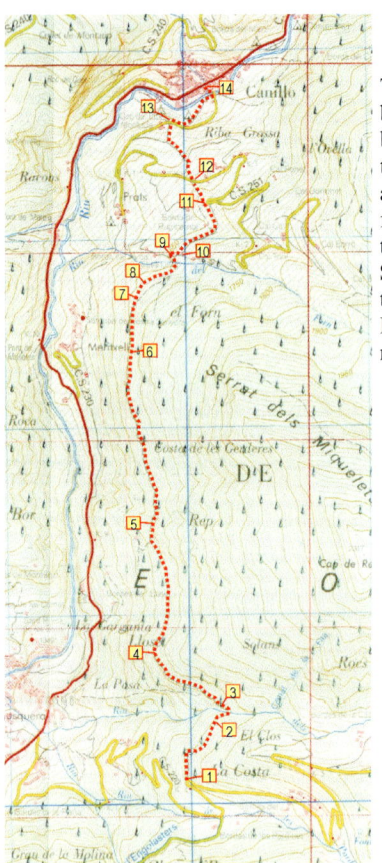

The trail continues descending between vegetable gardens, bringing us back to the road for the third time (Wp.13 80M) 25 metres above the 'Edifici Janramon', in front of which a path descends to the end of the lane leading to the **Sant Creus** chapel, where we cross the bridge and bear left onto the **Pista de Petanca** alley up to the main road (Wp.14 90M).

28 REFUGE DE PERAFITA

A classic ascent: lush woodland, rushing torrents, and a lovely Alpine pasture. Generally treated as a simple linear walk, but adapted here into a very satisfying loop thanks to a little known but easy path crossing the **Costa Verda/Bosc del Rodol** woods. **Cabana de la Perafita**, the old shepherds' hut near the main refuge, is a good place for observing marmots. Normally so shy of human company, they take to their heels in total disarray, banging into rocks, somersaulting over tufts of grass and diving down holes, they're remarkably domestic in the vicinity of the *cabana*, peering out of their burrows like a clutch of curtain-twitchers scrutinizing a neighbour with a dubious hobby.

| 5 | 4½ H | 9 km | 970m / 970m | ↻ | 0 |

Short Versions
(a) **Riu Madriu** - fork left at **Entremesaigües** and right at the 3 hours 40 mins point (signposted 'Perafita') for pleasant picnic spots below the **Rámio** meadows.
(b) **Fuente de Boïgot** - fork right at Wp.2 and climb via **Font de Boïgot** to **Font Pixadera**, returning via **Entremesaigües** N.B. I haven't done the **Font de Boïgot** path, but it's an official itinerary and should be waymarked throughout.

Strolls
(a) **Pont Sassanat**
(b) **Entremesaigües**

Access: by car

The walk starts from the CS101 on a signposted trail ('Entremesaigües, Rámio, Camí de la Muntanya' / 'GR7 Refugio de l'Illa, Portella Blanca d'Andorra' / 'GR11 Refugio de l'Illa, Port de Vallcivera') between the CS101/CS200 junction and the cobbled lane followed by the GR7 on its climb from **Escaldes**. If the roadside parking spots are taken, there's plenty of room beside the abattoir 150 metres down the CS101. The ascent follows one of the many variants of the GR11 (red-and-white waymarks), the descent a local path (yellow waymarks).

Climbing towards Entremesaigües

We begin on a broad paved trail, the **Camí de la Muntanya** (Wp.1 0M), climbing between mossy boulders and lush, largely deciduous woodland. After passing a very minor branch descending on the left to the **Riu Madriu** and a major, waymarked branch climbing to the right (Wp.2 10M), we cross onto the right bank of the torrent via **Pont Sassanat** (Wp.3 15M) and continue

Walk! Andorra 127

climbing along the waymarked route (splinter paths soon rejoin the main trail) to the hamlet of **Entremesaigües,** where we turn right on the GR11-10a for 'Collada de la Maiana / Estany de la Nou / Perafita / Claror' (Wp.4 35M).

Re-crossing the torrent via **Pont de Entremesaigües**, we climb past the remaining fields and the **Font Pixadera** 'spring-in-a-rock'. The path, which is lined with wild strawberries, climbs steadily to steeply, tunneling through the woods to the confluence of two ancient rockslides (Wp.5 55M).

After crossing the rockslides, we continue climbing through the woods for a couple of hundred metres before emerging in the open alongside the **Riu de Perafita**, where there are several fine plunge-pools.

Riu de Perafita

We continue climbing in and out of the woods, generally following the torrent but occasionally bearing left for an easier climb. There are few easily identifiable landmarks, but the way is always clear and well waymarked. After swinging left to cross a boulder slide (Wp.6 85M), we climb past a succession of natural jacuzzis. We then climb above the predominantly broadleaf woodland and the gradient eases before emerging in the open, 50 metres below a canvas shanty wrapped round a large rock within sight of the high sierras to the south (Wp.7 105M).

A gentle to steady climb leads to a GR arrow painted on a rock (Wp.8 120M), where we bear left, away from the torrent, to climb steeply in a generally easterly direction through the remaining pine woods. This last stretch of the climb seems interminable, but believe me, it's worth pushing on to the **Rasa de Perafita** pasture. Emerging above the treeline on a long grassy slope (Wp.9 135M), we maintain an easterly direction, trudging up the slope (there's no path, but an obvious natural way and regular waymarks), doubtless pausing once in a while to enjoy the magnificent views back towards **Pic Negre**. We eventually pass a large felled tree with a waymark at its base, 50 metres beyond which is a traditional stone-walled, grass-roofed hut (Wp.10 155M), the **Cabana de la Perafita**, that functions as an annex to the main refuge, 250 metres to the west.

From the main refuge, the GRP heads southwest to the **Refuge de Claror** and east to cross the **Collada de Maiana**, while the GR11.10 crosses the **Collet de Sant Vicenç** into Spain. Both paths are signposted and waymarked, and offer various opportunities for longer walks, one obvious and attractive option being to cross the **Collada de Maiana** and return to the start via the **Madriu** valley (see Walk 30). For the present though, we take the yellow-waymarked route to the west of **Cabana de la Perafita**.

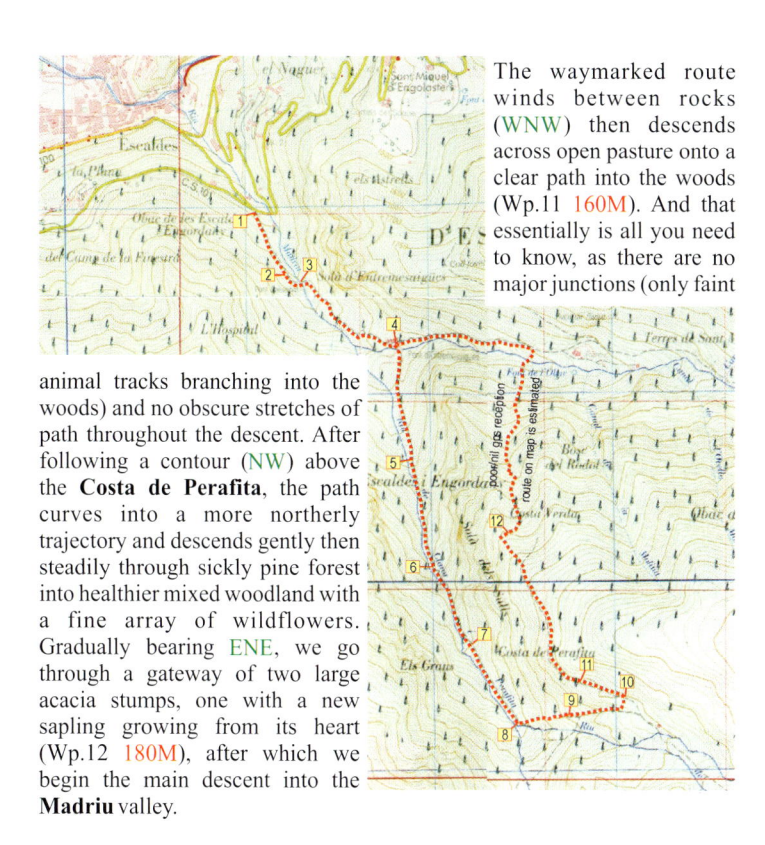

The waymarked route winds between rocks (WNW) then descends across open pasture onto a clear path into the woods (Wp.11 160M). And that essentially is all you need to know, as there are no major junctions (only faint animal tracks branching into the woods) and no obscure stretches of path throughout the descent. After following a contour (NW) above the **Costa de Perafita**, the path curves into a more northerly trajectory and descends gently then steadily through sickly pine forest into healthier mixed woodland with a fine array of wildflowers. Gradually bearing ENE, we go through a gateway of two large acacia stumps, one with a new sapling growing from its heart (Wp.12 180M), after which we begin the main descent into the **Madriu** valley.

After a steep zigzagging descent alongside a major rockslide, the path swings sharp left behind a large outcrop of rock (195M) and GPS reception becomes very sketchy. The gradient eases as we cut back and forth, our path a ribbon of roots and dirt curling across the mossy forest floor, eventually crossing an affluent and, 50 metres later, the main **Riu Madriu** (215M). Bearing left after the bridge, we climb past the **Rámio** meadows to rejoin the GR7 (220M), which we follow down to **Entremesaigües** (230M) and our outward route.

29 PRAT PRIMER VIA COLLADA DE CAÜLLA

An interesting itinerary characterized by steep climbs interleaved with glorious contour-line paths enjoying superb views despite the heavily wooded slopes they traverse. **Prat Primer** is normally approached by a strikingly unimaginative linear route following the **Riu de la Comella**, which is a pleasant descent and a nice short walk to **Borda de la Plana**, but would be dull done in its entirety two ways. The full circuit by contrast couldn't be more varied, beginning with an easy stroll along a dirt track then climbing through one of the finest pine forests in the principality, after which we benefit from those famous contour-line traverses - such a paradise for red fruit gathering you're half inclined to throw a skin over your shoulder and have done with the modern world altogether.

As for the oblique arrival in the **Comella Valley**, that presents a spectacle you will not forget in a hurry. The **Bosc de Palomera** (heavily suggestive of Russian folk tales - all you'd need would be a couple of wolves loping along through the shadows and you'd be away) is particularly recommended in hot weather when the tall shady trees are a godsend. The path traversing **Collada de Caüll** is the **Carretera Certeresos**, dubbed a 'road' as it's an old logging trail, said to have been broad enough for two ox-drawn carts to pass abreast. Doubtless the oxen were a bit leaner back then.

The entire itinerary is waymarked with yellow dots and, briefly, GR red-and-white stripes; however, there are such a profusion of waymarked and signposted paths, I'm afraid you have to spend a little bit of time with your nose buried in the book. Alternatively, given that everything *is* waymarked, you could spend a very happy afternoon simply wandering at will and seeing where you fetched up.

Short Versions	Stroll
(a) Bosc de la Palomera - there's an almost infinite variety of short walks to be pieced together from the newly waymarked paths crossed in the course of the climb (see text) **(b) Cortal de la Plana** (in reverse) - a pleasant spot for a picnic	Font de l'Astrell dirt track (see text)

Access: by car

To reach the start, take the turning south at km4.2 of the CS101 into the **Comella Parc Conjunt Residencial** and park immediately on the left in the **Punt de Berenada** car park, currently a patch of wasteland, though given the proximity of a large *Área Recreativa*, I guess it will soon be daubed with a coat of tarmac. The signposted 'Camí de Prat Primer' beside the car park is our return route and Short Version (b).

From the car-park (Wp.1 0M), we walk up the road for 250 metres till it ends at a barrier blocking access to the **Font de l'Astrell** dirt track, immediately after which we pass the first signposted path, doubling back on the left to the Camí de Prat Primer. We now simply follow this track to its end, generally climbing gently but occasionally strolling on the level, soon coming within sight of the high whitish crags passed at Wp.8 and, ahead of us, the fold concealing **Collada de Caüll**.

En route, we pass the **Camí de Collet de la Trapella** (Wp.2), **Camí dels Estarragalls** (Wp.3 15M), **Camí del Bosc Negre**, **Camí de Collet de la Trapella** (again)/ **Font de Ferro** / **Font de Cuc** (Wp.4), a picnic area and *mirador* (a possible destination for the stroll) (Wp.5), and finally **Camí del Planells dels Maians**, and **Camí de Font de Sansa** (Wp.6).

The *mirador* at Wp.5

At the end of the dirt track, we pass below a large reservoir and, ignoring a waymarked trail descending through the woods (NNW), double back to the left (Wp.7 35M) on a narrower trail climbing steadily (S) behind the reservoir. One hundred and fifty metres later, we pass a signposted branch descending to 'Font de l'Astrell'. Veering right, initially on the level then climbing steadily again, we pass below the higher of the two whitish crags seen earlier, where a waymarked path on the right (Wp.8 45M) descends to a second *mirador* below the lower crag (another possible picnic stop on a short walk).

The Bosc de Palomera

We then cross a small *coll* behind the lower crag and climb through the **Bosc de Palomera** woods to another signposted junction (Wp.9 50M). The **Camí dels Maians** doubles back to the left, but we follow the **Camí de Pica Romana** (SW) till it joins the GR7 (Wp.10 55M). Sticking with the **Pica Romana** stretch of the GR, we climb through the woods (SSW), passing a signposted link with the **Camí de Costa Seda** (Wp.11 60M).

We leave the GR (now called the **Camí de Manyat**) 100 metres later at a small rocky *coll* (Wp.12) and double back to the left, climbing (NE) for a further 100 metres to yet another junction of waymarked routes (Wp.13 65M) where we bear right for the 'Serrat del Planell del Ras', beginning our first really steep climb amid more open woodland along a shoulder of **Serra de la Creu**. After passing a first small clearing (Wp.14 75M), the gradient eases and fine views open out over **Sant Julia** shortly before a T-junction with a much clearer path (Wp.15 80M). Both directions lead to **Collada de Caüll**, but we turn left following the waymarked route. An apparent Y-junction 30 metres later is merely a shortcut across a bend in the path, after which we resume climbing, following a grassy path winding across a long clearing where the first abundant raspberries appear.

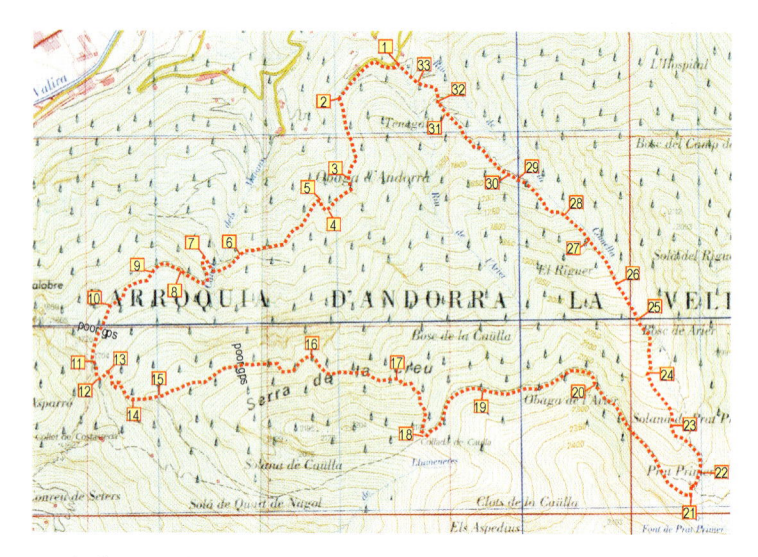

Dipping back into the woods again on the northern side of **Serra de la Creu**, we come to the first of the really long contour-line paths that are such a characteristic of this walk, and strawberries appear alongside the path - if you're walking in autumn, adjust timings according to appetite. We follow the contour, largely on the level but broken by brief climbs, the diminutive model village of **Andorra La Vella** way below us, birch and acacia gradually mixing in with the prevailing pine.

After crossing a small rise overlooking the undulating creases of successive folds and valleys in the southern massif (Wp.16 95M), our contour line, interrupted by a couple of brief but steep climbs, approaches the crux of the first 'valley', in fact no more than a watershed littered with loose debris, where we pass a meagre spring and reach a junction of paths (Wp.17 105M).

The path directly ahead should rejoin the described itinerary at Wp.30; there may also be a link with our outward route at Wp.9; we, however, turn right on the **Camí de Collada Caüll** and start climbing steeply, initially slipping and sliding all over the place, but soon finding our footing on a firmer surface. Nonetheless, it's still a long hard slog, trudging alongside a shrub riddled rockslide (more jam-making opportunities!) before we reach the **Collada de Caüll**, where there's a small meteorological station and a location-less location table (Wp.18 130M) - whether the latter stems from a philosophical crisis, a sudden lack of confidence or mere vandalism is unclear.

From the *collada*, we take the clear path to the northeast, the **Carretera Certeresos**, initially on the level then almost imperceptibly shading into a gentle climb. After going through a small green gate (you wouldn't squeeze many oxen through it) (Wp.19 135M), we follow a contour curving round the

Obaga de l'Avier, eventually bearing SE into the **Comella Valley** (Wp.20 145M) for our final approach, high above the spectacular pasture of the **Solana de Prat Primer**, to the **Refuge de Prat Primer** (Wp.21 160M).

As ever, these Andorran shepherds really had an eye for a picturesque plot of land - the refuge is superbly situated and a good base for longer walks. To the south, the **Camí de Bou Mort** climbs via the **Collada de Prat Primer** to **Pic Negre** and the GRP, while the clear path on the eastern flank of the valley curves round **Pic de les Asclades** to join the **Perafita** path (Walk 28).

The Refuge de Prat Primer

The descent is relatively straightforward, so apart from the succession of junctions at the end, description is largely for the purposes of time keeping. 150 metres north-east of the refuge, at the confluence of several watersheds, we pick up a faint but discernible cairn-marked path (Wp.22) descending across the broad sweep of pine spotted pasture. After a short stretch of clearer path (Wp.23 170M), we meander across the **Solana de Prat Primer**, crossing a low but distinct grassy 'lip' (Wp.24 175M).

We then follow a stonier, more unstable path descending to the right of a boulder slide clustered round a distinctive sheared *menhir*. Winding between banks of raspberry bushes (no impediment, you'll probably be completely sated by this stage), we descend steeply, gradually coming within earshot of then alongside the tiny **Riu de la Comella** (Wp.25 185M). After continuing our steep descent on a slightly fainter but more stable path, we come to a second loose rocky section (Wp.26 190M). Two hundred and seventy-five metres later, the path divides briefly (Wp.27) then, 200 metres after that, crosses the **Riu de la Comella** (Wp.28) and descends through shadier woodland to the **Cortal de la Plana** shepherds' cabin (Wp.29 210M).

Following the grassy path behind the cabin, we pass a branch of the 'Camí de l'Avier' on the left 70 metres later (Wp.30). Staying on the main trail, which soon becomes stony again and is quite badly eroded in places, we descend through the woods, forking right at successive junctions (Wp.31 220M & [80 metres later] Wp.32). After passing some 50 metres from a works hut, we bear right at a final junction of paths (Wp.33) a few minutes short of Wp.1.

30 TOUR OF THE SOUTH: ENGOLASTERS TO ILLA, THE AGOLS & MADRIU VALLEYS

It's a hard call in a country so full of great walks, but it's tempting to say of this itinerary, "If you only have time to do one walk in Andorra …". Untenanted, unspoiled, unvisited, populated principally by tubby fluffy bees and iridescent butterflies, the upper reaches of the **Agols Valley** seem like the nearest one's likely to come to a patch of paradise …until, that is, you start descending the **Madriu Valley**. This is one of the Pyrenees' undisputed Great Places and if there was a topographical Miss World, Andorra would probably feel bound to propose **Madriu** as its candidate! Not that there's anything especially vapid or witless about this particular spectacle. It's just that it's such a splendid place you can easily understand why the UN garlanded it with a metaphorical sash round the shoulders and gave it a peck on the cheek by declaring it a World Heritage Site. Add to that an extensive selection of wild fruit including raspberry, bilberry, redcurrant, and hazelnut, and talk of Eden doesn't sound so far-fetched!

The **Refuge de l'Illa** is popular, particularly with fishermen, and can get crowded at weekends. It's said to sleep sixty, but you'd have to be feeling pretty convivial as it looks full with thirty. That said, last time we were there, a Friday, the only other visitors were a middle-aged Catalán couple with their pet ferret! Still, best to do the walk during the week. Good pathfinding skills are required in the final approach to the **Refuge de Agols** as the waymarking is, at present, not up to the usual high standard encountered in Andorra. <u>Do not venture onto the plateau above **Cap de la Coma dels Llops** in mist or low cloud</u>. My thanks to Joan Pere Adellach who suggested this little known and, as far as I am aware, otherwise unpublished approach to **Illa**.

DAY ONE
ESTANY D'ENGOLASTERS to REFUGE DE L'ILLA via CAP D'AGOLS

5 | 5¼ H | 14 km | 1250m / 200m | one way | 0

Stroll	Short Versions
Camí de les Pardines, also known as **Camí Grau de la Molina**, and also as **Canal d'Engolasters**. Start from the **Pardines** end of the track at km3 of the CS220 and walk to **Engolasters**. Access: by car or (adding 300 metres climbing) on foot via the GR11 **Encamp** to **Engolasters**	(all start as per the stroll) (a) **Bordes de la Molina**; there are superb views back towards the **Casamanya** and **Estanyó** peaks from Wp.6. (b) **Agols** - Wp.7 enjoys comparable views, but is a prettier picnic spot (c) **Refuge de Agols** N.B. there is an alternative descent from the refuge, rejoining **Camí de les Pardines** at its eastern end. I haven't walked it, but it is signposted from the dirt track and, I believe, waymarked..

Walk! Andorra

The walk starts from the public car-park at the last bend in the CS200 (the car-park at the end of the road is private) where there's a mapboard for the 'Circuit de les Fonts' and waymarks for the GR11 (Wp.1 0M). We reach the **Estany de Engolasters** either by climbing to the end of the road and taking the trail descending to the lake-shore track from the **Camp del Serrat Restaurant** car-park or by following the 'Llac i Cel Restaurant' road on the left immediately after Wp.1. In either case, we follow the dirt track along the southern side of the lake, passing below the **Llac i Cel Restaurant**, immediately after which the GR11 descends to the left on the **Camí del Riu Blanc** for **Encamp** (Wp.2 15M).

We leave the GR at this point and continue on the pedestrianized dirt-track between **Engolasters** and the **Bordes de les Pardines**. We stroll along the track, passing the **Camí de Confòs** and an alternative, unmarked route to the **Refuge d'Agols** via **Planell de l'Alia**. Sticking to the dirt track, we soon see the **Funicamp** cable-car and **Pic de Maians** (see Walk 25), easily identifiable by the chair-lift station on the summit and the broad ski-piste scarring the slope (worth noting as this is a useful landmark later on).

Camí de Ses Pardines

We then curve into the deep sweep of the **Grau de la Molina** gorge and, immediately after crossing a bridge over the **Riu de la Molina** (Wp.3 45M), fork right on the **Camí de la Molina** for the 'Bordes de la Molina 1750m' and 'Els Agols 2400m'. We now climb steadily to steeply on a broad dirt track winding through the woods then climbing alongside the **Riu de les Agols** before curving NE to loop round the first of the **Bordes de Molina** houses (65M). The track then climbs more steeply past the second, newly-built house after which a gentler but still steady climb leads to a level stretch of track curving SW to the third house, currently a ruin, 75 metres before which (Wp.5 75M), we leave the track, forking left on a tiny, yellow-waymarked path winding through the rhododendron.

This path continues the steady climb, passing a signposted branch on the left for 'Serrat de Codinet' and 'Prat de Gilet' (Wp.6) before crossing an affluent of the main stream. We then traverse a pretty little meadow before re-crossing two channels of the affluent behind a signboard for 'Els Agols' (Wp.7 85M), where we join a cross-country race itinerary, currently marked with flimsily planted orange flags and plastic bunting tied to the trees. We now climb alongside the stream between delightfully healthy pine set in a lush plinth of dense undergrowth to a slightly more overgrown stretch (Wp.8 115M). Climbing the flank of the valley, initially maintaining our SSE direction but soon veering E, we zigzag up through the woods to a gateway formed by two massive blocks of granite (Wp.9 135M).

After an agreeable, level stroll through the woods on a clear path, we climb gently to a slightly more obscure way between low cliffs and a long strip of boulders (Wp.10 145M) leading to a dry-stone wall tucked into the lee of an overhanging rock to form a tiny storm shelter (Wp.11 155M). Ignoring (if you happen to see it) a faint animal track heading toward the torrent (invisible under a blanket of wild carrot, but clearly audible), we continue climbing, curving round to the left, onto a small *coll* (Wp.12 158M) at the head of the **Serrat de Codinet**, from where we can again see **Pic de Maians** to the NE.

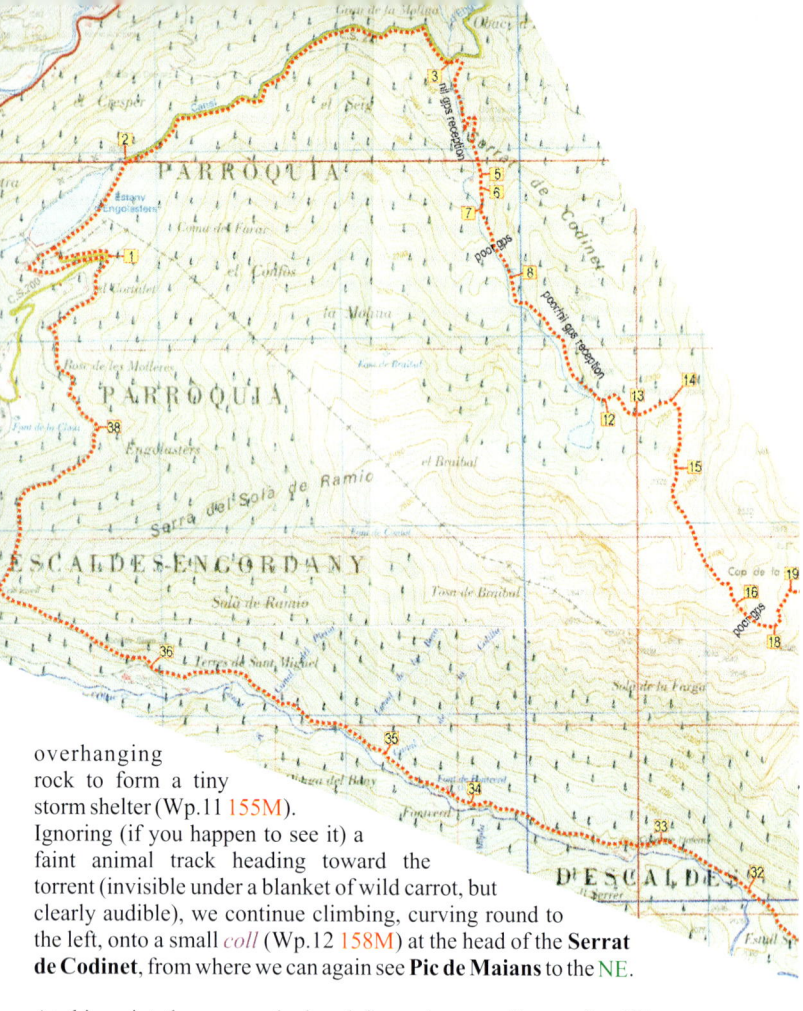

At this point the waymarked and flagged routes diverge for 200 metres. Though the latter is currently easier to follow, the flags and bunting are pretty impermanent. We therefore follow the waymarks, currently very faint, but hopefully due to be repainted. Descending 50 metres NE (towards **Pic de Maians**) we pass a couple of very ancient yellow waymarks before veering right (SE), passing a rock with a waymark cunningly camouflaged by lichen. We then follow a very faint path winding through scattered pine and clumps of rhododendron, intermittent waymarks confirming we're on route if not actually helping us find it. After crossing a narrow gurgling spring (Wp.13 165M), we rejoin the flagged route on a reasonably clear way (ENE), bringing the grass-capped chimney of the refuge into sight. The **Refuge de les Agols** (Wp.14 170M) is beautifully situated and a superb overnight stop if you happen to make a late start, the only drawback at the time of writing being that the piped *fuente* wasn't flowing, so you would have to walk a couple of hundred metres to find a source.

To the south of the refuge, a signboard indicates a grassy path (not, at present, waymarked with yellow dots as suggested) climbing (S) to 'Cap de les Agols 2601m' and 'Refugi de l'Illa 2480m'. The path climbs steadily, passing the first ancient pale blue waymarks, which we follow all the way to the top. After passing the head of a first small spring, we traverse a small meadow and climb past a second, gushing but invisible spring below a long rockslide (Wp.15 185M). A natural way then crosses sheets and blocks of granite to recover the grassy path as it goes through a mini-valley defined by large flat planes of granite. We then cross a succession of muddy springs and the dawning realization that the path climbs the steepest part of the crest appears to be confirmed - happily, this is a misapprehension.

Towards the head of the valley, as the climb begins to steepen, look out for a rock on your left with two large, reasonably clear, blue waymarks (Wp.16 200M). From this point, we gradually curve round to the east, climbing the obvious way up the **Cap de la Coma dels Llops**. Throughout the remaining climb, it's important to follow the initially faint then increasingly clear blue waymarks, as there is little else to guide us apart from brief stretches of cow-path amid a chaos of rocks.

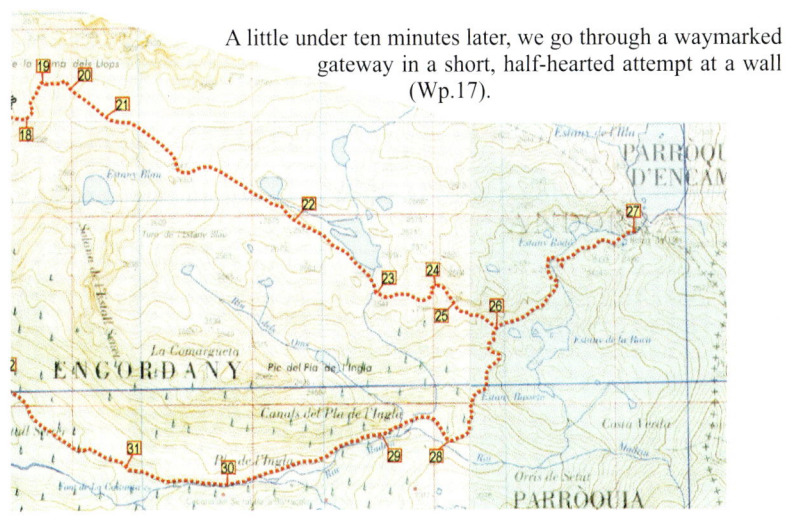

A little under ten minutes later, we go through a waymarked gateway in a short, half-hearted attempt at a wall (Wp.17).

The way takes a more pronounced easterly turn, then curves northeast, passing the first of what appear to be homages from the waymarker to his dear old dad, the word PAPI written in large blue letters (Wp.18 215M).

After the third PAPI, the gradient eases off, at which point you may see cairns marking a way (Wp.19 225M) climbing toward the three craggy summits visible on the crest to the south. You can either follow these cairns as we did, or for a slightly simpler ascent, continue along the blue waymarked route until it veers sharp right (S) up a shallow gully along a narrow shoulder. In either case, we pass just to the left of the easternmost craggy 'summit' (in truth a mere outcrop when you see it more closely) (Wp.20 240M), after which we cross a broad plateau scattered with great lumps of granite, as if some giant child has thrown a tantrum with his building blocks, gradually bringing into view the extraordinary, knife-like ridge defining the principality's southern frontier.

Midway across the plateau we come to a final, more emphatic PAPI on a blade of granite also marked with arrowed directions for 'Estany Blau' and

Walk! Andorra 137

'L'Illa' (Wp.21 245M). This is sitting-on-top-of-the-world time and a brief break is strongly recommended so that you can take in the grand spectacle that surrounds us, the blade of granite being perfectly angled as a backrest. Our onward route forks left (E), but I recommend continuing straight ahead (SSE) for 100 metres for the view over **Estany Blau**, very blue in fine weather.

Leaving the blue-waymarked route, we fork left at Wp.21, following an unmarked but clearly trodden way (E), soon bringing the interlocking lakes of **Estany Forcat** into view and beginning our long gentle descent (SE), the ground bubbling with thousands of frantically leaping grasshoppers. The path swings south briefly before curving back toward the first lake and descending to a grassy rise just above the marshy isthmus linking the two principal lakes (Wp.22 265M). The path disappears here, but maintaining direction (SE), we descend to cross the watershed about 50 metres below the largest lake (Wp.23 275M), at which point pathfinding becomes a bit complicated again.

There is an unmarked way, used by Andorran walkers and the local herdsman, leading directly to **Illa**. However, it crosses very convolute terrain mazed with interleaving gullies and is pretty well indescribable, so I've opted for a slightly less direct but simpler route. Climbing the small rise on the far side of the watershed, resist the temptation to descend the gullies immediately on the right, and continue to the east for 150 metres, passing two large cairns on your right, and bringing into view the **Estany de la Bova** lakes. Once you see these lakes, bear right (SE), descending a grassy swale for 100 metres before bearing left (ENE) into the next watershed where we come to a brief but clear stretch of cow path (Wp.24 285M) curving round a marshy area threaded with channels of still water. We now simply descend (SE) towards **Estany de la Bova**, passing a second stretch of clear path (Wp.22 288M) before joining the GRs7&11 (Wp.25 295M), 100 metres from the **Estany de la Bova** shepherds' cabin. We now simply turn left and follow the clearly waymarked GRs up to **Refuge de l'Illa** (Wp.26 315M).

DAY TWO
REFUGE DE L'ILLA to ESTANY D'ENGOLASTERS via MADRIU VALLEY & COLL JOVELL

Compared with the complicated itinerary of the first day, this is a delightfully easy descent for which description is virtually redundant, as we follow the well-waymarked GR11 all the way back to the **Circuit de les Fonts** car-park. The descent can be done in under three hours, but I strongly recommend you take your time and take as much pleasure as you can. Bathing is obligatory for all but the hydrophobic.

| 3 | 3H | 14.5 km | 150m / 1200m | one way | 3* |

* at **Engolasters**

Short Version
Madriu Valley (in reverse). Follow Walk 28 to Wp.4 then fork left and continue on the main trail along the **Riu Madriu**. **L'Illa** is perhaps a little far for a single-day linear walk, but you should definitely go to the **Fontverd** refuge, preferably push on to the junction with the GRP, and ideally continue to **Pla d'Ingla**.

Stroll
Circuit de les Fonts (see mapboard at the start of Day One).

After retracing our steps to **Estany de la Bova** (Wp.27 15M), we continue on the waymarked route, descending steadily across successive levels of pasture to the first stand of trees, just above the stream (Wp.28 30M). We then pass below a small tarpaulin covered cabin (not marked on most maps) and behind the **Refuge de Riu dels Orris** (Wp.29 40M). Our descent continues, passing a log bridge leading to the unmarked way up to **Port de Setut**, after which we cross one of the most beautiful parts of the walk, the long, flat **Pla de l'Ingla**, a place so perfectly formed an eighteenth century divine would doubtless have cited it as proof positive of the Argument by Design. At the end of the *pla*, we pass the bridge to **Cabana del Serrat de la Barracota** and go through the first of three green metal gates (Wp.30 55M).

We now stroll along a shady riverside path patched with enough sunlight to encourage us into the innumerable plunge-pools and natural jacuzzis, after which the river drops away from the path and we descend gently through the woods, crossing two affluents (Wps.31 & 32 61M & 75M) before rejoining the bank of the main stream, where the plunge-pools and jacuzzis are even better. Immediately after a third log-bridge we pass a signposted junction beside two rather flimsy bridges (Wp.33 85M), at which point the GRP crosses the river and climbs via the **Collada de la Maiana** to **Perafita** (see Walk 28).

We then pass another delightful little cabin (again not marked on other maps; the upper-floor is unlocked and equipped with wooden decking so that it doubles as an emergency refuge) and go through the second green metal gate. After a long, exposed, curving contour, the path divides briefly and the river once again drops away below us. The path levels out in a small meadow full of wildflowers then winds through the woods, passing the scaffolding of an abandoned summer hut and descending to a Y-junction (Wp.34 105M). The branch on the right leads directly to the **Refuge de Fontverd**, but we take the fork on the left, crossing the meadows just below the refuge. Soon afterwards, we go through the third gate, 300 metres after which, we ignore the yellow waymarked 'Camí del Solà' (Wp.35 115M) to 'Coll de Jovell', and continue down the **Madriu Valley** until we come to the Y-junction of the two GRs (Wp.36 135M), at present without a signpost but clearly waymarked. The GR7 continues along the **Madriu** to join Walk 28 at **Entremesaigües**, but we branch right, climbing gently and crossing successive rockspills bisected by beautifully tailored paths. After curving round a large boulder onto a platform overlooking **Entremesaigües**, we come to the final, steeper climb to **Coll de Jovell** (Wp.37 145M) and the end of the **Camí del Solà**.

The GR descends from the *coll*, immediately passing a signposted path on the left to 'Font de la Closa' and 'Pla de Engolasters'. Forking right at a Y-junction with a yellow waymarked path fifteen minutes later, we join the **Circuit de les Fonts** at the **Font dels Collalets** picnic area (Wp.38 165M) amid small cliffs popular with local climbers. We now simply follow this broad, level trail back to the start, ignoring all branch tracks and trails.

Estany de Engolasters, the start and end of the route

WAYPOINT LISTS

GPS Waypoints for the 30 walking routes included in **Walk! Andorra** are quoted in Latitude/Longitude for the WGS84 Datum; the default datum for GPS receivers. Before loading waypoints into your GPS please read 'Using GPS in Andorra' on page 38.

Waypoints are quoted to four places of decimals, as recorded during Charles Davis' research. If your GPS will only accept three places of decimals then you should 'round off' the third decimal place; e.g. .0178 would 'round off' to .018, while .9224 would 'round off' to .922.

The edited GPS Track and Waypoint files for **Walk! Andorra** can be downloaded from our **Personal Navigator Files (PNFs) CD** (version 2.01 onwards) via your PC into your GPS receiver; assuming you have a GPS-PC lead. For more information on our PNFs CD see our websites:-

www.walking.demon.co.uk & www.dwgwalking.co.uk

1
ESTANYS DE TRISTAINA

Wp	N	E
1	42 37.8988	1 28.8829
2	42 38.1502	1 29.1931
3	42 38.3032	1 29.2081
4	42 38.4544	1 29.2669
5	42 38.6842	1 29.5141
6	42 38.8912	1 29.3935
7	42 38.9860	1 29.1241
8	42 38.8480	1 28.8889
9	42 38.6962	1 28.8745

2
ROC DE LA CAUBA & COLL DE LES CASES

Wp	N	E
1	42 33.7080	1 30.0270
2	42 33.7200	1 30.1662
3	42 33.7008	1 30.3588
4	42 33.7692	1 30.6450
5	42 33.8556	1 30.8010
6	42 33.6744	1 30.9096
7	42 33.5928	1 30.7914
8	42 33.9960	1 30.6408
9	42 34.1058	1 30.3510
10	42 34.1454	1 30.3342
11	42 34.2330	1 30.2280
12	42 34.3008	1 30.1620
13	42 34.4244	1 30.1506
14	42 34.5798	1 30.0324
15	42 34.2612	1 29.1876

3
PIC D'ENCLAR & PIC DE CARROI

Wp	N	E
1	42 31.8396	1 30.0162
2	42 31.8210	1 29.9160
3	42 31.7868	1 29.6694
4	42 31.6362	1 29.1900
5	42 31.4952	1 28.8726
6	42 31.4532	1 28.7844
7	42 31.4070	1 28.6554
8	42 31.3536	1 28.5132
9	42 31.1790	1 28.2678
10	42 30.9792	1 27.8628
11	42 30.8262	1 27.9210
12	42 30.7650	1 27.9762
13	42 30.5988	1 28.1022
14	42 30.6696	1 28.3050
15	42 30.7404	1 28.5576
16	42 30.8400	1 29.0646
17	42 30.8424	1 29.1102
18	42 30.8496	1 29.2488
19	42 30.8514	1 29.2968
20	42 30.8406	1 29.3568
21	42 30.8292	1 29.4858
22	42 30.8592	1 29.6598
23	42 30.8490	1 29.7588
24	42 31.3104	1 29.9814
25	42 31.5528	1 29.5938

4
PIC DE LA BASSERA (aka PIC DELS LACS)

Wp	N	E
1	42 32.7786	1 25.1844
2	42 32.7204	1 25.1844
3	42 32.6514	1 25.2522
4	42 32.5368	1 25.2048
5	42 32.4336	1 25.3140
6	42 32.3838	1 25.5060
7	42 32.3082	1 25.4832
8	42 32.3334	1 25.4490
9	42 32.2290	1 25.3074
10	42 32.2278	1 25.2192
11	42 32.1276	1 24.9786
12	42 32.1246	1 24.8316
13	42 32.3556	1 24.8664
14	42 32.5128	1 24.9774
15	42 32.6004	1 25.0272

5
STORM IN A TEA CUP: PIC ALT DE LA CAPA

Wp	N	E
1	42 33.1155	1 27.2654
2	42 33.1695	1 27.2432
3	42 33.3855	1 27.2792
4	42 33.5031	1 27.3314
5	42 33.5343	1 27.3698
6	42 33.5919	1 27.8390
7	42 33.6213	1 27.7784
8	42 33.6501	1 27.7010
9	42 33.6621	1 27.6458
10	42 33.6801	1 27.5612
11	42 33.6879	1 27.4370
12	42 33.7347	1 27.2822
13	42 33.7767	1 27.2516
14	42 33.8865	1 26.9396
15	42 33.8343	1 26.9036
16	42 33.5547	1 26.9114
17	42 33.2439	1 26.9042

140 *Walk! Andorra*

WAYPOINT LISTS

6
PIC DE SANFONS

Wp	N	E
0	42 32.7210	1 27.1368
1	42 33.9606	1 26.6682
2	42 33.9684	1 26.6136
3	42 34.1574	1 26.6448
4	42 34.3728	1 26.2998
5	42 34.3908	1 26.2398
6	42 34.4478	1 26.0604
7	42 34.5408	1 25.9110
8	42 34.6992	1 25.7784
9	42 34.7742	1 25.7130
10	42 34.8786	1 25.6500
11	42 35.0106	1 25.5936
12	42 35.0646	1 25.6326
13	42 35.1180	1 25.6512
14	42 35.1384	1 25.6482
15	42 35.1738	1 25.6380
16	42 35.2506	1 25.6608
17	42 35.2668	1 25.8210

7
PIC DE COMA PEDROSA

Wp	N	E
0	42 32.7206	1 27.1370
1	42 33.9603	1 26.6678
2	42 33.9681	1 26.6138
3	42 34.1571	1 26.6450
4	42 34.3725	1 26.3000
5	42 34.3905	1 26.2400
6	42 34.5924	1 26.3322
7	42 34.6542	1 26.3106
8	42 34.7334	1 26.2512
9	42 34.8150	1 26.2320
10	42 34.8636	1 26.0352
11	42 35.1480	1 26.1846
12	42 35.1900	1 26.3142
13	42 35.2464	1 26.4318
14	42 35.3322	1 26.5482
15	42 35.3754	1 26.5806
16	42 35.5068	1 26.6214
17	42 35.4762	1 26.3388
18	42 35.3304	1 26.2500
19	42 34.7982	1 26.5356
20	42 34.8006	1 26.9238
21	42 34.7910	1 27.1212
22	42 34.9008	1 27.6522
23	42 34.9854	1 27.8802

8
ESTANY FORCATS

Wp	N	E
1	42 34.7712	1 28.6968
2	42 34.9932	1 28.2000
3	42 35.0616	1 28.2492
4	42 35.1792	1 28.0452
5	42 35.3922	1 27.6966
6	42 35.4750	1 27.7272
7	42 35.6370	1 27.6294
8	42 35.8422	1 27.7878
9	42 35.9508	1 27.7590
10	42 36.0138	1 27.6876
11	42 35.9856	1 27.4410
12	42 35.9472	1 27.2442
13	42 35.9070	1 27.0042
14	42 36.0120	1 26.8278
15	42 35.4294	1 27.9054
16	42 35.2326	1 28.8426
17	42 35.0730	1 29.1780
18	42 35.0449	1 29.2074
19	42 34.6692	1 29.1240
20	42 34.5432	1 28.8996

9
CAMINO REAL: EL SERRAT TO ARANS

Wp	N	E
1	42 36.9690	1 32.2944
2	42 36.8340	1 32.2602
3	42 36.6420	1 32.3004
4	42 36.5904	1 32.2830
5	42 36.3390	1 32.1618
6	42 35.9574	1 31.8744
7	42 35.7510	1 31.7010
8	42 35.1894	1 31.4442
9	42 35.0064	1 31.3428
10	42 34.9356	1 31.1484

10
ESTANYS DE L'ANGONELLA

Wp	N	E
1	42 35.7750	1 31.5942
2	42 35.8374	1 31.4052
3	42 35.8662	1 31.3668
4	42 36.0858	1 31.1412
5	42 36.1974	1 30.9972
6	42 36.3396	1 30.6006
7	42 36.3570	1 30.5814
8	42 36.4104	1 30.3468
9	42 36.4410	1 30.0882
10	42 36.5256	1 30.0228
11	42 36.4488	1 29.7840
12	42 36.4596	1 29.5368
13	42 36.4500	1 29.3190
14	42 36.4218	1 29.1984
15	42 36.4620	1 28.9110
16	42 36.5310	1 28.8996

11
PORT DE INCLES & ESTANYS DE FONTARGENT

Wp	N	E
1	42 36.1338	1 41.1762
2	42 36.2526	1 41.2824
3	42 36.6276	1 41.5548
4	42 36.8160	1 41.7372
5	42 36.9246	1 41.9634
6	42 37.0176	1 42.1134
7	42 37.1670	1 42.2946
8	42 37.3128	1 42.4314
9	42 37.5036	1 42.4794

12
REFUGE DE COMA OBAGA

Wp	N	E
1	42 35.7648	1 31.5978
2	42 36.0258	1 32.0058
3	42 36.2688	1 32.3148
4	42 36.3162	1 32.3670
5	42 36.4140	1 33.0474
6	42 36.4614	1 33.0030
7	42 36.5112	1 32.9142
8	42 36.5886	1 32.8668
9	42 36.6312	1 32.8536
10	42 36.7512	1 32.8428
11	42 36.7812	1 32.8542
12	42 36.8706	1 33.0006
13	42 36.9780	1 32.9238
14	42 37.0776	1 32.9220
15	42 37.0872	1 32.4798
16	42 37.1388	1 32.4102
17	42 37.0632	1 32.2788
18	42 36.9642	1 32.2032
19	42 36.6936	1 32.1516

13
PIC DE FONT BLANCA

Wp	N	E
1	42 37.9986	1 30.6858
2	42 38.0520	1 30.8292
3	42 38.1102	1 30.8952
4	42 38.1486	1 30.9660
5	42 38.1708	1 31.0518
6	42 38.1954	1 31.2036
7	42 38.2254	1 31.2678
8	42 38.2608	1 31.3446
9	42 38.2956	1 31.3914
10	42 38.3538	1 31.3890
11	42 38.4036	1 31.3608
12	42 38.5926	1 31.4400
13	42 38.6232	1 31.4622
14	42 38.6664	1 31.4988
15	42 38.6664	1 31.5792
16	42 38.5836	1 31.7964

Walk! Andorra

WAYPOINT LISTS

17	42 38.7930	1 32.0334	25	42 35.4000	1 32.8044			
18	42 38.9814	1 32.0586	26	42 35.3874	1 32.5710			
19	42 38.4534	1 31.2906	27	42 35.3466	1 32.1444			
20	42 38.4576	1 31.2726						
21	42 38.4330	1 31.1952						
22	42 38.3676	1 30.8784						
23	42 38.3496	1 30.7836						
24	42 38.2584	1 30.7998						
25	42 38.2056	1 30.8598						
26	42 38.2482	1 31.0338						
27	42 38.2656	1 31.0866						

18

ESTANYS DE LES SALAMANDRES

Wp	N	E
1	42 35.0454	1 39.1194
2	42 35.0622	1 39.2928
3	42 35.3544	1 39.3612
4	42 35.5026	1 39.4974
5	42 35.6562	1 39.5112
6	42 35.9562	1 39.5982
7	42 36.1986	1 39.7626
8	42 36.1740	1 39.5538
9	42 36.0414	1 39.4608
10	42 36.0588	1 39.4008
11	42 36.1266	1 39.4116
12	42 36.1236	1 39.2124
13	42 36.0132	1 39.1614
14	42 35.8518	1 39.1788
15	42 35.6244	1 39.3204
16	42 35.5224	1 39.2328
17	42 35.5212	1 39.2904
18	42 35.5044	1 39.3624
19	42 35.4618	1 39.3714
20	42 35.4438	1 39.4116

14

PORT DE SIGUER & ESTANY BLAU

Wp	N	E
1	42 37.5468	1 33.1068
2	42 37.7124	1 33.4254
3	42 38.1504	1 33.6336
4	42 38.4018	1 33.6558
5	42 38.5302	1 33.6324
6	42 38.6202	1 33.5946
7	42 38.7288	1 33.5094
8	42 38.8086	1 33.5730
9	42 38.9016	1 33.6480
10	42 38.9706	1 33.6690
11	42 39.1746	1 33.8112
12	42 39.2064	1 34.1292

16

VALL DE RIU & RIU MONTAUP

Wp	N	E
1	42 34.3572	1 36.0498
2	42 34.5696	1 36.6018
3	42 35.0586	1 36.6456
4	42 35.4402	1 36.9090
5	42 35.7348	1 36.7938
6	42 35.8590	1 36.8772
7	42 36.0108	1 36.5472
8	42 36.1866	1 36.4494
9	42 36.2154	1 36. 3216
10	42 36.2064	1 36.2580
11	42 36.0414	1 35.7132
12	42 35.9628	1 35.6286
13	42 35.8800	1 35.5716
14	42 35.7846	1 35.5506
15	42 35.6190	1 35.4204
16	42 35.6298	1 35.2554
17	42 35.6340	1 35.0826
18	42 35.5044	1 34.9374
19	42 35.3928	1 35.0076
20	42 35.3160	1 35.1144
21	42 34.4502	1 35.3922
22	42 34.3638	1 35.5200

15

PIC DE CASAMANYA & VALL D'ENSEGUR

Wp	N	E
1	42 33.3666	1 34.2984
2	42 33.6150	1 34.3422
3	42 33.8166	1 34.1268
4	42 34.1004	1 34.0392
5	42 34.4520	1 33.9570
6	42 34.5762	1 34.0008
7	42 34.7148	1 33.9924
8	42 34.8816	1 33.9858
9	42 35.0766	1 33.9288
10	42 35.2974	1 34.3512
11	42 35.4858	1 34.4664
12	42 35.5132	1 34.4775
13	42 35.5300	1 34.4841
14	42 35.5450	1 34.4607
15	42 35.5564	1 34.4409
16	42 35.6560	1 34.4907
17	42 35.6442	1 34.3326
18	42 35.6814	1 34.1838
19	42 35.6268	1 34.0968
20	42 35.5818	1 33.9186
21	42 35.5314	1 33.7536
22	42 35.4618	1 33.7644
23	42 35.4594	1 33.3072
24	42 35.4168	1 33.0054

17

PIC DE LA SERRERA via THE RANSOL VALLEY

Wp	N	E
1	42 36.7230	1 38.2656
2	42 36.8514	1 37.9842
3	42 36.9804	1 37.6650
4	42 36.9732	1 37.5210
5	42 36.8994	1 37.4334
6	42 37.0440	1 37.0650
7	42 37.1982	1 36.7962
8	42 37.0740	1 37.6050
9	42 37.0404	1 38.2896
10	42 37.1058	1 38.3286
11	42 36.9354	1 38.3076
12	42 36.6894	1 38.4648

waypoints 13 to 23 unreliable

24	42 37.1694	1 36.5388
25	42 37.2846	1 36.5112
26	42 37.2660	1 36.3684
27	42 37.3380	1 36.3042
28	42 37.5342	1 36.1542

19

ESTANYS DE JUCLAR & A NEAR NOAH EXPERIENCE

Wp	N	E
1	42 36.1218	1 41.2290
2	42 36.0684	1 41.7636
3	42 36.1122	1 41.8830
4	42 36.1068	1 42.1800
5	42 36.1494	1 42.2976
6	42 36.1728	1 42.4824
7	42 36.1788	1 42.7578
8	42 36.2868	1 42.6966
9	42 36.4308	1 42.8808
10	42 36.4374	1 42.9534
11	42 36.5190	1 43.2522
12	42 36.6036	1 43.4082
13	42 36.7542	1 43.5054
14	42 36.8742	1 43.8102
15	42 36.9150	1 44.1594
16	42 36.8640	1 44.2146
17	42 36.8274	1 44.2320
18	42 36.7962	1 44.1888
19	42 36.7956	1 44.2230
20	42 36.7584	1 44.2614

WAYPOINT LISTS

20
ESTANYS DES SISCARÓ & CAP DE PORT

Wp	N	E
1	42 36.1182	1 41.2284
2	42 36.0684	1 41.7636
3	42 35.9454	1 41.9346
4	42 35.7888	1 42.2466
5	42 35.7300	1 42.1980
6	42 35.4030	1 42.2598
7	42 35.4048	1 42.1380
8	42 35.2704	1 42.1668
9	42 35.1998	1 42.2544
10	42 35.2482	1 42.5202
11	42 35.1696	1 42.6378
12	42 35.1798	1 42.9666
13	42 35.1702	1 43.1538
14	42 35.1774	1 43.3332
15	42 35.0628	1 43.3086
16	42 34.9422	1 43.0596
17	42 34.8948	1 42.8706
18	42 34.8390	1 42.6546
19	42 34.8192	1 42.3288
20	42 34.8180	1 42.0828

21
NORTHERN TRAVERSE: INCLES TO EL SERRAT

Wp	N	E
1	42 35.7048	1 40.4070
2	42 35.8218	1 40.2438
3	42 35.9568	1 40.3608
4	42 36.2790	1 40.4772
5	42 36.4350	1 40.2816
6	42 36.4830	1 40.2744
7	42 36.6858	1 40.3386
8	42 36.4728	1 40.0728
9	42 36.5490	1 39.8784
10	42 36.5682	1 39.8058
11	42 36.6972	1 39.7470
12	42 36.7902	1 39.6804
13	42 36.9030	1 39.5316
14	42 36.9306	1 39.3486
15	42 36.9768	1 39.0372
16	42 37.1118	1 38.3352
17	42 37.0872	1 37.9050
18	42 37.1796	1 37.8060
19	42 37.2966	1 37.6374
20	42 37.3956	1 37.4196
21	42 37.3686	1 37.2396
22	42 37.2528	1 36.8784
23	42 37.1934	1 36.7944
24	42 37.1694	1 36.5388
25	42 37.2846	1 36.5112
26	42 37.2660	1 36.3684
27	42 37.3380	1 36.3042
28	42 37.5342	1 36.1542
29	42 37.1532	1 36.0930
30	42 37.0878	1 35.8878
31	42 37.1880	1 35.3094
32	42 37.3728	1 34.7964
33	42 37.4508	1 34.8072
34	42 37.4202	1 34.3794
35	42 37.3572	1 33.8412
36	42 37.2822	1 33.4992
37	42 37.3062	1 33.2460
38	42 37.3788	1 33.0834
39	42 37.3866	1 32.7720
40	42 37.2516	1 32.5518

22
CIRC DELS PESSONS; ESTANY DE LES FONTS

Wp	N	E
1	42 31.7976	1 41.8206
2	42 31.8318	1 41.6604
3	42 31.7208	1 41.5830
4	42 31.5774	1 41.4810
5	42 31.5504	1 41.4330
6	42 31.5000	1 41.3568
7	42 31.4958	1 41.3172
8	42 31.4472	1 41.3382
9	42 31.4040	1 41.1546
10	42 31.4106	1 41.0376
11	42 31.3554	1 40.8210
12	42 31.1418	1 40.4274
13	42 31.0890	1 40.2828
14	42 31.0092	1 40.0428
15	42 30.8028	1 39.8274

23
CAMÍ DE GALL: SOLDEN TO CANILLO

Wp	N	E
1	42 34.6626	1 39.7818
2	42 34.6524	1 39.5832
3	42 34.5804	1 39.5310
4	42 34.5054	1 39.2274
5	42 34.5588	1 38.9316
6	42 34.7191	1 38.4348
7	42 34.6662	1 38.0922
8	42 34.6602	1 38.0382
9	42 34.4442	1 37.5156
10	42 34.3974	1 37.4088
11	42 34.1940	1 36.7164
12	42 34.1988	1 36.6198
13	42 34.8982	1 36.2658
14	42 33.9258	1 36.1086

24
THE LAZY MAN'S MOUNTAIN: SENDER DE LES TRES VALLS

Wp	N	E
1	42 33.8476	1 39.8749
2	42 33.9648	1 38.8782
3	42 34.0830	1 38.6904
4	42 34.0380	1 38.5308
5	42 33.9432	1 38.4654
6	42 34.1286	1 37.5930
7	42 33.9192	1 37.0410
8	42 33.8550	1 36.7128
9	42 33.6708	1 36.5568
10	42 33.5442	1 36.7650
11	42 33.3468	1 36.9768

25
PIC DE MAIANS

Wp	N	E
1	42 33.3468	1 36.9768
2	42 33.5442	1 36.7650
3	42 33.6798	1 36.7116
4	42 33.6684	1 37.2120
5	42 33.3738	1 37.6728
6	42 33.2820	1 37.8042
7	42 33.1632	1 37.6818
8	42 33.1590	1 37.8558
9	42 32.8860	1 37.4628
10	42 32.7426	1 37.0728
11	42 32.8650	1 37.0026
12	42 33.0354	1 36.8010
13	42 33.1638	1 36.8868

26
REFUGE & ESTANY D'ENSAGENTS

Wp	N	E
1	42 32.1144	1 37.0176
2	42 32.0934	1 37.0398
3	42 32.0064	1 36.9120
4	42 31.9314	1 36.8682
5	42 31.8636	1 36.8568
6	42 31.6908	1 37.0548
7	42 31.5708	1 37.3044
8	42 31.5558	1 37.5060
9	42 31.3848	1 37.6818
10	42 31.2636	1 37.8384
11	42 31.0866	1 38.3490
12	42 31.0644	1 38.3814
13	42 31.0170	1 38.5170
14	42 30.9948	1 38.6310
15	42 31.0806	1 38.6292
16	42 31.1658	1 38.7042
17	42 31.2564	1 38.8038
18	42 31.6224	1 37.3596

Walk! Andorra 143

27
CAMÍ DE LA CANAL

Wp	N	E
1	42 31.9854	1 35.8932
2	42 32.1528	1 35.9790
3	42 32.2008	1 36.0120
4	42 32.3526	1 35.7588
5	42 32.7306	1 35.7564
6	42 33.2136	1 35.6514
7	42 33.3564	1 35.6514
8	42 33.4206	1 35.7078
9	42 33.4866	1 35.8200
10	42 33.4956	1 35.8632
11	42 33.6534	1 35.9622
12	42 33.7074	1 35.8932
13	42 33.8736	1 35.8110
14	42 33.9708	1 35.9454

28
REFUGI DE PERAFITA

Wp	N	E
1	42 30.2532	1 33.0642
2	42 30.0810	1 33.1830
3	42 30.0438	1 33.2754
4	42 29.8734	1 33.6114
5	42 29.5542	1 33.6972
6	42 29.2392	1 33.7926
7	42 29.0244	1 33.9354
8	42 28.8000	1 34.1280
9	42 28.8042	1 34.3278
10	42 28.8642	1 34.5438
11	42 28.9098	1 34.3668
12	42 29.3418	1 34.0872

29
PRAT PRIMER via COLLADA DE CAÜLLA

Wp	N	E
1	42 29.9106	1 31.8246
2	42 29.8038	1 31.5954
3	42 29.5848	1 31.6356
4	42 29.4918	1 31.5564
5	42 29.5170	1 31.5168
6	42 29.3550	1 31.1904
7	42 29.3532	1 31.0554
8	42 29.3214	1 30.9498
9	42 29.2974	1 30.8226
10	42 29.2032	1 30.6702
11	42 29.0532	1 30.6072
12	42 29.0004	1 30.6258
13	42 29.0298	1 30.6810
14	42 28.9410	1 30.7668
15	42 28.9434	1 30.8616
16	42 29.0652	1 31.4838
17	42 29.0070	1 31.8264
18	42 28.8528	1 31.9362
19	42 28.9746	1 32.1774
20	42 29.0028	1 32.6340
21	42 28.6704	1 33.0186
22	42 28.7406	1 33.0630
23	42 28.8786	1 32.9418
24	42 29.0190	1 32.8380
25	42 29.1804	1 32.8056
26	42 29.2848	1 32.7300
27	42 29.4102	1 32.6190
28	42 29.4876	1 32.5062
29	42 29.5818	1 32.3124
30	42 29.5986	1 32.2668
31	42 29.7618	1 32.0100
32	42 29.8026	1 31.9890
33	42 29.8626	1 31.9038

30
TOUR OF THE SOUTH: ENGOLASTERS TO ILLA, THE AGOLS & MADRIU VALLEYS

Wp	N	E
1	42 31.0596	1 34.2690
2	42 31.3488	1 34.3380
3	42 31.6296	1 35.6370
5	42 31.3122	1 35.7708
6	42 31.2672	1 35.7720
7	42 31.1994	1 35.7558
8	42 30.9996	1 35.8908
12	42 30.6582	1 36.2694
13	42 30.6174	1 36.3942
14	42 30.6696	1 36.5346
15	42 30.4458	1 36.5598
16	42 30.0780	1 36.7926
18	42 30.0168	1 36.9618
19	42 30.1296	1 37.0248
20	42 30.1080	1 37.1286
21	42 30.0222	1 37.2786
22	42 29.7270	1 38.0328
23	42 29.5176	1 38.3712
24	42 29.5326	1 38.6118
25	42 29.4816	1 38.6808
26	42 29.4186	1 38.8704
27	42 29.6994	1 39.3870
28	42 29.0904	1 38.6562
29	42 29.1054	1 38.3814
30	42 28.9614	1 37.7658
31	42 29.0094	1 37.3638
32	42 29.2572	1 36.8562
33	42 29.3868	1 36.5112
34	42 29.4906	1 35.7276
35	42 29.6454	1 35.3586
36	42 29.8704	1 34.4448
37	42 30.1031	1 33.8262
38	42 30.5682	1 34.2108

GLOSSARY

This glossary includes words found in the text (shown in *italics*), plus other local words that you may encounter.

CATALÁN	ENGLISH
a	
agua, con/sin gas	water, fizzy/still
aljub	ancient cistern/reservoir
alt	summit
área recreativa	picnic spot, usually with barbecues, toilets, water
atalaya	ancient watch-tower
avall	lower
avinguda	avenue
ayuntament	town hall
b	
baix	low
barranc	gorge, ravine
bassa (pl basses)	pond, pool or reservoir
bony	lit. bump, lump or bulge used in Andorra for a flattish summit
borda (pl bordes)	farm building in the mountains
c	
cabana	lit. cabin, most often used in Andorra for a traditional stone shepherds' hut

Catalán	English	Catalán	English
cala	creek, small bay, sometimes just a tiny coastal indentation	*lluc*	farm
		m	
		mercat	market
carrer	street	*mig*	middle
camí	road, path or way	*mirador*	viewing point, sometimes with man-made facilities, more often a natural place with a good view
camí real	royal road, once a major donkey trail		
campo	countryside, field		
ca/can/ca'n	house of (as *chez* in French)	*morro*	snout or muzzle, a rounded summit
carrer	street	**o**	
caseta	hut, cabin, small house	*obac, obaga*	shady side of the valley
cingles	cliffs, crags; most often used to describe the sort of short, abrupt cliffs that typically define the rounded summits of many Catalán mountains	**p**	
		parada	bus stop
		parc natural	natural park
		particular	private
		passeig	walkway
		peatones	pedestrians
ciutat	city	*penya/penyal*	rock or boulder, used for a knoll or pinnacle on a ridge
coll, collada, collet	saddle, neck or pass	*pic*	translates as 'hill' or 'height', though more often a peak or mountain
coma	coomb		
correos	post office		
cortal	a hamlet of bordes, or a shepherds' corral	*pista*	dirt road
		pista forestal	forest road
costa	coast	*pla*	plain, flat land
cova	cave	*plato combinado*	lit. combined plate, a restaurant dish including (usually)meat or fish, vegetables or salad, and potatoes
d			
dalt	high, upper		
e			
embalse	reservoir		
ermita	hermitage, small church, shrine	*platja*	beach
		plaça	town square
estany	lake	*port*	port, mountain pass
f		*pou*	well
fiesta	festival, public holiday	*privado*	private
font	spring, well	*prohibido el paso*	no entry
g			
grau	lit. grade/degree, generally used for a rocky access point into or over a cliff or steep slope	**r**	
		refugio	mountain refuge, some offering basic overnight accommodation
h		*rota*	mountain smallholding with cabin
horno de calç	lime kiln		
hostal	hostel, simple accommodation	**s**	
		san/sant	saint
l		*santuari*	monastery, hermitage
lavadero	public laundry area	*senda*	footpath, trail

APPENDICES

Please note: Telephone numbers are shown in red. To dial from outside Andorra, use the code 00 376. Websites and email addresses are shown in green.

A USEFUL ADDRESSES & RECOMMENDATIONS

If you have the time, there's a tremendous amount of information about Andorra on the internet, but a lot of sifting is required. A basic Andorra/accommodation search elicited 781,000 sites - not bad for a place that's only got 30,000 hotel beds and 65,000 permanent residents! With such a glut of information, you might be excused for giving up and going to the travel agent, or just turning up and finding accommodation on the spot, which is not a problem. Otherwise, the following websites may be of use:-

www.andorramania.com
http://eurohot100.com/andorra/
www.andorra.starttips.com
www.andorraonline.ad
www.encamp.ad
www.vdc.ad
www.andorraantiga.com
www.pyrenees.guide.com
www.2camels.com/budget_accommodation/andorra.php3
www.andorra.com
www.hola-andorra.com
www.turisme.ad
www.arinsal.com
www.turismescaldes.ad
www.vallordino
www.pyrenees-pirineos.org
www.pyrenees-online.fr

Global booking services including sections on Andorra:
www.virtualtourist.com/vt/155   www.hotelguide.com
www.hotelstravel.com

Though clearly not a priority for the present publication, for information on skiing in Andorra consult www.skiandorra.ad

Emergency phone numbers:
Local Police   110   Fire & Ambulance   118
Medical   116   Mountain Rescue   112

Recorded weather forecast:
French 848 853   Spanish 848 852   Catalán 858 851

Helicopter rides: Heliland 837 929   Helitrans 807 566

Recommendations are by no means comprehensive and are not intended as a detailed guide to all services. Rather, they merely reflect our own largely haphazard and possible eccentric tastes and experiences:

Camping Mitxeu in **Llorts**: friendly, spacious, very clean, well-situated, good basic facilities, very cheap, and with pleasant river-dipping. The best campsite in the principality, largely because it's run as a kind of social club by its owner, who's ready to do anything to help. It's currently threatened by a singularly dim road-building scheme, but if it survives that, you won't find better hosts elsewhere.

Camping Borda d'Ansalonga further down the valley and **Camping Xixerella** near **Pal** have more facilities, but are both very crowded during the Summer and considerably more expensive. Of the more attractive campsites, **Camping Xixerella** is the only one open all year round.

Camping d'Incles at the end of the **Incles** valley, isn't really a campsite **at** all, but a 'zona de acampada'. It has a cosy bar and superb location, but is run down and only marginally maintained. **Camping Font de Ferrossins** lower down the same valley has better services. Plus, more campsite websites:

www.camingansalonga.com www.campingcasal.com
www.campinginternacional.com www.paradorcanaro.com
www.campingvalira.com www.campingxixerella.com

For affordable luxury (€20-35 per person depending on the season) **Aparthotel Montarto** (www.hotelmontarto.com) and **Aparthotel Els Meners** (elsemeners@andorra.ad) in **Canillo** are highly recommended, while the English run **Alba Hotel** in **El Tarter** (www.thealba.com) provides **unbeatable value** (€30 per person half board or €30 for two people self-catering in a studio-flat - though the latter option presupposes you're equipped for camping as the kitchen battery is minimal; full self-catering is not available in August, when B&B costs €23 The walker friendly **Alba** is also recommended for its relaxed, accommodating approach to hotel keeping. And to cap it all, one of the waiters is involved in waymarking local paths, so you literally can't go far wrong there!

Gourmets and gourmands MUST visit the excellent **Borda d l'Horto** restaurant on the CG2 between **Canill**o and the **Ransol** turn-off. The **L'Era del Jaume** in **Llorts** is less imperative, but only by comparison with the **Borda de l'Horto**, and is also highly recommended. **Llac i Cel** at Engolasters is absolutely frantic but friendly under pressure; the food is good, despite the frozen chips. No frozen chips at the **Borda Xixerella** restaurant opposite the campsite of the same name; even the new potatoes are nicely diced and browned, and the meat (*a la brasa* or, if ordered in advance, a *civet*) is excellent.

B REFUGES

In theory, with the exception of **Roca de Pimes** and **Refuge de la Serrera**, all refuges have a water supply in the vicinity. However, pipes freeze, sources change course, springs dry up. It's entirely possible you will arrive at a refuge and find you have to walk several hundred metres to the nearest running spring. Always take an adequate supply of water with you.

The only manned refuge is **Coma Pedrosa**. The manned section sleeps 60, is open from mid-June to September (depending on the weather), and charges €7 for a bed, €11.50 for a meal, €3 for a shower. When it's closed, there's an unmanned section that sleeps 10.

The following list of free, unmanned refuges features the name of the refuge, its altitude and capacity. The capacity numbers are the official ones. In some cases, you'd have to be pretty chummy to fit that number in.

		Altitude in metres	Capacity
1	**Agols**	2230	6
2	**Angonella**	2235	6
3	**Cabana Sorda**	2295	20
4	**Claror**	2280	20
5	**Coma Obaga**	2015	15
6	**Còms de Jan**	2215	10
7	**Ensagents**	2425	14
8	**Fonts**	2195	10
9	**Francoli**	1865	10
10	**Illa**	2480	60
11	**Fontverd**	1880	14
12	**Juclar**	2315	50
13	**Montmalús**	2445	10

14	**Perafita**	2200	10
15	**Pla de l'Estany**	2050	10
16	**Pla de les Pedres**	2150	5
17	**Portella**	2265	6
18	**Prat Primer**	2235	10
19	**Rialb**	1990	10
20	**Riba Escorxada**	2075	6
21	**Riu dels Orris**	2230	10
22	**Roca de Pimes**	2160	10
23	**Serrera**	2200	5
24	**Siscaró**	2145	10
25	**Sorteny**	1965	25
26	**Vall del Riu**	2160	10

C LONG DISTANCE PATHS

The following notes are designed to help anyone planning a long-distance walk incorporating several of our day-itineraries. The number preceding each path indicates how many days you might expect to spend on each route. // indicates a *possible* end to each day, in each case at or near a refuge, hotel or campsite unless otherwise specified.

8-9 days Taking the itinerary anti-clockwise from the south, the **GRP** starts in **Juberri**, not the most obvious beginning as there's no public transport to the village, and begins with one of its least interesting sections, climbing via the **Rabassa** cross-country ski-station to **Pic Negre** before a more attractive descent via **Refuge de Claror** to **Refuge de Perafita** // N.B. Not only is this traditional first day of the GRP a bit dull, it's very long. You could divide it by two, stopping at the **Refuge de la Rabassa**, or hitch to the ski station and start there. Otherwise, a more logical and more interesting approach to **Perafita** would be from **Andorra La Vella** via **Prat Primer** (Walk 29) or **Riu de Perafita** (Walk 28). From **Perafita**, the GRP crosses **Collada de la Maiana** to join the GR11, climbing **Vall de Madriu** to **Estany de l'Illa** //. It then follows the GR7 via the **Collada** and **Circ dels Pessons** (Walk 22) before (another less exciting stage) heading north via **Refuge Pla de les Pedres** // and **Port Dret** to **Refuge del Siscaró** (Walk 20) //. After descending to the **Vall d'Incles**, it climbs via the **Riu del Manegor** (Walk 11) to **Refuge de Cabana Sorda** and crosses into the **Ransol Valley** and the **Refuge dels Còms de Jan** (Walk 21) //. It then crosses the **Coll de la Mina** and descends the **Sorteny** and **Valira del Nord** valleys to **Llorts** (Walk 21) //. Following a stiff climb past **Refuge de l'Angonella** (Walk 10), it crosses into the **Arinsal Valley**, passing below the **Les Fonts** and **Pla de l'Estany** refuges (Walk 8) //. It then climbs via **Refuge de Coma Pedrosa** (Walk 7) // to **Collada de Sanfons** (Walk 6) and descends to **Coll de la Botella** (Walk 5) from where a relatively dull section leads to **Collada de Montaner** and a pleasant descent to **Sispony** (Walk 3) //.

N.B. Remember that when the GRP follows another GR the conventional red-and-white GR stripes take precedence over the red-and-yellow GRP stripes.

5 days Again starting in the south, the **GR7** arrives in Andorra from **La Seu d'Urgell** and climbs to **Juberri**, from where it follows the road back down towards **Sant Julià** before branching north to cross the **Aubinyá** residential area. It then winds along the contour above **Sant Juliá** via **Llumeneres** and **Certés** before traversing **Bosc de Palomera** (Walk 29) and descending to **Andorra La Vella** //. The only accommodation I know in this first Andorran stage is the **Coma Bella Hotel**, near the spring of the same name and east of the GR7, so if you intend doing this route entire, you'll probably have to camp out somewhere. For this reason, the first Andorran overnight stop is not indicated above. On the presumption that the route is begun in **La Seu d'Urgell**, I have counted an overnight stop at **Camping Frontera** on the Spanish side of the border. From **Andorra La Vella**, the GR7 climbs to **Entremesaigües** (Walk 28 - take a taxi to the junction of the C200/CS101, the walk up from the city is only for purists) before joining the GR11 for the long haul up the **Vall de Madriu** to **L'Illa** (Walk 30) //. From **L'Illa**, the path crosses the **Collada de Pessons** into the **Circ de Pessons** (Walk 22) before curving round to **Porteilla Blanca d'Andorra** (another night out somewhere along this stretch) and descending via the **Vall de Campcardós** (a great smugglers' favourite) to **Porta** in France //.

6 days The **GR11** suffers a serious identity crisis in Andorra, splintering all over the place, so I will stick to the principal path. It arrives in Andorra from the west via the **Portella de Baiau** (a horrendous little scramble and itself a full day's walk from the nearest road - **Areu** in Spain). If you do arrive this way, a stopover in the snug **Refuge de Baiau** on the Spanish side is strongly recommended //. From the *portella*, the GR descends via **Refuge de Coma Pedrosa** to Arinsal (Walk 7) // then crosses **Coll de les Cases** (Walk 2) to **Arans** and **La Cortinada** //. After a steady climb over the **Coll d'Ordino**, it descends to **Encamp** // then climbs again via **Estany d'Engolasters** and **Coll Jovell** before following the **Vall de Madriu** to **L'Illa** (Walk 30) //. It then crosses **Port de Vallcivera** into Spain, passing the **Refuge de Malniu** en route to **Puigcerda** //.

5-7 days The **HRP/ARP** has always struck me as a fairly fluid sort of route, evolving according to the audacity of the latest walker to have tackled its more dangerous sections and taken the trouble to construct a few cairns. Depending on your source, it arrives in Andorra either via **Pas de la Casa** and **Port d'Envalira** or (a more interesting option) via the **Port d'Incles** (Walk 19) then climbs via **Cabana Sorda** (Walk 11) onto the crest defining the western line of **Estany de Cabana Sorda**, at which point things get decidedly hairy. After crossing the **Pic de la Coma de Varilles** (NOT recommended! See Walk 21 for an alternative version, also identified as the HRP in some publications) and passing below **Pic de la Pala de Jan**, it descends to the **Estanys de Ransol**, where it insinuates itself into the GRP (Walk 21), which it follows to **El Serrat**. It then climbs toward **Tristaina** before leaving Andorra, depending on your source, either via **Port de Rat** or **Pic de l'Estany Forcat** above **Tristaina**. If following this route, the obvious stop-off points would be **Refuge dels Còms de Jan** (some way off the HRP, but accessible) //, **Refuge de Sorteny** //, and **Cabana de l'Eucasser** (at the end of the asphalted section of the CG3) //. However, those three days in Andorra give no logical start or finish to the walk. **Port d'Incles** can be reached by following the GR10 from **Merens-Les-Valls** in France, stopping over in the **Refuge de Rulhe** //. From **Port de Rat**, the HRP crosses into Spain via **Port de Boet**, from where paths lead down to **Refuge de Vallferrera** //, the GR11 and **Areu** //. Alternatively one could descend directly to **Etang de Soulcem** in France and the D108 in the hope of hitching a lift down to **Tarascon**. Another option, if favouring the **Pic de l'Estany Forcat** pass, would be to descend to **Estany d'Izourt** in France to rejoin the GR10. This all sounds rather haphazard, but to be honest, the sort of person capable of following the HRP for any distance will consider the logistical hassles and the route's general mutability totally inconsequential.

D CABLE CARS & CHAIR LIFTS

The following cable-cars and chair-lifts are open in summer:
  Arinsal-Pal (every day in July and August, weekends in June and September until Sept. 12th)
  La Caubella to **Pla de la Cot**
  Coll de la Botella to **Port Negre** (see Walks 6 & 7)

Arinsal to **Comallemple**
See www.palarinsal.com for up-to-date information
Ordino-Arcalis
Port de Creussans (15th June to 30th September)
See www.vallordino.com for up-to-date information
Grand Valira (10th July to 12th September)
Encamp to **Collada Solanelles** (not too far from the start of Walk 26)
Canillo to **El Forn** (see Walk 25)
Soldeu to **Espiolets** (see Walk 24)
See www.grandvalira.com for up-to-date information

E MOUNTAIN BIKE ROUTES

The following suggestions have not been tested. They are ideas culled from on the ground observation, sightings of cyclists who still seemed to be in one piece, and the study of maps and local publications. For more details, ask in local tourist information offices and ski-resorts. The latter, in particular, are likely to be updating and extending mountain-bike itineraries. Most of the cable cars listed above also accept mountain-bikes. Where local publications assess difficulty, I reproduce their assessment. Where longer itineraries overlap with shorter itineraries, I cross-reference the two rides. Bikes can be rented in **Sant Julià Pal**, **Ordino**, **Encamp** and **Soldeu**.

A=Mountain Activities booklet (see Bibliography)
For these itineraries, the first number is the booklet itinerary number, the second the distance, the third the climb, the fourth the descent, the fifth the time. The final initials assess first the physical difficulty then the technical difficulty. (*Difficulty in all itineraries is estimated as follows: VD=very difficult D=difficult Av=average E=easy VE=very easy)

West

Itinerary Number		Distance	Climb	Descent	Time	Difficulty*
1	**Aixovall - Os de Civís (Spain) - Pal - La Massana**					
	A1	24km	1100m	700m	3h30	VD / D
2	**Aixovall - Os de Civís - Pal - Sispony** (c.f. **Pal-Arinsal** itineraries below)					
	A8	18km	1100m	750m	3h	D / D
3	**Sant Julià de Lòria - Borda de Gasto - Santuari de Canòlic - Bixessarri - Sant Julià**					
	A2	24km	980m	930m	2h30	D / VE
4	**La Massana - Pal - Escàs - Sispony** (c.f. **Pal-Arinsal** itineraries below)					
	A3	9km		600m	20'	E / D
5	**La Massana - Coll de Montaner - Bordes de Setúria - Coll de la Botella - La Massana** (cf **Pal-Arinsal** itineraries below)					
		42km				D

The following itineraries have been signposted in the **Pal-Arinsal Mountain Park**. In the circuits, the numbers refer to distance, time, and climb, in the descents to time and altitude descended.

Circuits:		Distance	Time	Climb	Difficulty*
6	**Caubella**	2.3km	25'	40m	VE
7	**Joan Guardia**	4.5km	1h10	200m	E
8	**Cubil**	6km	1h30	400m	D
9	**Llobatera**	3km	1h	50m	E
10	**Roc de l'Àguila**	4km	1h30	500m	D
11	**Setúria**	5km	1h30	500m	E

12	**Pallars**	16km	2h	650m		VD
13	**Collada de Montané**	10km	2-3h	800m		VD
14	**Os de Civis**	12km	2-3h	400m		VD
Descents:			**Time**	**Descent**		
15	**La Serra**	25'		40m		VD
16	**Escàs**	1h10		400m		VD
17	**Sispony**	1h10		400m		VD
18	**Cardemeller** 40'		500m		VD	
19	**Port Negre**	45'		500m		VD
20	**Comallempla**	25'		40m		D
21	**Les Marrades**	1h10		400m		E
22	**Arinsal**	20'		950m		VD
23	**Cortals de Sispony**	40'		700m		VD

The remaining itineraries are a mixture of published and unpublished routes. The codes are as above.

24 Walk 9: **Camino Real**: El Serrat - Ordino

North
Itinerary
Number**Distance****Climb****Descent****Time****Difficulty***

25 **Coll d'Ordino - Beixalís - Vila**
A7 11km 200m 900m 1h E/D

26 **Coll d'Ordino - Collada de Beixalís - Ordino**
  29km   VD

27 **Encamp - Bordes de Beixalis - Vila - Camino de la Solana - Encamp**
  16km   E

28 **Vall de Ransol** (CS260)
  6km   E

29 **Vall d'Incles - Soldeu - Canillo** (c.f. Walk 23: **Cami de Gall**)
A9 12km 250m 450m 1h50 D/D

South
Itinerary
Number**Distance****Climb****Descent****Time****Difficulty***

30 **Andorra La Vella - Cortals de Sansa**
  9km   VD

31 **Andorra La Vella - Rec de l'Obac - La Comella**
A6 12km 700m 650m 1h10 Av/VD

32 **Engolasters - Meritxell**
A4 8.5km 100m 200m 1h15 Av/VD

33 Walk 23: **Camí de Gall** (c.f. Itinerary 29 above)

There are numerous high tours and descents possible using the **Grand Valira** cable-cars (**Encamp**, **Canillo**, **Soldeu**) which charge €18 per rider+bike. The following suggestions are by no means comprehensive.

34 Walk 24: The Lazy Man's Mountain
35 **Espiolets to Soldeu** (either via the dirt track or, for the more daring, one of the ski-pistes)
36 **Espiolets - Grau Roig - Soldeu**
37 **Collada Solanelles - Pic de la Portella/Maians - El Forn - Canillo**
38 **Grau Roig - El Piolet - Llac des Pessons - Grau Roig**
39 **St. Julià de Lòria - La Rabassa**
  29km   D
40 **La Rabassa - Pico Negre - Prat Primer - La Comella**
A5 14.4km 600m 1200m 2h30 D/VD

F CLIMBING ROUTES / VÍAS FERRATAS

I'm no climber and most of the routes itemized here would have me crawling round the ground quietly babbling to myself. This is simply a digest of published information to give you an idea of what's possible. For further details, contact the local tourist offices. The Mountain Activities booklet (see Bibliography) gives further details of location, orientation, necessary equipment and the type of rock on the first 8 climbs. There are also climbing walls in **Canillo**, **Caldea-Escaldes**, **Ordino**, **Encamp** and **Pas de la Casa**.

Climbing routes:
Andorra La Vella
1 Solà d'Enclar — Grade 4-7
2 Pirámide — Grade 4-8a
3 Llastra de l'Obac — Grade 5-6b

Escaldes-Engordany
4 Roc de la Guilla — Grade 5-7a + 7c
5 Boulder de Coll Jovell — Grade 4-8a
6 Agujas de Engolasters — Grade 4-6b

La Massana
7 Sant Antoni de la Grella — Grade 5-7c

Canillo
8 La Cascada — Grade 3-6a

Arcalís
9 Creussans — Grade 5-6b
10 Balma de Arcalís — Grade 5-6a

Encamp
11 Pic de Ríbuls — Grade 5-6a

Vías Ferratas
1 Sant Julià de Lòria: Tossa Gran de Aixovall — Av
2 Andorra la Vella: Sant Vicenç d'Enclar — Av
3 Escaldes-Engordany: Roc d'Esquers — Av
4 Encamp: Clots de l'Aspra — E
5 Canillo: Canal de la Mora — E
6 Canillo: Roc del Quer — D
7 Canillo: Racons — VD
8 Canillo: Canal del Grau — D
9 Canillo: Bony d'Envalira — E
10 Canillo: Collada dels Isards — VD

G BIBLIOGRAPHY

The **Guia Azul** (Ediciones GAESA) was a mine of information for the facts and figures featured in the introduction, saving me hours trawling through libraries, virtual and otherwise.

I also made use of the **Ecoguía de Andorra** (Anaya), another series covering some of Spain's great natural areas and dedicated to promoting sustainable tourism, a laudable project marred by walk 'descriptions' so short on directions and so long on rhapsodies about the flora, fauna and architecture, one gets the distinct impression they were researched in the library.

Andorra Mountain Activities is a useful booklet. Includes maps (after a fashion) of some of the mountain-bike itineraries detailed above and details of climbing routes. Free from most Tourist Offices. N.B. This is the green booklet, not the white one with the same name, which includes similar information, but with more walks less coherently integrated.

36 Interesting Itineraries on the paths of the Vall d'Ordino and the Parish of La Massana is the nearest thing to a classic on walking in Andorra. Very sketchy descriptions, but includes some ideas not incorporated in the present publication. €2 from the Ordino and Massana tourist offices.

Bibliophiles may care to consult their local second-hand book dealers for early accounts of Andorra, published in the nineteenth century by the English Alpinists who pioneered Pyrenean tourism, notably **Guide to the Pyrenees**, for the use of mountaineers (1867) by Charles Packes and **Through The High Pyrenees** (1898) by Harold Spender.

For anyone interested in the geology, ecology, biology and anthropology of the Pyrenees the essential guide is by the French naturalist and academic, Claude Dendaletche, published in French and Spanish: **Guide du Naturaliste dans les Pyrenees Occidentales** (Delachaux & Niestlé) **Guía de los Pirineos** (Omega). A bilingual (French & Catalan) book, **Histoires de Pierres**, co-produced by various local agencies in Languedoc-Roussillon collates local legends and anecdotes concerning common toponyms. There is no specific reference to Andorra, but it's useful to the extent that Andorra partakes of a common Pyrenean culture in which myths and superstitions are repeated from one end of the chain to the other and local customs tend to infiltrate neighbouring communities.

Editorial Trabucaire based in Perpignan produce books of special local interest, including scientific monographs (**Les Tremblements de Terre dans les Pyrénées Orientales et en Catalogne** by Gérard Soutadé is particularly interesting), local history and ethnology, and novels.

For anyone able to muddle their way through Catalán and interested in learning more about the colourful career of Boris Skossyreff, Antoni Morell has written a novella on the subject, **Boris I, Rei d'Andorre** (Proa Butxaca). This book is part of a family saga portraying the history of Andorra in the twentieth century. The other volumes are **Set Lletanies de Mort** and **La Neu Adversa**.

INDEX OF PLACE NAMES

	TEXT	MAP
A		
Agols (refuge)	6, 134-136	
Aiguassos	81	
Aigües Juntes	60	
Alba Hotel	21	
Alt de Covil	49	
Alt de Griu	123	*121*
Alt de la Capa	47	*56, 58, 61*
Andorra La Vella	10, 18, 21, 22, 32, 67, 87, 124, 132	
Angonella (refuge)	69	
Ansalonga	45, 67	
Aparthotel La Neu	67, 75, 77	
Arans	4, 5, 47, 67-69, *84,* 83, 84, 87	
Arans Hotel	87	
Arcalis	42, 71, 78	
Arinsal	11, 22, 45, 47, *45, 65,* 57, 60, 62, 63, 66, 69	
B		
Baladosa		*100, 103, 107*
Bassa del Raco		*70*
Basses de l'Estany Negre	61	*58, 61*
Bony de la Pleta de Jan	108	
Bony de l'Estany Mort	108	*93, 106*
Borda de -		
Janramon	91	*89*
la Plana	130	
Roig	91	*89*
Horto	31, 115	
Borda del Pugicernal	125	*126*
Bordas de la Coruvilla	64	
Bordes de -		
Fenerols	48	
la Molina	134, 135	
la Mollera	69	
l'Armiana	88, 91	
l'Ensegur	68, 83, 87	
les Pardines	135	
Montaup	88, 91	
Percanela	64, 66, 69	
Bordes del -		
Horto Restaurant	115	
Torner	66	*65*
Prats Nou	66	*65*
Bosc de -		
Campeà	121	
Castellar	78	
la Font del Pi	87	*84*
la Mollera	70	
la Palomera	130, 131	
Bosc del -		
Barrer d'Areny	66	*65*

	TEXT	MAP
Pa de Rodo	52	*53*
Rodol	127	*129*
Soleador	69	*70, 76*
Bretxa d'Arcalis	71	
Bringué Hotel	77, 110	
C		
Cabana -		
de Castellar	78	
de la Perafita	127, 128	
de la Vall del Riu	88, 90	
de l'Eucasser		*42, 108*
del Serra de la Barracota	139	
dels Planells de Rialb	82	*82*
Cabana Sorda (refuge)	72, 95, 96, 105, 106	*107*
Cabanas de la Plata de les Romes	81	
Cal Daina Hotel	87	
Camí de -		
Collada Caüll	132	
Collada de Montaner	48	
Gall	6, 114, 124	
la Canal	6, 124	
la Llebre	125	
la Muntanya	127	
lesPardines	124, 134	
Munyat	131	
Pica Romana	131	
Port Incles	72, 73	
ses Pardines	135	
Camí del -		
Bosc de Campeà	121, 123	
Coll Turer	55	
Maians	131	
Camí Vell de Tristaina	78	
Camíno Real (Camí Ral)	4, 67, 75	
Camp de Serrat	135	
Camping d'Incles	72, 102	
Canillo	6, 10, 20, 21, 22, 32, 83, 89, 91, 114, 116-119, 124, 125	*114, 126*
Canya de la Sucarana	69, 70	*70*
Cap -		
d'Agols	134	
de la Coma dels Llops	134, 137	*137*
de la Serrera		
de Port	5, 102, 104	*103*
de Rep	120	
de Tossa d'Entor	95, 97	*95*
Casamanya - see Pic de Casamanya		
Cascada de la		

	TEXT	MAP		TEXT	MAP
Vall de Riu	116		l'Estany Més Avall	70	70
Castellar woods	78		la Devesa	56	56, 58, 61
Certés	11		la Font		
Circ de Pessons	6, 29, 111, 113	112	de Miquelets	60, 61	58, 61
Cirque de Rialb	81		l'Alt de la Capa	56	56
Clots d'Encarners	90, 91	89	les Enles	56	56, 58
Clots de			l'Estany del Mig		42
Estany Segon	98	101	Perafita	129	129
Clots de la Serrera	110		Port Dret	104	103
Coll d'Arenes	83, 85-87, 90, 91	85	Costa del Congost	65	65
			Costa del Port		56, 58
Coll de -			Costa Rodona	42	42
Jou	45, 46		Costa Verda	127	
Jovell	138, 139		Creussans	42	
Juclar	98		**D**		
la Botella	49, 52, 55, 57, 60		Devassa	116	
			E		
la Mina	92, 94, 105, 109		El Forn	118, 119	
			El Serrat	4, 5, 22, 67, 74, 76, 77, 80 92, 105, 108, 110	76, 108
l'Alba	98, 100, 101	101			
les Cases	3, 45, 47	45			
Turer	55, 56	56			
Coll d'Ordino	83, 88		El Tarter	21, 22, 95, 115, 117	118
Coll Pa	50				
Coll Petit	57, 59	58, 61	El Vllar	88	114
Collada de -			Els Llacs	52-54	52
Caüll	6, 130-132		Els Plans		115
Ferreroles	74		Encamp	10, 21, 32, 117, 125, 134, 135	136
Juclar	23, 100	101			
les Vaques	84	85			
Maiana	128, 139		Engolasters	6, 29, 124, 134, 135	136
Maians	120				
Montaner	48, 49	49	Engordany	10, 21, 32, 67	
Montmalús	113		Ensagents (refuge)	6, 121	
Pessons	113		Entor	95, 96	
Prat Primer	133		Entremesaigües	127-129, 139	129
Sanfons	57		Envalira	29	
del Clot Sord	97	95	Erts	11, 45	45
Estanys Forcats	66		Escaldes	10, 21, 31, 32, 67, 127	129
Meners	92				
Collada d'Entinyola	123		Espiolets	117	
Collart	115		Estany(s) -		
Collet de -			(de) Forcats	2, 19, 64, 66, 112, 113, 138	65, 112
Coma Pedrosa	62	58			
Font Podrida	66	65	Blau	5, 79, 81, 82, 138	82, 137
Llosa	47	45			
Sant Vicenç	128		de (Més)Mas		
Coma -			Amunt	43, 71	42
de Ransol		106	de Baix	102-104	103
del Mig	79		de Cabana Sorda	105-107	107
dels Llops	122	137	de la Bova	137-139	
Estret	84, 86	84	de l'Alba	101	
Obaga (refuge)	74	76	de les Canals		
Pedrosa	57, 58, 60, 61, 64	58, 61, 65	Roges	102-104	103
			de les Fonts	6, 111, 113	112
Comella Valley	130, 133		de les Truites	58, 60, 62, 63	58, 61
Comís Vell	78, 80	79	de l'Estanyó	74	
Còms de Jan			de l'Illa		137
Refuge	92, 94, 105-108		de l'Isla	72	73
			del Cap des		
Cortal de la Plana	130, 133		Pessons	111, 113	112
Cortals de Sispony	48, 49	49	del Meligar	113	112
Costa de -			del Mig	43	42
l'Estany Més			del Querol	95-97	95
Amunt		70	dels Meners		

Walk! Andorra 155

	TEXT	MAP		TEXT	MAP
de la Coma	109	*93, 106*	Juclar (refuge)	99	*101*
d'Engolasters	134, 135, 138	*136*	**L**		
d'Ensagents	6, 121		La Coma		
Esbalçat	4, 19, 78, 80	*79*	(restaurant)	42	
Gnioure	80		La Comarqueta	104	*103*
Gran de la Vall			La Comella		*112*
del Riu	88, 90	*89*	La Cortinada	67	
Moreno	121		La Era del Jaume		
Mort	92, 94, 108	*93, 103,*	(restaurant)	67	
		106	La Mandurana	116	
Negre	57, 58, 62	*58, 61*	La Massana	10, 21, 45, 46,	
Primer	43, 110, 112,	*42, 112*		67	
	123		La Neu Aparthotel	65, 75, 77	
Primer de Juclar	99	*101*	La Passera	75	*76*
Rodó	113	*112, 137*	La Portella	120	*120*
Roig	80		La Rabassa	49, 81	
Segon de Juclar	100, 123	*101*	La Serreta	89	
de Baiau	57, 59	*58*	La Seu d'Urgell	21, 31, 32	
de Fontargent	4, 72, 73	*73*	La Valira d'Orient	22	
de Juclar	5, 19, 98, 101, 119		Lac del Forn	120	
de la Vall del Riu	88		L'Era del Jaume		
de l'Angonella	4, 19, 69	*70*	(restaurant)	74	
de les			Les Canyorques	61	
Salamandres	5, 95, 96, 106		Les Costes de l'Alt	56	*56*
de Ransol	92, 93, 105,	*93, 106*	Les Salines	67, 76, 77	*68, 76*
	109		Les Tallades	77	*76, 108*
de Tristaina	2, 3, 19, 29,	*42*	Llac des Pessons	112	
	42		Llac i Cel		
des Siscaró	5, 19, 102		(restaurant)	135	
F			Llorts	22, 67-69, 74,	*68, 70,*
Font -				76, 77, 83,	*76, 84*
de Boïgot	127			108, 110	
de l'Astrell	130		Lloset		*126*
de Miquelets	61	*58, 61*	**M**		
del Port de			Madriu valley	6, 46, 113,	
Cabús		*52*		119, 128, 129,	
del Sucre	49	*49*		134, 138, 139	
del Travenc	98, 99		Mas de Ribafeta	47	*45*
del Vi	49	*49*	Meritxell	125	
dels Clots			**O**		
de Llosa	93, 94	*93, 106*	Obaga de l'Avier	133	
dels Comellassos	105		Ordino	10, 11, 22, 42,	
Freda	81			67, 71, 83, 84	
Pixadera	127, 128		Os de Civis	49	
Fonts del Collalets	139		**P**		
Fontverd (refuge)	139		Pal	22, 55	
Funicamp	124		Pales de les Basses		
G			de les Salamandres	106	*95, 107*
Grau de la Molina	135	*136*	Pardines	134	
Grau Roig	113	*112*	Pas de la Casa	15, 17, 21, 22,	
Grau Roig Hotel	29			49	
H			Pas de l'Angonella	70	
Hotel Alba	21		Pas de les Vaques	104	*103*
Hotel Arans	87		Perafita (refuge)	6, 127	
Hotel Bringué	77		Percanela	66	
Hotel Cal Daina	87		Pic -		
Hotel del Serrat	67, 77		Alt de la Capa	4, 46, 55, 56	
Hotel Grau Roig	29		d'Anrodat	73	
Hotel Subira	110		d'Arbella	43	
Hotel Tristaina	77, 110		de Carroi	3, 48, 50, 51	*49*
I			de Casamanya	2, 5, 20, 46	*84, 85*
Illa	134, 138			49, 69, 79,	
Illa (refuge)	6, 133, 138	*137*		83-85, 86, 90,	
Incles	5, 95, 105			91, 117, 119,	
J				125, 134	

156 Walk! Andorra

	TEXT	MAP		TEXT	MAP
de Coll Pa		49	Portella -		
de Coma			Blanca d'Andorra	15, 23	
Pedrosa	4, 60, 62, 92	58, 61	de Baiau		58
de Encampanada	118, 119	118, 120	de Pessons	113	
de Font Blanca	4, 78, 80	79	de Rialb	78, 82	
de la Bassera			de Sanfons	57	
(Pic dels Llacs)	4, 46, 52, 53	52	Prat Primer	6, 46, 130	132
de la Cabaneta	90, 109	93	Prat Primer (refuge)	133	
de la Coma de			Presa de Ransol	115	
Varilles	95, 106		**R**		
de la Portella	119, 125		Rámio	127, 129	
de la Serrera	5, 79, 92-94,	93, 106,	Ransol	88, 92, 93, 95,	93, 115
	97, 105, 108,	109		124	
	109		Ransol Valley	5, 29, 92, 97,	93
de les Asclades	133			106, 107, 109,	
de les Fonts		89		118	
de l'Estanyó	79, 86, 90, 92,		Rasa de Perafita	128	
	109, 134		Recs de Obac	124	
de Maians	2, 6, 119, 120,	136	Refuge de -		
	125, 135, 136		Agols	6, 134-136	
de Medacorba	57, 66, 92		Cabana de		
de Noé	98, 100		Castellar	78	
de Pessons	113		Cabana Sorda	105, 106	107
de Port Negre	57	56, 58, 61	Coma Obaga	4, 74, 75	
de Ransol		107	Coma Pedrosa	60	
de Sanfons	4, 57	58	Còms de Jan	92, 94,	
de Setúria	52, 54	52		105-108	
de Tristaina	43	42	Fontverd	139	
del Mig	85		Illa	6, 133, 138	137
del Port Vell		58, 61	Juclar	99	101
del Solà d'Erts	46		la Serrera	108, 110	
d'Enclar	3, 48		l'Angonella	69	
d'Escobes	98, 100		Perafita	6, 127	
Negre	128, 133		Prat Primer	133	
Negre d'Envalira	22, 49		Rialb	81	82
Pirámide			Riba Escorxada	118	
Pista (de)			Riu dels Orris	139	
Pla de l'Estany	63, 64, 66		Siscaró	102	100, 103
Pista de Petanca	126		Sorteny	86, 110	82, 108
Pla de l'Estany	64-66, 69		Refuge del Pla		
Pla de l'Ingla	138, 139	137	de l'Estany	65	
Planells de l'Alia	135		Refuge		
Planells d'Entor	95, 97	95	d'Ensagents	6, 121, 122	
Pont de/ d'			Restaurant -		
Arans	87	84	del Lac des		
Baladosa	72, 98, 102	100, 103,	Pessons	111	
		107	La Coma	42	
Collart	115		La Font d'Arans	68	
Entremesaigües	128	129	Lulu	116	
la Farga	67	68, 76,	Piolet	111	
		108	Rialb (refuge)	81	82
de les Mines	75	68, 76	Rialb valley	81	82
de les Moles	68, 75	76	Riba Escorxada	117	
de Puntal	110	108	Riba Escorxada		
Sassanat	127		(refuge)	118	
Port de -			Riu de/d' -		
Cabús	52, 53, 55	52	Valira d'Orient	10, 12, 115	84, 114
l'Arbella (l'Abeille)	43		Areny (d'Areny)	60, 63, 65	61
Setut	139		Bor	117	118
Siguer	5, 81, 82	82	Aiguarebre	70	
d'Incles	4, 72, 73, 106	73, 95	Cabana Sorda	105, 106	107
Dret	104	65	Cebollera	110	109
Negre	52, 56, 60	56, 58	Collart	115	
Negre de Pallars	57, 59	58	Coma		
Vell	57, 82	58, 61, 82	Pedrosa	60-62	58, 61

Walk! Andorra 157

	TEXT	MAP		TEXT	MAP
Ferreroles	74, 75		Miquel d'Enclar	32	
Jan	94, 107	106	Miquel		
Juclar	99	100, 101	d'Engolasters	32	129
l'Angonella	70	70, 76	Romà de Juberri	32	
l'Estany			Romà de les Bons	32	
Esbalçat	79		Romà dels Villars	32	
Riu de la/les -			Coloma	32	
Cebollera		109	Santuaro de Meritxell	32, 125	
Coma del Forat		42	Sedornet	69	
Coma del Mig	79		Seig valley	120	
Comarqueta	90	89	Sender de les		
Comella	130, 133	132	Tres Valls	6, 117, 119	
Molina	135		Serra de/del/de la		
Serrera	110	109	Cabana Sorda		107
Vall del Riu	88, 89	90	Casamanya		85
l'Ensegur	86, 87	84	Creu	131, 132	
Agols	135		Cap de la Coma	71	
Cebes	110	109	Corrals		56
Portelles	94	93, 106	Estanys	88, 90	89
Maians		132	Codinet	136	
Montaner	48, 49, 51		Serrat de la Burna	69	
Riu de/del/dels/d' -			Serrera (refuge)	108, 110	
Perafita	128	129	Setúria	52, 53	52, 58
Rialb	81	82	Siscaró (refuge)	102	100, 103
Siscaró	102	100, 103	Sispony	48	
Sorteny	108, 110	108	Solà de Coma Obaga	75	76
Tristaina	67, 77	76, 79, 108	Solà de Encampanada	118-120	118, 120
			Solà del Jordà	122	
Bancal Vedeller	66	65	Solana de Prat Primer	133	132
Comís Vell	78	79	Soldeu	6, 22, 97, 105 114, 117	115, 118
Forn	117, 125	126			
Manegor	72, 73		Sornás	67	
Montaup	5, 88, 91	89	Sorteny	108	93
Port Dret	65, 66	65	Sorteny (refuge)	86, 110	108
Querol	87	68, 84, 95	Sorteny Valley		108
Seig	117-119	120	Sorteny Visitors'		
Valira		89	Centre	110	
Cortals	124		Subira Hotel	110	
Estanys		89	**T**		
Llacs	53	52	Torregols del Alt	62	58, 61
Meners	92	93, 106	Torrent de la Fon		
Orris		137	de l'Altar	52	
Pessons	112	112	Torrent de Ribal	66	65
Engolasters		126	Torrent Prego	124, 125	
Ensagents	122	121	Tossa del Cap del		
Incles		100, 107, 115,	Siscaró	102, 103	103
			Tristaina	78	42
Riu L'Avetar	115		Tristaina Hotel	77, 110	
Riu Madriu	127, 129		Turó de Jan	108	106
Riu Sec	49		Valira del Nord Valley	78	
Riu Valira Nord	67, 77	68, 76	Valira Nord valley	87	
Roc de la Cauba	3, 45, 46	45	Vall d'Angonella	74	
Roc del Forn	125		Vall de Agols	46, 134	
Roc del Quer		126	Vall de Perafita	46	
Roca de Àliga	56		Vall del Riu	5, 19, 88-90, 125	
Rocky Mountain			Vall d'Incles	72, 96, 98, 102, 105, 117	
Café	66				
S					
Sant -					
Cerni de Nagol	32				
Climent de Pal	32				
Creus	126				
Joan de Caselles	32, 88				
Julià de Lòria	10, 32				
Martí de la					
Cortinada	32				

HOW TO GET HOLD OF OUR PUBLICATIONS

Ask in any bookshop, order from amazon.co.uk, via our websites, or order direct from us by mail order, using the form below.

If you are ordering direct from us, please:
- complete your details in BLOCK CAPITALS
- write the full title(s) of the publications you require
- enclose your payment (please note that post & packing is free)
- make your cheque payable to:

Discovery Walking Guides Ltd.
and post to:
**Discovery Walking Guides Ltd.
10 Tennyson Close
Northampton NN5 7HJ**

TITLE(S) ORDERED   ITEM COST

I enclose my cheque for this **TOTAL**
(free post & packing)

YOUR NAME

ADDRESS

POST CODE

*TEL Nº

**email   @

* for order enquiries only   ** for enewsletters and updates

DISCOVERY WALKING GUIDES LTD. TITLES LIST

GPS NAVIGATION

GPS The Easy Way
Manual £4.99

PERSONAL NAVIGATOR FILES
Version 2.01 Downloadable GPS records for all Walk!/Walks Guidebooks + GPS Utility Software
CD £7.99

SPANISH MAINLAND

Sierra de Aracena - a Walk! Guidebook
Guidebook £11.99
Sierra de Aracena
Tour & Trail Map £2.99
34 Alpujarras Walks
Guidebook £9.99
Alpujarras Super-Durable
Tour & Trail Map £7.99
Walk! Axarquia
Guidebook £11.99

CANARY ISLANDS

Walk! Lanzarote
Guidebook £11.99
Lanzarote Super-Durable
Tour & Trail Map £7.99
Lanzarote Indestructible Map £4.99
Lanzarote Plant&Flower Guide £2

Walk! La Gomera (2nd edition)
Guidebook £11.99
La Gomera Super-Durable
Tour & Trail Map £7.99
Drive! La Gomera
Touring Map £2.50

35 Tenerife Walks
Guidebook £9.99
Tenerife Super-Durable
Walkers' Maps £4.99
Tenerife Paper Edition
Walkers' Maps £2.99
Tenerife Indestructible Map £4.99

Drive! Tenerife Touring Map £2.50

Tenerife Plant&Flower Guide £2

Gran Canaria Mountains
Tour & Trail Map £5
Gran Canaria Plant&Flower Guide £2

Walk! La Palma
Guidebook £11.99
La Palma Super-Durable
Tour & Trail Map £7.99

BALEARIC ISLANDS

Walk! Mallorca (North & Mountains)
Guidebook £11.99
Mallorca North & Mountains Super-Durable
Tour & Trail Map £7.99
Walk! Mallorca West
Guidebook £11.99
Walk! Menorca
Guidebook £11.99
Menorca Super-Durable
Tour & Trail Map £7.99

ANDORRA

Walk! Andorra
Guidebook £11.99

PORTUGAL, INCLUDING MADEIRA

Madeira Super-Durable
Tour & Trail Map £7.99
35 Madeira Walks
Guidebook £9.99
Drive! Madeira
Touring Map £2.50

Algarve - Loule Walking Guide £5
Algarve - Silves Walking Guide £5

MALTA & GOZO

Malta & Gozo Walking Guides £5